PURDAH

Purdah, which can be formal law or informal custom, involves keeping women segregated from society, restricting their independence, and obliging them to dress in clothing that fully covers them. First published by Kegan Paul in 1932, this was a seminal book for the women's rights movement in general, and the Indian Woman's Movement in particular, and remains highly relevant today, as Indian, Islamic and Asian women continue to feel the conflict between modernity and tradition. Swiss by birth and married to an Indian, the author had a unique opportunity to see life in India from the perspective of women in *purdah*. Beginning in the Vedic period, she shows how the institution of *purdah* developed over time, describes *purdah* as long practiced in India, and then details the various reform and suffragette measures undertaken to eradicate it and the effect of the Nationalist movement on Indian women's freedom. There are clear parallels with the status of women in other countries. In recent decades, *purdah* is once again reasserting itself in parts of India and elsewhere as conservative forces gain ground. This important work gives insight into the roots and strength of *purdah*.

KEGAN PAUL
BOOKS OF RELATED INTEREST

SIAMESE HAREM LIFE
Anna H. Leonowens

INDIA AND BEYOND: ASPECTS OF LITERATURE,
MEANING, RITUAL AND THOUGHT
Edited by Dick van der Meij

HINDU MANNERS, CUSTOMS AND CEREMONIES
Abbé J.A. Dubois

PURDAH

*The Status of Indian Women from Ancient
Times to the Twentieth Century*

FRIEDA HAUSWIRTH

Routledge
Taylor & Francis Group

LONDON AND NEW YORK

First published in 2006 by
Kegan Paul Limited

Published 2016 by Routledge
2 Park Square, Milton Park, Abingdon, Oxfordshire OX14 4RN
711 Third Avenue, New York, NY 10017, USA

First issued in paperback 2016

Routledge is an imprint of the Taylor and Francis Group, an informa business

Distributed by:
Marston Book Services Ltd
160 Milton Park
Abingdon
Oxfordshire OX14 4SD
United Kingdom
Tel: (01235) 465500 Fax: (01235) 465555

Columbia University Press
61 West 62nd Street, New York, NY 10023
Tel: (212) 459 0600 Fax: (212) 459 3678

British Library Cataloguing in Publication Data
Hauswirth, Frieda
Purdah : the status of Indian women. – (Kegan Paul Asia library)
1. Women – India – History 2. Women – India – Social conditions
3. Feminism – India
I. Title
305.4'2'0954'09
ISBN 0710307845

ISBN 13: 978-1-138-99698-4 (pbk)
ISBN 13: 978-0-7103-0784-2 (hbk)

AUTHOR'S FOREWORD

It is expected that the present volume will be the precursor of a book envisaged but not yet written. I had hoped that an occasion would present itself for an early return to India, for the purpose of making on the spot a protracted study of the Indian Woman's Movement of this century, particularly of the developments of the immediate, most vital present. Pending this, I have acceded to the demand to share with others such knowledge as I have at my command.

It has not been my intention, within the short compass of this book, sharply to separate historical fact from legend, as both equally express the truths relevant to the present. Nor have I aimed at a consistent chronological presentation of later historical factors involved in the determining of women's position. The value of the book will lie mainly in a viewpoint and presentation conditioned by fresh personal experience; that, at least, is what friends think, who urge that my life has placed me in a position which leaves me comparatively free from the racial, national, or imperial bias to which most ordinary white sojourners in India are prone.

Born and brought up in Switzerland, I completed my academic studies at Leland Stanford University in California, then attended the California Institute of Art, and later went to India as the wife of a Hindu graduate in agricultural industries of the University of California.

In India, by virtue of this unusual position, I had the chance of being for eight years in intimate contact with Indian family life in all grades of society and in many different sections of the country. In the welter of social and British-Indian problems and conflicts, it has been my endeavour to side not with partisans, but only with truth, as I saw it. This truth I tried to express in my former book, *A Marriage to India*, as well as in the present one. *Leap-Home and Gentle-brawn*, a series of linked tales to appear this autumn, will, beneath their superstructure of fiction, also be based on this foundation of actuality and experience.

I hope that in *Purdah* the exceptional opportunities that I have had of seeing life in India from an unusual standpoint may put before the reader a few new considerations, new angles of approach to the complex question of the status of Indian women. If I have succeeded in this, I shall be satisfied.

The appended list of books touching on the subject under consideration is in no sense a bibliography. I have merely included those few books to which I am, in varying degrees, indebted for refreshing my memory or for new information, hereby gratefully acknowledged. Beside the writers mentioned in footnotes, I have drawn particularly upon the works of Margaret Cousins, N. Macnicol and S. N. Dutt for biographical matter. My thanks are likewise due to those members of the Round Table Conference who have supplied me with information covering the three-year period since my departure from India, and to my many friends in India who helped me to my understanding of their Motherland long before any thought of recording it in writing crossed our minds.

F. H. D.

Cambridge,
March 1932.

CONTENTS

PURDAH: THE STATUS OF INDIAN WOMEN

I

INTRODUCTION

A FEW years ago an occidental woman went all over India in a mad scramble for "material". She covered her field kangaroo-fashion in great erratic leaps; she searched dark corners; her eyes saw just what they wanted to see, her heart found just what could quicken it. The rest she, for her purposes, ignored.

This investigator stopped whenever she came across an evil cesspool, pounded the ground with booming noise, turned up her eyes and called the heavens and the wide earth to witness and to condemn such appalling, unparalleled iniquity. "Behold, O my white people. Compared to these Indian sinks our Western cesspools are indeed but heavy-perfume phials!" And a good deal of truth her indictment indeed contained.

The earth listened to her ominous thumping. Breathless shivers of mingled horror and pharisaical delight ran up and down the spine of the entire

reading world. Then up rose a mighty cry of voci-
ferous sympathy for the poor far-off victim of this
exposed iniquity—for the downtrodden, long-suffer-
ing, helpless womanhood of India. More and more
emphatic, increasing in credulity and volume grew
the asseverations that the kind hand of Western
protection and interference could alone mitigate this
awful state of suffering, could restrain, guide, and
redeem the guilty men and race of India.

Yet a mere three years later, over five hundred of
these very women, these much-abused, defenceless,
weak creatures, gathered together in Bombay to give
the world a drastic little demonstration of just how
cowed they were and how abused they felt. But
while millions in the West had listened to the kan-
garoo's resounding indictment and been swayed by
it, hundreds only were reached by the direct voice
of protest of these Indian women themselves.

Strange to note, the demonstration of these
assembled women took the form of protest not against
the Tyrant Male of India, but against the Broad
Protecting Western Hand. Their timidity wore the
garb of sheer defiance : on a certain day they braved
the white-officered Bombay police for twelve hours
on end.

The worm had turned with a vengeance !

An edict had gone forth from the Government,
prohibiting the annual memorial procession in honour
of Tilak. The Government had its hands more than
full with non-co-operation troubles in Bombay, for
this was the fateful year 1930. The authorities
justly feared that all processions, in fact all gatherings
of any kind or size—no matter how avowedly peaceful
and non-political—might easily turn into breeding

centres of political agitation or flare up into active volcanoes of insurrection. At this time the women of Bombay decided to take it upon themselves to assert their right to hold peaceful processions on celebration days.

Their leader was frail and low-voiced, to outward appearance most representative of the unassuming, unassertive old type of Indian womanhood. But now the steel of unbending determination glinted through the soft enveloping folds.

On this Tilak day, August 1, Mrs. Hansa Mehta (a well-known social and educational leader, later member of an advisory committee of the Round Table Conference in London) led her defiant band, five hundred strong, with songs and banners through the streets of Bombay. Women of all ages, castes and conditions made up that throng, though the majority were young, highcaste, and educated. It was the heavy monsoon season, and even dead Tilak himself would doubtless have mourned to see his tenderest adorers out in such pelting rain.

An ever-increasing crowd of spectators lined the streets through which the women passed, and hundreds upon hundreds followed. For two whole hours the women paraded before the police received orders to stop the procession. Suddenly a wall of blue-clad, yellow-turbaned men blocked a street in front of the advancing group. Impossible to press forward and pass on. The women would not turn back. The police could not make way.

In this impasse Mrs. Mehta quietly and serenely sat down in the squashy yellow mud of the road; down sat her followers; down came the rain. The police ordered and expostulated in vain; all they could do was to shift from one foot to the other, feel uncomfortable and exasperated, and wait. For they had no orders to disperse the crowd by force. The authorities were wary and slow to act when faced by women-infringers of the law, for they feared the emotional repercussions of harsh dealings with this annoying sex.

The monsoon however seemed to side opportunely with the police and led them to expect confidently that the relentless and unusually intense downpour would soon accomplish what their verbal orders failed to do—send these silly refractory women home to dry clothes, warm shelter, fragrant curry, and children; to the homes which, but a few years ago, nothing could have induced them to leave. But in these days unheard-of things have come to pass; the world has been turning upside down, it seems. Even many of the mothers among Mrs. Mehta's followers did not go home; their babies were brought to them and fed in the street.

An hour passed, two, three—and still the women sat on. Despite the intense physical discomfort of the chilling monsoon, there they squatted, laughed, joked (even with the police) and sang, *sang* at the top of their voices, hymns, patriotic chants, and songs in memory of the patriot Tilak, far on into the sudden twilight and the deep long night.

Thousands and thousands of spectators gathered and remained to work themselves up more and more into admiration and partisanship. The realization grew that these women, soaked to the skin and chilled to the bone, were actually and seriously endangering their health. But no pleading, whether from their own supporters or from the police, could induce them to budge from their stubborn determination.

As night wore on, exhaustion and suffering became more apparent, but were borne away again and again on the wave of new outbursts of prayer and song. Many among the spectators realized in time the new mettle of these demonstrators and saw that they would not give way. These sympathizers remembered that the women had gone without food since the preceding noon. At four in the morning people appeared with great vessels of steaming coffee and served it out in leaf-cups to the squatting women, who drank together regardless of caste or creed.

Mrs. Mehta and her band were fully determined to force the issue : either acknowledgment of the right to hold peaceful processions, or arrest. When day dawned, it found them still on the same spot, hollow-eyed but undaunted. There they would have stayed on indefinitely, had not the old Congress leader, the revered Vallabhai Patel himself come in person at 6 a.m. to request them to go home, at least to change into dry clothing. As the women considered themselves in the light of Congress soldiers, they obeyed. They planned to go home in relays to eat and change, and then return again to their posts.

But meanwhile the police had received orders to disperse them by force, as the only means of preventing the demonstrators from carrying the day with ever-increasing approbation and immense triumph. A series of *lathi* charges followed, lasting for two whole hours, in which the surging, shifting crowd of spectators also came in for its share. There were numerous wounded and hundreds of arrests.

The leader, Mrs. Mehta, had gone home to change just before the news spread that a *lathi* charge was coming. The moment she was told of this new development, she went to the nearest police station and offered to surrender herself as the most responsible offender. She was refused arrest.

"For every one of us who sat there in the mud, ten are ready now to face such a task or worse, over again to-day," she asserted to me months later in a quiet London room. She did not raise her voice; it retained a low, smooth, steely coolness that bodes evil for opposing forces.

At the same time I heard of other surprising doings on the part of the women of India. Initiated by Gandhi, the Satyagraha, or soul-force movement, had captured the imagination of India's outcastes. More and more frequently organized bands of untouchables were trying at various places, by means of this non-violent protest, to compel the high castes to grant permission for the equal use of public wells, roads and access to temples. At Munshiganj untouchables had agitated and suffered for nine whole months in a campaign to gain admittance to the temple of Kali. During the scorching heat of the day, in drenching rains, they had lain in the road and made of their maltreated bodies a second living barricade before the wood-barricaded doors of the temple. But none of their suffering could move the petrified hearts of the orthodox caste men and Brahmins of the community. So finally the untouchables adopted the last resource left to Satyagrahis—the hunger strike. They vowed not to touch food or drink unless and until the gates were thrown open. This meant that continued refusal would place the blame for their death upon the heads of the heartless orthodox community. At this point an amazing thing happened. Two hundred high-caste women of the town revolted in favour of those patient sufferers, armed themselves with axes, saws and whatever tools they could lay their hands on, stormed and broke down the barriers, and threw the sacred doors of the temple wide open to the outcastes.

About the time these things took place in Bombay and Munshiganj, I heard by letter of equally astonishing changes in Calcutta, to which a previous personal experience of my own lent special colour. In 1921, after my arrival in that city, an old friend of my husband's repeatedly urged him to bring me, the foreign wife, to visit the family. My husband delayed for weeks to accede to this simple request. I then discovered that his unwillingness was in reality a half-teasing, half-resentful retaliation, induced by his irritation at the previous behaviour of his friend, Mohan. For many months Mohan himself had withheld from my husband the sight of his own wife's face. Thus I found myself in the amusingly annoying position of observing ' purdah ' for some time so far as this particular family was concerned.

The two friends, who both belonged to the Kshatriya caste, had studied together in Japan and California and had there shaken themselves free from old caste and religious limitations. Mohan, the first to return to India, in time gave way to continuous pressure by his mother and looked around for a wife. However, he had flatly stipulated that he would not marry a girl unless she was fully mature, educated to some degree at least, and unless he was given the opportunity to " have a look ". The circle which

would permit even the merest peep at an intended
bride was still very restricted in those days. But
at last news came of a girl who belonged to the
same caste (the mother's stipulation) and was " grown
up and accomplished ". So Mohan had set out on his
trip of bride-inspection. This first attempt to inau-
gurate such a modern and revolutionary marriage
arrangement within his orthodox group proved also
his last. Mohan was received in an outer room by
the grandfather. Some time later the girl herself
was summoned to appear. Mohan was dumb-
founded to see a shy little thing of at most thirteen
years come up timidly and lean against her grandfather in painful embarrassment.

" Show what you can do," she was ordered, and
she read in a halting childish voice a fable out of a
third reader. The grandfather's face beamed with
pride. He then went on to mention all the other
advantages of the prospective bride, distinctly stres-
sing her physical attractions. To lend his argument
convincing weight, he slipped his hand over the
body of the shrinking girl and gloatingly raised the
folds of her garment to show Mohan how enticing
and shapely were the slender limbs above the knee.

Mohan was speechless with embarrassment and
revolt. He ached with indignation at seeing a
child's feelings so violated, a girl shown off physically
like a young bullock for sale in the market-place, at
the shame she must feel, especially if, after all, she
were refused. Yet, with his Western ideas, he simply
could not bring himself to marry this particular,
or indeed any, child. He left as soon as he could
possibly get away without giving too much offence.
On his way home he swore that never again would

he be a party, however passive, to the humiliation by exposure and rejection of any other helpless Indian girl. Even orthodox Hindu marriage, he told his mother, seemed better than such a bastard innovation, and he asked her to go ahead with the choice and arrangement of both bride and wedding in the good old style all by herself.

Thus it came about that Mohan married a girl who had never before beheld the face of any man other than her father, brother, and nearest relative. And when my husband also returned to India, even he, close friend though he was, had not for many months been permitted to meet Mohan's wife—a situation against which he stormed as unpardonable backsliding.

But at last both friends relented, and I too met the entire family. Though wife and mother were still in purdah, big breaches had already been made in the veil in favour of a close circle of admitted friends.

Only eleven years have passed since then. In the light of that experience the news I recently had of this family, after my return to the West, was significant. Mohan, the pampered head of the household, was now coming home from a hard day's work in his factory to cook meals, feed youngsters and put them to bed himself, since every female member of the household—mother, sisters, and but lately secluded wife—were giving the whole of their time to work outside the house; in fact, to the boycott movement. All were, or had been, in jail. The old mother, over seventy years of age, was just then serving her third term; one daughter had organized a sweepers' strike. What an incredible revolution in thought and action is presented by the picture of this family alone. In the short space of eleven years, how unbelievably complete a change.

A new light this, in which Indian womanhood is to-day revealing itself in these three instances—defying the foreign government at Bombay, its own priesthood and caste system at Munshiganj, and the hoary purdah régime at Calcutta!

Our present concern is not to attempt to determine the rights or wrongs of this startling departure in the behaviour of Indian women, nor whether their insurrection against the existing order of things is justified in its objects or wise in its directions. Our purpose is to assert the facts, trace the sources, and gauge the significance of the change.

In hundreds of other families throughout the length and breadth of India, similar "incredible" changes are taking place. Tenderly nurtured women, physically under-developed because of the rigours of former seclusion, women used to soft silky garments, bejewelled, sheltered, economically dependent, women a short while ago too shy ever to speak freely to a stranger and too proud to grant a glimpse of their face even to the most august outsider—these women, dressed in plain rough garments, are now suddenly to be found in the streets of slums even, where they face staring crowds before liquor shops, plead with total strangers, brave the police and are ready to undergo unflinchingly the worst of hardships.

Such a state of affairs would have seemed unthinkable, fantastic even to imagine, a mere ten years ago. For it cannot be denied that Indian women generally have been gentle, retiring, and self-effacing to a degree unknown in the West.

Whence this astounding change?

"What are we coming to in these godless days when our very women grow shameless and unsexed?" the orthodox in India exclaim in consternation.

"What bug of perversity and subversion has bitten them?" the Westerner in India is asking in puzzled annoyance.

"What man has ever understood the conduct of woman?" moaned an ancient Hindu sage a full three thousand years ago.

It is doubtful whether then or now any comprehensive, conclusive answer could be given. Yet it is to the past indeed that we must turn to find an equivalent—in fact, any sort of satisfying explanation —of these complex, conflicting, present-day phenomena. We must recall to memory days long past, the days when Mahratta horsewomen gave dazzlingly skilful displays of mastery in riding and spearcraft, when a woman, the Rani of Jhansi, fought with ferocious valour against the British, or when the warrior queen Chand Bibi led her own army against the Mohammedan aggressor Akbar; or days even farther back, before the beginning of our own era, when a woman with a crowd of women followers defied the edict of her own town against the Buddha and sallied forth beyond its gates to greet the coming Lord.

For in the heart and brain of Indian womanhood, as elsewhere and everywhere, the shining force of life may slumber but cannot die. Ever and anon, its pent-up fountains must push through—no matter how deep the layers and accumulated weight of repression or stagnation—and reach the day, to sparkle with bubbling freshness that rejuvenates sick worlds.

Any particular incident of history, such as the present nationalist movement in India, may call forth and offer a definite field for expression to such pent-up forces, but it is not their actual cause.

For the past few centuries the womanhood of India has lain under the pall of a deep degraded slumber, kept down to some degree by a foreign government, but far more so by the weight of Indian custom. But for over half a century now, especially during the last ten years, and most of all in the two years just gone by, there has been a tremendous stirring in the mighty limbs of Mother India, a quickening and awakening of momentous promise. Nor is this all ; our day witnesses the most significant rousing of the consciousness of women in the history of the entire Orient.

It is a spectacle of confusing vastness and untold possibilities, this movement in India, embracing as it does an agglomeration of women of endlessly varied races, religions, tongues, of every degree of domestic and social development. It affects, and will continue to affect in ever-increasing intensity, women of the highest caste and culture, women who are illiterates, and those who still live in appallingly primitive conditions.

To understand, even in a small degree, the significance of the present-day women's movement in India, it is quite indispensable to reach back to the roots and origin of her race. In spite of Tacitus' emphatic witness to the independence, pride, and high standing of the women of the Germani, it may not be absurd to assert that no woman in all antiquity stood higher, or was surrounded by a richer mental and spiritual background, than the Aryan woman of ancient India. Though she stands to-day degraded, amidst clashing influences, old and new, from East and West, the Indian woman's fate and future, while stimulated by the recent influx of ideas and customs from the Occident, does not depend on that, but is deep-rooted, traceable, and predictable in the light of Indian history alone. More than in the case of any other people, the Indian woman's development has its roots in, is now feeling after, and will continue to express itself within, the currents of the ancient, exalted, religious and ethical conceptions of her race.

II

THE FREEDOM OF THE VEDIC PERIOD

To Brahma one single day comprises four billion three hundred and twenty millions of human years ; three hundred and sixty such days make up one single year of Brahma.

In such vast terms has the Indian mind been accustomed to view the life of man on earth and his slow evolution in an immense upward curve towards ultimate attainment and complete conscious identification with godhead. The life of man, like that of all things created, is merely Brahma realizing himself through extraversion ; therefore, at all points and in all stages, from stone to sage, divinity is immanent in all created things. Only after one hundred of Brahma's incomprehensibly immense years have passed comes the end of all experience, of existence, of time.

Underlying all the apparent fatalism of India, so much criticized by Westerners, there rests this tranquil lake of profound optimism, based on ultimate religious trust and faith ; this realization of the imminence of divinity in all life on earth, be its fugitive appearance good or evil. The Indian knows that the wheels of God grind slowly ; he also knows that they never cease turning and may not be hurried by the fretting will of man.

From time immemorial vast changes have swept over India, great conquests and civilizations, of which we have traces (still only partly deciphered at Mohenjo-Daro) that reach back even beyond the famous Aryan invasion that happened more than 3,500 years ago. The philosophic conception of life evolved in India from earliest days has proved itself of such tremendous underlying force, resistance, and elasticity, that it has withstood shock after shock of alien onslaught of life and thought through its power to adopt, absorb and surmount them. Dravidian, Mongol, Aryan, Greek, Scythian, Hun, Persian, Dutch, Portuguese, French, English—wave after wave of new invasion has broken against her shores, flooded her plains and valleys, without ever finally subduing, or even submerging for long, the individualistic stamp of culture that is India.

Thousands, both of foreigners and of India's own, have tried to interpret the ever-changing elusive flash of her life, refracted from millions of facets, to the Western world—every possible degree of truth and untruth about India has found expression. It is useless to pick out any particular isolated period in her development and to compare it, whether to her favour or disfavour, with conditions existing contemporaneously in some other part of the world. That leads only to fruitless and endless wrangling, or to pointing out by way of retort (as has been done in answer to Miss Mayo's wholesale indictments) the many blemishes of Western civilization. To lead to any understanding that is even approximately true, India's development as a historic whole must be kept in view, and the slow steady factor of time.

If we cannot tear ourselves away from comparisons

when studying the degraded state of Indian women of to-day, this time factor will make us bear in mind for instance, that less than a hundred years ago about ninety thousand English women between the ages of eleven and eighteen still worked in British factories for ninety hours per week. This may help us to return in a chastened frame of mind to Indian history and search after the reasons of the peculiar condition existing at present in India : deep physical and mental degradation of women in actual life side by side with a high idealization of womanhood in abstract thought.

To go back to the beginning of that first vast day of creation, Brahma, " seeing that the men fashioned on earth were lonely, further created that being who steals away a man's reason, yet is half of his personality —woman ". Then followed the days when gods still walked with men and were invoked " with the tenderness which a husband has for his wife " or " the faith which a wife has in her husband ", and when such " prayers of mortals became the spouses of gods ". Such men and women, living in close and reverent communion with the deified forces of nature, poured down, 3,500 years ago, as Aryan conquerors through the passes of the Himalayas into the fertile Indian plains. In hymns incomparable for their age and dignity they embodied their conception of the universe, their adoration, their life. They built no temples and worshipped no images ; their unsheltered altars were erected on the tops of mountains, a fact which in itself speaks volumes for the high dignity of that ancient worship.

Significant is the place given to female deities in this ancient worship, an honour equal to, if not exceeding, that of the gods. From the very dawn of Indian philosophy—embodied in the hymn known as the *Rig-veda*—the conception of the *duality*, male-female, of divinity held sway. Each god was closely linked with his *shakti*, or female principle; the god was energy, the goddess the form through which alone it could pour itself out and find expression; "... the female principle went forth throughout the universe as the abiding force of the creator in the world. ..." " Aum " is the mystic logos, and voice or speech is a goddess, the wife of the creator. It is she who sounds throughout the universe, whose vibration has created all things—" in unison with whom and by whom the creator accomplishes his creation ". The feminine principle is adored under many forms in Vedic days. We find the goddess *Indrani* exclaiming proudly, " I am the victorious one; may my husband recognize my strength, O gods! It is I who made the sacrifice from which the great and glorious Indra deriveth all his strength." Again, it is *Aditi* who embodies the whole realm of nature and is the " common mother of gods and men ".

Under whatever aspect the ancient Aryans worshipped the mysterious forces of nature, the feminine principle always received its more than generous share of adoration. The idea of all-encompassing motherhood as the highest principle was firmly accepted in Vedic times, transmitted to all later periods, and has throughout all ages formed the basis of the exceptional degree of reverence paid in India to the *mother*. This aspect is the clue for the deciphering of the reasons for the present-day attitude of Indian men towards their women.

But although modern Indian men still worship feminine divinities, and easily express themselves in mystic ecstasy over mother-worship, few among them have cared to follow that guiding thread to any practical purpose. Though the Vedas are still considered among the most sacred books of India, and as revealed scriptures their lesson concerning the true place of woman has been lost treasure until very recent days. Yet a thrill of mingled shame and pride will flash through Indian veins—shame for the present and pride of the past—once the significance of Vedic life and teaching is again universally revealed. For the Vedas speak of a life of freedom and strength lived by men and women as equal partners in a great task of home and nation building. In those days women were absolutely free to take part in every aspect of the mental and spiritual life of the race. It is known that they were even among the composers of the great sacred chants, the Vedas themselves. Women could also take part jointly with men in the performance of all religious ceremonies. Not only this, but women in Vedic times even had the right of offering the great horse sacrifice—that most exalted of religious functions—on their own initiative and in their own name. At a little later period, when a whole clan participated in sacrificial worship, it was the wife of the officiating priest who, after the fire was lit, advanced with female attendants to decorate the altar with garlands of flowers. Also at festivals, in kingly ceremonies, everywhere woman took an equally honourable part with man.

It is no wonder that in a society which pays high honour to goddesses in genuine worship, woman in the flesh should also fare well, unless and until some special corrupting influence should creep in. Such an influence was later to manifest itself in the Brahminic priesthood, but early Vedic days were free from its taint. Woman stood unfettered and high both in the home and in the communal life ; no slur attached to either sex as such. The earliest sages of India declared that " then only is a man perfect when he consists of three persons united, his wife, himself, and his son ". In the light of so high a conception of the closest of human ties do we first meet the Vedic family. Within it, the universally admitted teacher is woman. She was considered pre-eminently fit to impart religious instruction to her children. The Vedas give us further revealing glimpses ; nowhere in all these hymns is there even the faintest suggestion of the existence of any seclusion of women, or of child marriage. Monogamy was the prevailing condition of the married state ; lack of sons in high families alone led to isolated cases of polygamy. *Swayamvara*—the free choice of a husband by a grown maiden—was the accepted rule.

It is especially in the Vedic marriage rites which have been recorded for us in these ancient hymns that we fully realize what a high conception was held of the sacredness of marriage and the dignified estate of woman as an equal, beloved partner. The Vedic marriage-rites take their place among the highest and purest ceremonies ever drawn up and performed by mankind. Bride and groom were joined in the presence of their entire group before an altar erected in the open. The priest prayed over the maiden and offered her the sacred fire, which she was henceforth to tend. Then he pronounced a benediction over the joined hands of man and maiden. The husband addressed his wife : " I take thy right hand as a pledge for our happiness ; I wish thee to become my wife

and to grow old with me; the gods gave thee to me
to rule over our house together. May the head of
creation grant us a numerous race; may Aryaman
prolong our life. Enter under happy auspices the
conjugal home. May there be happiness in our home
for both humans and animals. . . . Come, O
desired one, beautiful one with the tender heart,
with the charming look, good towards thine husband, kind towards animals, destined to bring forth
heroes."

The priest then turned to her assembled people,
and pointed to the bride, saying: "Approach her,
look at her, wish her well, and return to your own
homes."

Upon arrival at the husband's house, now the joint
home of both, new ceremonies blessed her coming.
As she crossed the threshold she was addressed,
"Here may delight be thine through wealth and
progeny. Give this house thy watchful care. May
man and beast increase and prosper. Free from the
evil eye, not lacking wedded love, bring good luck
even to the four-footed beasts, thou gentle of mind,
bright of countenance, bearing heroes, honouring the
gods, dispenser of joy. Live with thy husband and
in old age mayest thou still rule thy household.
Remain here now, never to depart; enjoy the full
measure of thy years playing with sons and grandsons.
Be glad of heart within thy house."

After the bride had thus been admitted to her new
home with so dignified a welcome, the priest blessed
the family hearth: "Remain here, do not depart from
it, but pass your lives together, happy in your home,
playing with your children and grandchildren . . . O
generous Indra, make her fortunate! May she have

a beautiful family, may she give her husband ten children! May he himself be like an eleventh!"

What could be more tender than this concluding sentence! Or what more indicative of the fundamental Aryan attitude towards woman as *ma*, the *mother*,—even to her husband!

Another extract from the marriage ceremonies gives us further enlightment as to the secure position of the new wife within the joint family system which she has entered as a member: ". . . reign with thy father-in-law, reign with thy mother-in-law, reign with thy husband's sisters, reign with their brothers." Here, though no direct reference to the property rights of women is found in the Vedas, is a clear indication that marriage in no sense entailed irksome dependence or lack of opportunity to attain inner growth through responsibility on the part of the woman, nor even a trace of that abject subjection to a husband found in later times.

Widows could and did marry again if they so chose.

The Vedic age was also quite free from the taint of widow immolation. No *satis* are anywhere mentioned, no widows burned themselves on the funeral pyres of their husbands. On the contrary, the Vedas quote a priest at the burial of a man turning to the widow with this consolation: ". . . return to the home where thou mayest still find life awaiting thee. Find in the children who are left to thee him who lives no longer!" While to the dead man the priest speaks these beautiful words of farewell: "Go, seek the Earth, that wise and good mother of all. O Earth, rise up and do not hurt his bones; be kind and gentle to him. O Earth, cover him as a mother covers her infant with the skirts of her garment."—

So even in death we find the Indian hunger for the mother !

Liberal scholars and Indian reformers point to all the above-mentioned outstanding facts to prove their contention that nowhere in the actual life of Vedic days can any trace of the subjection or seclusion of womanhood be found, nor the faintest endorsement thereof in its religious teachings and philosophy. These reformers urge a return to the Vedas as the unpolluted and most sacred source of Hinduism, the repository of India's true revealed wisdom.

Present-day orthodoxy and the priesthood likewise are very apt at quoting sacred authority, but they do so in order to enforce the perpetuation of social iniquities and the latter-day degradation of women. For them, the Vedas are unfruitful trees ; they needs must quote the arbitrary laws formulated by Brahminism in post-Vedic days, the words of priests who had lost both vision and reverence, and had become corrupted and drunk with power.

III

RESTRICTIONS ON WOMAN'S FREEDOM: LAWS OF MANU

EVEN during Vedic days, Aryan society had become organized into caste divisions on lines of work, descent and colour. Highest among these stood the Brahmins or priests, who were arrogating to themselves supreme virtues and powers, claiming to an ever-increasing degree the right to act as sole intermediaries between gods and men, and to be the ultimate arbiters of religious, moral and social life. Monopoly of sacred lore, specialization of work, religious tabus were their high-road to power.

In the period which followed the great Vedic days, under this growing influence and ascendancy of the priests, society lost its homogeneity, religion its spontaneous quality of genuine worship. The latter turned into a vast mass of ritual, on the proper observance of which depended the fate of man. The Brahmin was becoming the acknowledged guardian of all things spiritual, and as such claimed and obtained supreme honour as well as material sustenance from all the lower castes. Through the mouth of the Brahmins the gods revealed that the one unforgivable sin on earth was the killing of a priest; whosoever should dare even to revile a Brahmin was " to have

his shoulder-blades smitten off, to be flayed alive, his
flesh cut in pieces, and be slain by a hundred-pointed
thunderbolt ''.

Next to the Brahmin stood the Kshatriya, the warrior and ruler, a high and noble status in a conquering
and expanding society, whose position and esteem
rested on valour and utility, instead of on artifically
fostered prerogatives such as those of the Brahmins.
It is in this caste that we find woman retaining longest
the impress of her free Vedic origin.

Below these was the third and last 'white' group
of castes, the Vayshiyas, peasants and traders.   This
completed the group of the twice-born, the members
of the Aryan invading race.   Still lower than these
was the vast mass of the Sudras, or labourers, drawn
from the dark conquered races.

Membership of these castes was hereditary.   During the *Brahminical Period* were laid down laws which
minutely regulated the rights, limits and work of the
numerous sub-castes as well as their interrelations
with the other castes.   But there remained one group
which still retained uncertain and incalculable elements,
that might, because of their emotional potency, at any
time prove a danger to the priestly power unless
hedged in and subdued by yet more special restrictions.
The Brahmins realized that their greatest rival in
influence and spiritual power was woman, especially
so long as she still remained surrounded by that double
halo—the mystery of her own life-bearing sex, and
this enhanced and sanctified by the ancient worship
of the female aspect of deity.   There could be no
uncontested or secure supremacy for Brahmins until
woman lost her high estate, stood degraded and
branded as an inferior being in the eyes of men, and

was moulded into a mindless slave to religious dictation.

The first step towards achieving this was to inculcate into the minds of fathers and husbands doubts and fears as to the wisdom of continuing to initiate women into the religious mysteries and the doctrines of philosophy. So began the slow, persistent and at last completely successful effort of the priests to wrest from woman her religious and cultural rights, her social and domestic equality and power. It was the unrolling in India—with variations peculiar to her—of the world-wide story of the struggle, unconscious, undefined and unacknowledged, yet none the less actual, between priest and woman to retain ascendancy over man,—a struggle that has its beginning in subterranean currents which probably modern research and sex psychology can alone fathom and interpret.

The Brahmins had not only regulated the position and work of each individual by restricting him to the caste into which he was born, but they also divided his life into four sections. The first was the period of study, of preparation for his work within his caste ; the second was that of the householder, or married state, with its necessary domestic and social functions, whose complete fulfilment was demanded ; third came the time of withdrawal from worldly concerns, of spiritual search, of retreat to the forest ; the last stage was that of the attainment of spiritual freedom, the complete conquest of all desire. The stage of retreat to the forest could be undertaken by husband and wife together, if their spiritual aims were similar, but the last road had to be walked alone.

There was a two-fold significance in this conception

of the progressive development of life by successive stages ; first, it fully recognized that a definite period of life is to be given over to sex and family experience as a matter of sanctified necessity and desirable growth. This saved India from a celibate priesthood with its concomitant contempt of sex and worship of virginity ; furthermore, the demand that the latter half of life should be spent away from worldly pursuits and in attaining freedom from all desire, made sex the strongest and most dreaded antagonist to be overcome within oneself.   So sex, with its stress on motherhood as its highest expression, always remained on the one hand a sanctified principle worthy of worship ; on the other it became the dragon in the path to final attainment.   Thus considered, it was but a step to further development, to reach on the one side an accentuated adoration of the female principle in divinity with its inherent tendency to ecstatic spiritual uplift, and on the other to accelerate the process of rendering powerless and degrading the woman of flesh and blood.

Certain it is that wife-degradation and mother-worship progressed hand in hand in Brahminical times and thenceforward throughout the following centuries down to our day.

The more the living woman was being deprived of freedom of thought and movement, and the dignified consideration that had been hers in Vedic times, the more did men and priests appear to be moved by an uneasy, unformulated feeling that the goddess in heaven and woman in the flesh might after all make common cause against the aggressor.

This restless uneasiness in turn seemed to drive men all the more back into the arms of the *physical mother*, that for ever sustaining and forgiving being, and to a very worship of her. This was carried to such a point that to address any woman as " ma " became the highest form of honour that could be paid her. But this did not prevent " ma " from being subject to the full force of laws discriminating against women ! It was during the Brahminical Period we are now considering that a number of lawgivers arose who crystallized all the repressive tendencies into such fixed laws and attempted to secure for these latter an ever-widening acceptance. They provided merciless punishments for their transgression, the most dreaded of which was that of being expelled from one's caste,— which implied virtually living death. But the power of resistance to priestly encroachment which lay hid in Vedic ideals was strong, and reflected itself even in the lawmaking. Never did lawgivers within one nation and period formulate more contradictory laws ! These mirror with surprising clarity the struggle going on between old free customs and new fear-born priest-initiated repression.

Most famous among these lawgivers was *Manu* to whom is attributed a code of laws which are most likely a compilation from various sources. Manu's original *Dharma Sutra* is lost, but a later compilation was made a few centuries before our era. It is Manu's code that has had the most negative effects, forging unbreakable shackles on Indian women for countless succeeding generations. Even to-day, it is his laws which keep millions helpless in the prison of Hindu orthodoxy. Manu for the first time legally assigned to woman her definite place in the scale of society. But his laws reflect a conflict even within himself between his valuation of woman as a spiritual entity

on the one side, and as a unit in society on the other.
He averred that a mother is more to be revered than
a thousand fathers, yet his laws place woman socially
on a level with the lowest of all groups in Aryan
society, the Sudra.

Manu starts with categorical "thou shalt nots"—
those sure signs of inner uncertainty.   First and most
important—Manu deprives woman of her power and
dignity as priestess and worshipper.   He lays it down
that no religious fast or ceremony or sacrifice shall
concern woman by herself, as apart from man;   she
must reach heaven henceforth only through service
to her husband.   She is to have no more direct dealings with godhead;   her husband is to be her supreme
guru (teacher) in all things;   she is never to falter in
her allegiance to him, to attain the highest virtue
only through implicit obedience to his wishes or
commands—be they good or evil, be the husband
"debauched or devoid of all virtues".   "If a wife
obey her husband, she will for this alone be exalted
in heaven."   In fact, woman is to regard and worship
her husband "as her god".   The *Skandá Purana* goes
even farther than Manu and enjoins: "Should a
woman still wish to perform religious ablutions herself,
she is to wash the feet of her husband and drink the
water"!   In any case, woman could not obtain
heaven through any merit of her own;   it was hers
only through her husband and as reward for having
duly worshipped him as a god on earth.   So deeply
ingrained did this belief become in later times that
even to-day orthodox Hindu women quite generally
perform the ceremony of "taking the dust of the
lotus feet" of their lords as their first act of worship
on rising each morning.   They would be shocked

beyond expression were the tables suddenly turned some merry morning, and the husband attempted to touch their feet instead!

Yet Manu, seemingly, does think of honouring women. He says that at times of ceremonies and festivals " they are ever to be honoured by gifts of ornaments, clothes and food ". We cannot help but suspect that this generous consideration is merely intended to make woman forget—as one gives a sweet to a hurt or fretting child—that she may no longer take a direct part in worship on such occasions. Though her own ancestress actually composed some of the Vedas, she is not even permitted to study them —to " Sudras, women and servants " they are sealed henceforth. Nor are the Vedas to be used any more by or for her in religious ceremonies.

The bright sacrificial fire of spiritual aspiration has indeed been trimmed and dimmed to a small and weakly hearth glow, and woman's whole concern from now on is to tend this.

But not only are her spiritual aspirations henceforth to flow exclusively through channels of masculine appointment, but to Manu and the priests of his time it seemed equally essential to curb her power of independent decision and freedom of will in all worldly things. He lays down the rule that girls and women of all ages are under no condition whatever, at any time or place, to act for their own mere pleasure; they are always to be dependent upon the nearest male relative or, failing him, upon the king. They are to be guarded day and night, as the only unfailing means to ensure purity of offspring, the belief being apparently current which a later writer so neatly expressed, that " neither shame, nor decorum, nor honesty, nor timidity, but the want of a suitor alone, is the cause of a woman's chastity".

No wonder then that we find the further injunction that woman is never to govern herself or manage her own affairs, nor is she to have a free hand in domestic expenditure. Even a grown son is to have power to rule his mother.

Such strict rules fully reveal how well aware was the great lawgiver of woman's disturbing emotional influence. Yet another of Manu's laws indicates that he dreads weakness even more in another aspect, though his restrictions make the woman alone pay the penalty : " One should not be seated in a secluded place with mother, sister, or daughter—the powerful senses compel even a wise man ! "

It is extremely interesting to follow Manu in the formulation of his laws of marriage. Here also, the positive lawgiver, concerned first and foremost with the cornering of power for the male, is swayed none the less by those haunting religious conceptions handed down from Vedic times which conceived of the deepest creative powers of the universe as acting only through the shape of the *mother*—that " goddess, mother of all things, supremely worshipped ". He starts with a propitiating compliment—" A spiritual teacher exceeds a worldly teacher ten times, a father exceeds a spiritual teacher one hundred times, but a mother exceeds one thousand times a father's claim to honour on the part of a child and as its educator."

But after this Manu merrily proceeds with his restrictions. Before the Brahminical period, members of various castes might still intermarry. Now Manu lays down the law that men may marry only those of equal rank, though they may still take as second wife a woman of lower caste. Woman is given no such privilege. He grants legality only to those marriages for which the girl obtains the consent of father or brother, with a single exception in favour of the warrior. Probably owing to the special exigencies of a society still expanding by means of conquest, the Kshatriya still retains his ancient right to contract a valid marriage by mere exchange of mutual vows. But in the case of all other forms of marriage, the woman's consent was no longer necessary. Parents now had the right to marry off their children, and were permitted to betrothe a girl even before her eighth year. Not only this, but Manu makes it legal for a man of thirty to marry a girl of twelve, or a man of twenty-four a girl of eight.

Manu recognized eight kinds of marriage as valid. In the first four of these the maiden was given away by her father with the usual rites ; the fifth was that based on mutual love ; the others were, where a price was demanded and taken by the father, forcible abduction and sexual intercourse " with a sleeping or unconscious woman ". The first four of these are fully approved by the lawgiver, the fifth is tolerated, the last three are disapproved, but retain claim to recognition ; and this is a measure of real protection for women.

Manu gives a husband the right to repudiate his wife for very trifling offences, but lays down the rule —retained to this day—that a Hindu wife can under no condition escape from the marriage bond. That affection, however, cannot be compelled, even Manu recognizes when he asks that in the case of a woman who " hates her husband " he should " wait one year . . . before repudiating her ". The lawgiver also relents somewhat in the case of a virtuous but unloved wife ; such a one is not to be sent away from the protection of the husband's roof. This of course implies that while the husband has the right to turn to another woman, the unloved wife must abstain from sexual activity for the rest of her life, or lose protection and security.

Manu, however, exhorts to mutual loyalty between husband and wife " where possible ", and even goes to the extent of saying that he considers perpetual celibacy preferable to a misfit union. He also assures a husband and wife who rightfully discharge their marital duties here on earth, that they shall not be parted even by death and shall be together in the world beyond. He does not state whether the wife will continue to wash her husband's feet there !

Besides giving a husband the right to repudiate an unloved wife almost at will, definite rules for special cases are laid down. A man might remarry if his wife " plagued him, wasted his money, was diseased, drank, opposed him, was sinful ". Surely a wide enough range of excuses for getting rid of an unwanted wife ; modern Reno has scarcely improved on this.

Since childlessness was considered to be the fruit of evil Karma accumulated in a previous existence, a barren wife might be repudiated in her eighth year, it being always taken for granted that the fault lay with her. A mother who had borne girls alone might be replaced in her eleventh year ; a mother whose children had all died, in her tenth.

Manu's laws established polygamy as a fully recognized institution. Where plurality of wives had until then been a very isolated phenomenon, the zenana now came into existence in most of the houses of the great, and grew to be the earmark of distinction and worldly power. Life in the zenana gave rise to that crop of great stories which fill the treasure-house of Indian literature to overflowing and leave so vivid a picture of those ancient days; stories of endless feminine scheming and intrigue, of rivalry, poison and sudden death, but also of great sorrow nobly borne, of sublime patience, devotion and self-abnegation.

There are other aspects of interest in Manu's laws relating to marriage. He permits a husband to strike his wife with a cord or a bamboo cane. He does not specify the thickness of the cane, but he stipulates that she is not to be struck " on any noble part ", but only on her back. It is, however, both refreshing and amusing to note that Manu " doubts the efficacy of such procedure ". Still, he was not averse to the experiment being made.

Manu considers the endless round of family and motherhood tasks, more efficacious than his own laws, the best means of ensuring a woman's virtue and of binding her to the home.

Since the husband is god to his wife, it is not fit that she eat with him. Her sons will not be born strong if she dare forget her place and eat in his presence. Manu enjoins that a woman must eat only after having served her husband; food left by him is *prasad*, bread of the gods; hence even to-day women frequently eat from what is left on the husband's plate, or still more often do not touch food till noon or later, because some man or even boy of the household has not been in for his.

Many other laws are concerned with the question of ceremonial purity. Those affecting women at the time of parturition have had a most evil effect, and are still working infinite harm to-day upon the majority of Indian women. Woman was declared unclean during childbirth and her touch inflicted pollution. For this reason none but the lowest of caste women, dirty and ignorant, would consent to be birth-helpers.

When Manu comes to the matter of children, he grows more tender. Here he gives the mother her innate rights, and places the nurture of her offspring entirely in her hands. He enjoins that children are to render to mother and father equal obeisance, love and respect. Legal guardianship, however, is the mother's under certain circumstances only, but she has joint power to arrange a daughter's marriage. Yet, though Manu did not omit to give most precise instructions concerning the education which men of the three upper castes were to receive, he refrains completely from any mention even of the need for education of women who, as mothers, are to nurture children and thereby to mould the men of the race. Of all Manu's sins of commission and omission, this withholding of education from women is one of the worst.

In Vedic days not only could and did the widow remarry, but the *Niyoga* union even permitted a widow without remarrying, if she so chose, to " produce two sons for herself and two for each of four other (presumably childless) men ". Manu, however, expressly forbids remarriage to the widow; he threatens infringement with the opprobrium of society and curses it with the everlasting ruin of the soul. After the death of her husband, a widow may not even presume to mention the name of another man; she is to renounce sex for the rest of her life, and is to mortify her flesh by rigid asceticism, and live on "fruits, roots, and flowers". Should she, despite these prohibitions, yet dare to become unfaithful to her dead husband, she is to meet with harsh blame and persecution on earth and the dread loss of her place by the side of her husband in heaven. Hence the millions of widows' lives shorn of vital interest, the death by poison and the leap into the well of later days!

But credit is at least due to Manu for not authorizing the terrible practice of a widow's turning *Sati* through immolation.

Before Manu's time, the remarriage of women had been permissible in the following cases; if the husband were lost, dead, impotent, expelled from caste, or became a religious ascetic. But from now on marriage, for woman, was to be an inviolable and indissoluble sacrament. Yet even Manu could not entirely refuse to allow for human failings. He no longer sanctions remarriage, but excuses a woman's adultery if her husband be insane, degraded, impotent, castrated, or sexually diseased; but not if he be 'merely' a drunkard or invalid, or if he neglect her. If, in these last instances, a wife commits adultery, the husband is not to have the right to reject her wholly, but may "neglect her for three months". Thus we have here the curious situation of denial of remarriage, but acceptance and excuse of adultery; hardly a progressive step.

There are still other aspects of the relationship between man and woman of which this amazing lawgiver treats. An earlier legislator, Narada, had already demanded that man be tested for virility before being given a wife in marriage. Manu, who drew up many laws highly valuable for their hygienic content, here also lays down others with a definitely eugenic bearing. Let him who marries " avoid such families as neglect religious rites, have no males, which possess not the Vedas, whose members are hairy, have piles, are afflicted with consumption, dyspepsia, epilepsy, leprosy " ; moreover, let a man " not marry a tawny (dark ?) maiden, or one without hair or with too much, or a chatterbox (!) or one red (-eyed or -haired) or one called after a star, tree or river, a bird, snake or slave, or one with a terrifying name ". (Let the name " of a woman be easy to pronounce, soft, clear, agreeable, propitious ; let it terminate in long vowels and resemble words of benediction ! ") " Let him marry a well-formed woman with a lucky name who walks like a swan or an elephant (sign of stately grace), with slender locks and teeth and a soft body."

By providing for rigid caste exclusiveness, Manu has already guarded against undesirable intermarriage, but here we have further definite proof that the white Aryan was opposed to an intermingling of his blood with that of the various aboriginal races of Mongolian or Dravidian stock. Manu's injunction may have been especially intended for the Kshatriya, the warrior.

Manu also precisely defined the property rights of woman. She is to hold so-called *sixfold property* in her own inalienable right, these being wedding gifts, bridal procession gifts, love gifts, gifts from brother, mother, father. Any property which she may receive as a gift after her wedding from either family or from her husband, is also hers. All such special property is inheritable in the first instance by

her children, secondly by her husband, thirdly by her
father's family. Yet Manu elsewhere decrees that
wife, son, and slave are to have no property ; the
wealth which they acquire or earn is for him to whom
they belong.

Content with having put woman in her place,
unable probably to foresee how later centuries would
make his laws weigh on the neck of women as the
harshest yoke ever wrought, Manu does not fail to
propitiate the female principle once more. "Where-
ever women are honoured," he states, "there the
divinities are pleased ; but where they are not
honoured, all religious worship is fruitless. Where
such homage has been withheld, there houses are
cursed by the women of the family and perish
utterly as if wiped out by great magic."

What depths of contradiction lie hid in the laws of
those times ! Nothing better exemplifies the existence
of two currents flowing down side by side through
the centuries—on one side that of the free, high Vedic
tradition, on the other that of a highly intuitive intellectual priesthood out for absolute power—than the
following two delightfully revealing examples which
we quote in conclusion. It will be recalled that
Manu granted the husband the unfettered right to
give his wife a sound thrashing whenever he might
choose to think she needed one ; but another contemporary lawgiver admonished men : "Do not
strike your wife even with a flower, though she be
guilty of a hundred faults ! "

This explains why, in the great epic days of the
Ramayana and the *Mahabharata*, which do not precede,
but follow, Manu's law-making, we yet find those
grand legends full of the most sublime stories of

womanly love, grace, and conjugal devotion ; peerless pictures of female heroism and tenderness, and even of free independence, as well as of high attainment in scholarship and the arts.

IV

WOMEN IN EPIC DAYS

LUCKILY it took many centuries for Brahminical power to consolidate. The differing strata of Aryan society submitted to varying degrees, but the great masses of non-Aryan people came hardly at all under direct Brahminical influence and retained to a large extent their own animistic beliefs. This meant a very unequal diffusion of Brahminical influence through the already conquered sections. On the other hand, Aryan life itself became affected to a certain extent by the faiths and customs prevailing among the conquered races. To check the spreading of Brahminism still further, other foreign invaders occasionally swept down into India from the North-West, leaving traces of their influence. So the attempt to enforce universal acceptance of Brahminical laws, such as Manu's, met with numberless obstacles.

The greatest check came from the warrior caste, not so much in the form of any clearly conscious or concerted opposition, but because the spirit and courage which had carved out the Aryan kingdom did not easily bend even under a priestly yoke. While the Brahmins were doing their best to make the living Vedic faith a thing of dead routine, the Kshatriyas still held to the right to develop independent philosophical thought, to exercise criticism, and to take part in dialectic disputes. While under Brahmin influence harsh laws were passed denying women all right of mental training, we still find woman taking an active part at kingly courts and in intellectual life. Even among the Brahmins themselves there were still those who held on to the old Vedic forms of free aspiration and defied the lawmakers of later periods. Thus we find the great sage Yajnavalkya giving his wife the highest instruction in religion and philosophy, and considering it no diminution of his dignity to dispute publicly on an absolutely equal footing with the redoubtable woman dialectician, Gargi, over the profoundest philosophical problems. We also find that the women of royal houses still retain the right of succession to the throne, that women are known as poets and painters, and one even as a great mathematician and writer on logic; that they sing, dance, and play musical instruments, and that young girls of high birth are permitted to act in social plays such as those of Kalidasa.

This vivid and spirited life of the Kshatriyas found perfect expression in the literature of the great epics and a little later in the classical drama. These depict for us types of the highest and noblest womanhood. No literature of any race or epoch is richer in such records. The two great epics, the *Mahabharata* and the *Ramayana*, contain inexhaustible semi-mythical semi-historical material in tales that centre around great dynasties, their wars and victories. They show us an India which, a thousand years before our era, had already attained a very high peak of culture—beautifully planned cities such as Ayodhya, artistry and elegance in dress and adornment, brilliant pageants and tournaments in which learning, moral and intellectual achievement ranked even higher than physical development and prowess at arms. Though Draupadi, daughter of the king of Panchala, is promised to Arjuna, the wielder of a magic bow, other suitors for the hands of high-born maidens are still often required to pass tests of intelligence and accomplishment. Maidens still choose their own mates freely, even against the will of their parents, as did the famous heroine Savitri. When death took away her beloved husband, she followed undaunted, until her devotion, astuteness, and unanswerable arguments trapped death itself into surrendering his victim. A lovely story of outwitting the very gods is also told of the princess Damayanti who had set her heart on a certain suitor. During her *Swayamvara*—the rite of choosing a husband from among an assembled group of suitors by throwing a garland around his neck—the gods themselves, enamoured of Damayanti's beauty, came down to earth to defeat her choice. They assumed the exact appearance of Nala, the favoured suitor, even to the holding of a fresh lotus blossom in one hand, and sat on the right and left of him in a long row so that none of the onlookers were able to single out the human lover. But instead of a flustered and hopelessly discountenanced bride, the assembled multitude saw Damayanti step up at the appointed moment with graceful poise and unhesitatingly throw the garland over the right wooer's shoulder. She alone had been keen enough to perceive that one single lotus out of the many in the hands of the row of wooers was drooping slightly and her quick intuition had leapt to the conclusion that a lotus could wilt only at a human touch ! Many are the stories which tell of the dignified gentleness, tact, gracious beauty and accomplishments of the women of the epic period, and of the loftiness of mind among men. One story eloquently shows us this spirit still prevailing in Kshatriya society. The wife of a fallen king, whose husband had deserved death and been justly struck down, unhesitatingly lifts up her tiny orphan son in her arms and holds him out towards the conqueror : " . . . let the child of thy fallen foe be defended by thee ; let him become as thy own son." The answer comes immediately from the victor, " Yes, he who was Srigala's son shall become mine," and he himself crowns the son of his fallen enemy.

The relationship between fathers and sons also still often stood on a spontaneous and tender basis, free from the stain of enforced respect and ceremonial touching of feet in salutation, and from the unquestioning obedience which the Brahminical system sought to impose. One ancient writer exclaims charmingly, " than for a son, *even though he be covered with dust*, to run to his father and embrace him, what greater pleasure can exist ? "

The relationship between husband and wife likewise is still one of confidence, trust and joy. " . . . consumed by the troubles of the soul, afflicted by reverses, men find pure delight in their wives, as creatures suffering from heat find it in the freshness of water."

In the immortal story of Sakuntala, the heroine further defines this high ideal. The wife . . .

" is an object of honour in the house ; it is she who rears the children. The bride is the breath of life to her husband, and she is all devotion to her master. She is the half of man, the best of his friends, the source

of well-being, wealth and happiness, the root of the
family and of its perpetuity . . . sweet-spoken wives are
ever partakers in joy, ministering helpers in hours of
sorrow and sickness . . . men who have wives accomplish well the sacred ceremonies and fulfil the duties of
head of the house . . . such men are filled with joy and
the happiness of salvation is assured to them. Wives
are friends in the wilderness, giving consolation by their
gentle discourse ; they are like fathers in the serious
duties of life, they become like mothers in times of distress . . . whoever has a wife is sure of support ; that
is why wives offer the best of refuge in life."

Sakuntala, the forest-reared maiden, that "lotus
in water, sparkling flame of life ", had married for
love by a mere exchange of vows. Beautiful words
of sanction were spoken over her union : " a soul
unites itself by love to another; a soul finds refuge
in another ; a soul gives itself to another ; such is the
rule traced out for thee by divine law ". What a
difference between the spirit of this union and present-
day marriage in India !

In those olden days married devotion was carried
to heights which to us moderns seem almost fantastic,
such as certainly no Brahminical edict could ever
ensure. Only love freely given and steadied by a
profound understanding and sympathy could have
induced Queen Gandhari to go through life with
voluntarily bandaged eyes because she did not wish to
enjoy a privilege denied to her blind husband.

The epic of the *Ramayana* depicts the type of wife-
hood that was the flowering of the Vedic ideal. It is
doubtful whether any other single character in all the
world's literature has had such immense formative
influence upon endless generations as that of Sita.

Even to-day, Sita is held up to every girl in India as the supreme model for her to emulate.

The tale, briefly told, is this. The old king Dasaratha is tricked into promising to Kaikeyi, a younger wife, that her own son Bharata shall inherit the throne instead of the legitimate heir Rama, son by the first wife Kausalya. In addition, Rama is to be banished to the forest for fourteen years. Though " sworn to a miserable woman " by " a crazy old man weakened by love and overruled " by her, the oath must be kept ; a king's word is sacred. To the overwhelming sorrow of the entire kingdom, accompanied by his wife Sita and his brother Lakshman, both of whom refuse to leave him, Rama prepares to go into exile. During their sojourn in the jungle, the demon Ravana, king of Ceylon, parts them by a trick and carries off Sita to Lanka in Ceylon. Despite Ravana's endless and enticing temptations, Sita does not falter for one single moment in her loyalty to Rama. The latter, inconsolable for the loss of his cherished wife, moves heaven and earth to regain her and after many years succeeds. But at the last moment doubts assail him as to Sita's having remained faithful during the long period of imprisonment. He humiliates her publicly at the moment of the reunion ; but though insulted, she retains her devotion and dignity, undergoes the fire-test of chastity, and comes out victorious.

This epic most vividly depicts the closest of human ties, those between wife and husband, mother and son, brother and brother. The dialogue between the personages in the noble drama and their actions express the loftiest thought and sentiment that intimately related human beings have ever harboured. No northern or Greek epic rises to their plane. No finer ethical sentiment could be voiced than that found in Rama's exhortation to his grief-stricken mother Kausalya, who is torn by the conflict between duty to her husband and love of her son. With all her heart she desires to follow into exile the son whom her husband's folly has banished. But without a trace of rancour for the injury inflicted upon himself, Rama pleads with her that a wife's place is always and under all circumstances by the side of her husband, and asks her, for very love of him, to remain behind and comfort with her pity his remorse-scourged king and father. Rama goes even farther and pleads with her to love her very rival, Kaikeyi, and that rival's son, Bharata.

When Rama's young wife, the beautiful and tenderly nurtured princess Sita, expresses her desire to follow him into exile, he, wishing to protect her from the dangers of an unknown fate, exhorts her too to stay behind ; but he assures her, " I leave my soul here with thee, only with my body shall I go into the forest ; . . . stay here, none the less shalt thou dwell in my heart ; . . . and in remaining here, my well-beloved, thou shalt not be further from my thoughts." But Sita does not wish to be spared any hardship ; " separated from thee, I should not wish to dwell even in heaven ! I swear it to thee by thy love and by thy life ! Thou art my lord, my guru, my way, my very divinity. With thee I shall go, I have resolved on it absolutely . . . even hell with thee cannot be otherwise than a sought-after heaven. Did not my father and mother leave me in thy hands, ordering me to have no other habitation but my husband's ? "

" Then come, follow me if it so please thee, my beloved ! I wish ever to do that which rejoices thy heart, O woman worthy of all reverence," her husband exclaims, and later adds, " it is as impossible for me to leave Sita as it is for the wise man to abandon his glory."

Equally noble are the sentiments expressed by others. Bharata, the unwilling usurper, refuses to ascend the throne which his mother has procured for him by fraud. He places Rama's sandals upon it during the latter's exile, as token of the real holder of the kingship. The third brother, Lakshman, insists upon following the exiled pair into the forest to serve and watch over them unceasingly as their self-appointed minister. He is the perfect incarnation of brotherly devotion, this faithful lad who reveres his sister-in-law Sita so humbly and touchingly that when, during her enforced flight, she drops her jewels one by one in the hope of thus giving the brothers a token of her fate and whereabouts, Lakshman is able to recognize only her anklets, because he has never dared raise his eyes to her face!

This epic also shows that a distinct spirit of chivalry still existed in those days. " Restrain thy anger . . . reflect above all that she is a woman ! " Bharata exclaims to the man about to punish a wicked dwarf for her fateful intrigues. Another admonishes, " Even in thy anger, O hero, beware of ill-treating a woman."

Rama is depicted as the model of kingly virtue, wisdom and justice during the greater part of the epic. But towards the end his attitude and action is disappointing to Western readers. Both Sita and Rama have undergone untold miseries, she in her confinement, he in his attempts at rescue. Both are longing for reunion. Yet when Sita is at last freed and word is brought to Rama of this, he suddenly shows a

meanly jealous and suspicious streak entirely unworthy
of either himself or his noble wife, and he does not
hesitate to manifest this in public, nor to humble her
publicly. While she is devoured by eagerness to rush
to him and throw herself in his arms, he coolly sends
her word that she is to attire herself carefully and then
to come to him *on foot*, like a penitent, exposed to the
gaze of the motley army. Sita, timid and ashamed,
cries bitterly, and can only call out in a broken voice,
" My husband ! " But Rama does not answer, nor
take a single step to meet her. Even Lakshman, grief-
stricken, covers his face, and the whole multitude
weeps over her undeservedly inflicted indignity. But
Rama thinks of nothing and fears nothing but the
possible stain on his blameless honour, should anyone
ever dare to insinuate that Sita might not have retained
her purity while in the demon's power. (How like
the preoccupation with personal honour of Nora's
husband in Ibsen's play 2,500 years later !) Rama's
first words are concerned with this alone ; no greet-
ing, no reassurance to his suffering wife ; " The hardship I have borne (nothing is said of hers !) in the war
with my friends was borne to vindicate my honour,
not suffered for thy sake ! " he flings at her. " The
sight of thee is most irksome to me . . . there is
nothing left in common between thee and me."
    Rama even goes so far as to suggest to the queen
that she had better choose some other husband. Sita
answers with dignity, " You wish to give me to some
other man, like a dancing-girl ? I, born noble and
married noble ! I am not what you think me to be ;
put more confidence in me, for I am worthy of it, I
swear it by your own virtue ! " She then voices a
complaint that has echoed and re-echoed in the heart

and on the lips of woman throughout the ages down to our own day : "Blindly swayed by anger like a fickle-minded man, thou hast placed above all qualities my one quality that I am a woman,"—just this disproportionate stress on physical chastity only, no real esteem for character or the virtues of mind and heart ! In those ancient days, and until our own, no matter how mean and cramped or even lewd of thought, how ungenerous of heart, how selfish of action—a woman was a 'good' woman provided she remained physically chaste.

Sita of her own accord chooses trial by fire and proudly walks into the flames of the burning pyre. The goddess Agni herself bears the indicated Sita out of the fire in her arms, triumphant. But this is not enough ; her father-in-law who has died meanwhile —that same old king Dasaratha, whose polygamous weakness was the original external cause of all the suffering endured, has to stick his head out of heaven and add his opinion before the assembled multitude. Unctuously he once more enjoins Sita : "Thy husband must always be in thy eyes as the supreme divinity ! " In the face of such aggravated provocation on the part of men, there was indeed need of special—both priestly and posthumous—exhortation to obedience.

Whether these characters or happenings are purely legendary or not does not matter ; fiction or history, they reflect the thinking of those ages. What is still more important, these epic stories have been an actual moulding factor of thought and morals throughout succeeding centuries. The attitude of later ages towards these characters is in itself revealing. For instance, Hindu men to this day laud Rama for the attitude he adopted in the end towards Sita. They say that it was his duty, as a just and blameless king, to re-establish before his people beyond cavil or possible breath of slander the purity of their queen. But we may read into the incidents another meaning. This over-emphasis on the physical aspect of womanhood, this lack of confidence which is its natural result, attributed even to the noblest of Hindu kings, explains to some degree why it was possible for laws such as Manu's in time to gain complete ascendency, and to wrest from woman all other interests in life but those of sex and home-making.

Though no more eloquent testimony to the heights which Indian women are capable of reaching can be found than in the lives of these women of the *Ramavana*, this epic itself bears clear evidence of negative forces at work. It is true, no more glowing eulogy of the advantages of voluntarily monogamous union in which husband and wife complete and elevate each other, can be found than in the married life of Rama and Sita ; but there is the warning example—so little heeded in later days—of king Dasaratha, all of whose troubles are due to the conflict of affections and interests arising from plurality of wives, and whose zenana contained the respectable number of three wives and three hundred and fifty other women.

The *Ramayana* also draws for us a vivid picture of the unavoidable evils of the zenana. The women's quarters seethe with intrigues, jealousy and defamation which heap unalleviated sorrow on a neglected wife's head. As comic relief we discover the " chamber of anger ", that special room set apart for a woman to retire to when she wanted to brood over a grievance or nourish a complaint, and where she had to be

placated and coaxed to come out again. Another evil
is also already clearly indicated—the devastating influence on the lives of others of an unscrupulous or
ignorant woman who has too much power in her
hands, an aspect which was in later ages to become so
marked in the repressive influence of the mother-in-
law and the oldest woman as unquestioned head of
the house.

We also find in the epic period the beginning of the
seclusion of women, but it is still confined to princely
houses and is distinctly a mark of honour and not a
symptom of fear. We have " Sita, of whom lately
even the Gods themselves could not obtain a glimpse ",
and who dreads being exposed to the vulgar gaze of
the soldiery. Yet such seclusion was by no means
strict, for we read that " neither house nor raiment nor
the restricted space of a zenana nor the etiquette of
courts nor any other kingly ceremonial can veil a
woman from the gaze of others ; the only veil of a
woman is her virtue. In ill luck, in marriage ceremonies, when a maiden chooses her husband, during
sacrifices, in public assemblies, a woman's face is for
all to see ".

There is proof in this epic that a custom has crept
in which was entirely absent in Vedic times ; Sahamarana, or widow immolation. Rama's mother,
Kausalya, expresses the wish to burn herself on the
pyre of her dead husband, and by this act of Sahamarana become a *Sati*, exist as " perfect woman ".
Sakuntala also says : " If a husband go to another
world and fall into the realms of darkness, a faithful
devoted wife follows him into that region." The
custom was already being viewed with favour. A
widow conferred a coveted mark of distinction on her

family by turning *Sati*, and furthered her own future interests since the Brahmins asserted that " she who voluntarily burns herself with her deceased husband will reside in Swarag (heaven) for as many thousands of years as there are hairs on the human body ". It is therefore not surprising that in the other epic, *Mahabharata*, we find the two mothers of the Pandava brothers, Kunti and Madri, disputing hotly with each other as to which one is to have the privilege of turning *Sati*. The best beloved wife exclusively arrogates to herself this honour.

But widow immolation was still very rare in epic days, and entirely confined to royal houses and the highest caste. It was still a genuine and deep-felt desire not to be separated even by death from her loved mate, for " in the heart of a wife neither son nor father holds the same position as a husband ". There was no taint as yet of the frightfulness of enforced immolation of later days.

While tracing with a feeling akin to awed delight the exquisitely devoted and noble lives of some of the heroines of this Indian epic, we cannot fail to recall that these belonged to the Kshatriya, and only a sprinkling to the Brahmin caste. There remained the vast voiceless unsung substratum of low castes, and beneath these the countless millions who made up the unabsorbed Dravidian peoples and aboriginal tribes who were to form for thousands of years that most degraded mass of " untouchables " upon whom no Aryan light of culture ever shed a kindly beam. We must surmise that low-caste Hindu women were already degraded, while the indigenous races had never risen at all from the clutches of their own fear-dominated religions. The very marriage rites evolved by priests for caste members are indicative of this even in pre-epic days, when caste intermarriage was still permissible. A Kshatriya woman marrying a Brahmin held an arrow in her hand, the simple sign of recognition of almost equal rank ; a Vaishya woman marrying a Brahmin held a whip as symbol of his mastery over her ; but a Sudra woman must touch the hem of his robe in token of most abject subjection.

Several other factors, inherent in Hindu society and already distinctly traceable, were bound to aid in the degradation of womanhood. Briefly enumerated, the most important are these : the need for sons rather than daughters in Vedic days ; the evolving of the theory of the transmigration of soul in Brahminical days ; the joint family system ; child marriage ; the theory of Karma.

As the Aryan invader had gained his foothold in India step by step by the steady subjugation and pushing back of the indigenous dark tribes towards the south, there was special need of stalwart sons. Their birth was hailed with particular joy. So already in Vedic days it is " the bearer of heroes ", the " mother of many sons " who received the greatest honour, while the birth of daughters led to disappointment. " A son is another self, a spouse is a friend, but a daughter is a source of affliction." Throughout succeeding ages, this feeling became more and more accentuated, until it was to lead to the frightful practice of widespread infanticide.

The theory of the transmigration of the soul, formulated in post-Vedic days, also contributed greatly to the special rejoicing over the birth of a son, for concomitantly with the idea of transmigration rose this other, that only a son had the right and power to perform funeral sacrifices and later propitiatory rites. As these rites were considered absolutely essential to the welfare of the departed soul, and had as their result to shorten its period of suffering in purgatory and to accelerate the attainment of heaven, it was most desirable that the first child should be a son, and that he should be born to his parents as early as possible. If the first child proved to be a daughter, there was cause for mourning and invective and her unwelcomeness reacted as a further belittling factor upon all later daughters.

This eagerness to have a son at the earliest possible moment to insure the proper performance of family ceremonies, acted as a powerful impetus to bring into existence the factor of child-marriage. Marriage arranged before puberty became quite general. The custom was spreading especially rapidly among the Brahmin caste, so that it was soon possible to enforce by legislation that a girl's marriage must take place even before her breasts developed ; if she were not married until menstruation had begun, the most terrible punishment would fall upon all offenders, both the family which she joined, and her own father, grandfather, and great-grandfather, who would be reborn as " insects in ordure ". For people who seriously believed in the transmigration of the soul, this prospect was indeed a sufficient deterrent.

With such early marriage, another factor immediately arose to act as a strong retarding and warping influence in the girl's development. She entered still unformed into the family of the husband. In such joint families, father, father's brothers, their sons, their sons' sons and the wives and children of all these lived under the same roof or within the closest possible group. Such joint living involved the need for enormous discipline, with great stress on respect for Dharma—conformity to law—for all members of the vast household, often comprising a hundred beings or more. The young bride entering it was bound to unquestioning obedience not only to her husband, but to every older member of the husband's family, not only males, but also sisters-in-law and especially the mother-in-law and oldest woman of the family. This meant an enormous limitation on her chance of developing any sense of independence or responsibility and laid a premium on conformity, self-effacement, and humility.

But most far-reaching, because operating forcefully upon the entire race, was the factor of religion, the doctrine of *Karma*, in determining the position of Indian women. The scope of this book will not allow of more than the most superficial consideration of the vast subject of Indian religion and philosophy. But some knowledge of this one aspect at least is absolutely essential to any understanding of the problem under consideration. The law of Karma had early become an unquestioningly accepted and fundamentally determining dogma of Hindu belief. It proclaimed the law of cause and effect to be absolute and universal, the supreme principle in operation in all created things. According to it, not even divine intervention has power to prevent a human being from suffering or enjoying the inescapable consequences of his thoughts and actions; their accumulated balance of virtue or burden of sin is carried over from one life to the next rebirth, and numberless reincarnations alone can enable each being to reach the ultimate perfection that is the destiny of all.

Theoretically, this law of Karma is one of the
loftiest conceptions and interpretations of life, with
its stress on the high dignity of absolute self-determination. On its positive side it makes for the most
sensitive awareness of human responsibility in thought,
word, and deed, and acts as a high ethical and moral
impetus towards right living. But then this belief
in Karma has a negative side, and this seems to have
been the one to operate most heavily against the welfare and progress of Indian women. It was so easy
for men, striving both consciously and unconsciously
for power and ascendancy, to lay at the door of a
woman's Karma all blame, not only for her personal
failings, but also for the very evils which resulted
from the forcing of women into unnatural surroundings by men. If a mother bore girls only, it was
because she had neglected her duty as mother of sons
in a previous birth, and must meekly bear her punishment now ; if her husband died, it was because of her
former infidelity and criminal wickedness, and no curse
too terrible could be flung at her, in particular if a
child widow ; if a woman's children died, it was not
because she bore them out of an immature body, or
reared them in sunless and airless rooms, but once
more because of her sinfulness.

For the truth of all these endless interpretations,
men pointed to religious authority ; the assurances
and anathemas of priests sufficed ; woman herself was
no longer permitted to study the sacred scriptures to
obtain direct confirmation and guidance. Since her
mental faculties were not trained in any other way
which would have compensated for the loss caused by
this exclusion from the accumulated stores of the
wisdom and knowledge of her race, her mind was

bound to become a welter of abject fears and super-
stitions and limited preoccupations. She became a
prey to the dread of giving new offence, and grieving
over the past, and her life became a round of acts of
propitiation, atonement, and—by means of charms and
gifts to Brahmins and religious mendicants—precaution against future evil.[1]

[1] Quotations in the preceding chapters are largely drawn
from Clarissa Bader's and Lajpat Rai's works mentioned in the
bibliography.

V

THE FIRST GREAT REVOLT

FIVE hundred years before our era, Brahminism at last obtained such a hold that the daily life of all the castes became circumscribed by and linked to innumerable religious rites and tabus, with the Brahmin enthroned as indispensable functionary and arbiter. But despite this priestly stranglehold, the spirit of India, though numbed, was not yet completely crushed. In the period of darkness the seed of strength lay hidden and grew.

Just as we found that it was the Kshatriya who had held out longest against Brahminical imposition in post-Vedic days, so now men sprang from this same indomitable caste to head revolts that aimed at overthrowing the Brahmins' rule in order to escape from its maze of dead and meaningless formalism into a life of direct aspiration and independent thought. The Sikh and the Jain religions were the outcome of two such insurrections, and each did away with some flagrant defect of the old system ; but another, which preceded, was the most significant of all, the tremendous puritan movement of Buddhism. Tracing the characteristics of its spread and development, we cannot but be struck by the similarity of some of its symptoms to present-day happenings in India. The Kshatriya prince Siddhartha, though born to a throne and reared in luxury, was affected by the realization of the sorrow and suffering of humanity to such a degree that he turned away from the very threshold of ultimate peace, vowing that he would not rest until the whole world had heard the teaching of the redeeming truth. Mahatma Gandhi, though on the road to great material success, was so gripped by his knowledge of the poverty of the lowly that he vowed not to rest until his work and striving had brought them relief. He could take no joy in the possession of wealth or position, as long as sixty million of his people were forced to subsist on one meal a day; he went so far as to hope that if he must be born again, it might be as one of the lowest of the low, among the untouchables.

As by Buddha, so by Mahatma Gandhi, the starved spirit of India was shaken and touched so profoundly that it changed the entire outlook and aspect of India.

The future Buddha, while still a prince, opened war on the corrupt Brahminical power by issuing a defiant declaration against the priestly tabus surrounding its sacrosanct caste system. He avowed that he would choose a wife even from among the Sudras, lowest of castes, provided her character was noble. His bride's father responded in kind; his daughter is to be given to Siddhartha, not because he is a prince, but because of his noble qualities: " it is a law in our family to give our daughters only to men of high attainment, and never to men who are strangers to accomplishments ".

When Siddhartha attained enlightenment after a long period of penance and searching after truth and came forth as the great teacher Buddha, he reduced to nought both the spiritual hold over the masses of the Brahmin priests and the caste divisions they had artificially strengthened. He taught that there is a direct way, an eightfold path to attainment, that truth suffices without the help of priests. He also broke down the restrictions that hedged round women and made it possible for them once more to come forward and stand free and equal beside men. Among the very first to challenge the Brahminical anathema were women; Buddha's own wife and aunt joined him as disciples in the light of open day, to aspire once more unhindered to knowledge and learning.

Buddha went from city to city, teaching this new revelation, The Law. Men and women of all castes followed in his footsteps. But a most dramatic incident occurred as he reached a certain city. The frightened priests had caused the gates of this city to be shut against his coming. But the city contained people held in threefold confinement—the women, kept prisoners by walls, by priest-craft, and by man-made laws. These had heard of the promised hope and craved for freedom; hundreds of them banded together, defied alike religious and civil authority, broke down a gate, and marched forth jubilantly to welcome the coming Lord.

There exists no more concrete or revealing testimony as to the marvellous boon bestowed by Buddhism upon the women of India, than a close study of the rock-cut temples and monasteries of Ajanta in the Hyderabad Deccan, which date from the second century B.C. to the fifth A.D. Hundreds of frescoes still adorn the walls, on which thousands of people are presented in the manifold occupations of life, from a king's reception of foreign ambassadors to a woman grinding spices on a curry stone. No painted records of any land or any period surpass, and few equal, the gracious beauty of the women drawn on those walls. Nor among all the thousands of figures of women can a single one be found in a position indicative of social or sexual degradation. There is not a trace, either in painting or in sculpture, of obscenity, such as Brahminical art so often exhibits. Queens ride forth in state or dally lovingly side by side with their kings in unaffected ease ; mistress and handmaiden alike walk among men unveiled and unafraid, yet with a curiously delicate modesty. Tenderness between mates, between parents and children, men and animals, is depicted in innumerable ways. These frescoes reveal a highly spiritual, yet materially richly endowed peak of civilization which is equalled in freedom of spirit, though not in material beauty, only by what we know to have existed in Vedic days.

Thousands of monks and nuns thronged the monasteries ; they possessed all that was best and highest in the learning and art of the time, and this marvellously fertilizing stream of culture and aspiration flowed from these centres throughout India, and overflowed south, west, north and east, even to the limits of China and Japan.

But the harsh and soulless restrictions of Brahminism, which had driven a revolting India into the refuge of Buddhism, were, curiously enough, to prove in the long run the very factor which should defeat the usurping faith itself. Intense reaction against the degraded life lived under Brahminical sway caused the new women converts to overshoot the mark, and Buddha, instead of checking this excess, opened a door which permitted this high flood of aspiration to lose itself unfruitfully in desert sands : he granted women the right to join monastic orders.

His own foster-mother was the first to entreat him to give women the same right as men to join the monastic orders. As their life had been made so dreary with household drudgery unrelieved by any intellectual interest, their will so completely subjugated to that of men, their outlook so hopeless, women, in order to escape the feeling of horror at the idea of rebirth into an endless chain of similar lives, flung away all earthly interests at the promise of finding in strict asceticism complete and final liberation. Thousands of women turned into Buddhist nuns. This means of escape was a marvellous boon, especially to widows, childless wives, and to mothers whose children had died ; it was their only means of avoiding the social obloquy, curse and lonesome isolation laid on them by Brahminical society. But this wholesale retreat into the ascetic life had the serious result of withdrawing from the domestic sphere the vital energies and reformative powers of the mentally best-endowed and spiritually most aspiring of women. As mothers, shedding their influence within the home, such intellectually reawakened and socially freed women would have had an infinitely more telling effect upon the growing generations than they could possibly have as nuns. Thus much of the regenerative influence of Buddhism in turn bore sterile fruit and made it easier for Brahminism to revive again.

Buddha himself was fully aware of this danger, though he did not deny the right of self-determination to these women, nor block their choice of the path of total renunciation. But he expressed the prophetic opinion that no religion which allowed women to abandon domestic life would or could endure.

Though the people at large, and women in particular, were completely won over by the rebel power of Buddha, there remained one class in India that had gained nothing and lost all by its advent—the Brahmins. Owing to the persistent efforts of the priests, and to certain wonderfully subtle constructive minds among them, such as, for instance, Sankarachariya, Hinduism at last was able to demonstrate to the satisfaction of the Indian intellect the ultimately sterile pessimistic nature of Buddhism. Great thinkers were able once more to reassert and exalt the deep philosophical truths of Hinduism, its comprehensive and tolerant intellectual view of life, its high spirituality. All these constructive aspects again took hold of the minds of men. But all the negative forces of Hinduism were once more directed against women ; Brahminism, revived, forged for them new social shackles far more binding than any that had been welded before. From this time forward, with only minor further checks, inevitably the slow but steady degradation of woman's status went on apace throughout the centuries, to come to a halt only in our own day.

VI

MOHAMMEDAN INFLUENCE: ENHANCEMENT OF RESTRICTIONS

IN the eleventh century began the Mohammedan invasion of India—a factor quite as significant for Indian women as had been the coming of Buddha. But while, among the many external stimuli acting at various times upon Brahminical society, Buddhism had liberated them, Mohammedanism was the one outstanding single factor to work wholly against the interests and progress of Hindu women. The blame for this lay by no means entirely with Mohammedan conquest, religion, or society, but to a far greater extent with the particular trend of Hindu reaction to Moghul influence. Polygamy and the strict veiling of women were common Moghul practices; if adopted, they could but intensify already existing Hindu evils. On the other hand, the law of the Koran gave an unusual degree of property protection and social privilege to Mohammedan women— widow remarriage, divorce and remarriage for wives, were common; if these were accepted even in a modified form, they would work for the emancipation of Hindu women. But Hindu men adopted the worst and rejected the best among the customs affecting women.

This was, to a large extent, inevitable and inherent in the tendencies already existing in Hindu society. Hindu men and priests conjointly had laid down and brought to universal acceptance among high castes the law that marriage—for woman—was an indissoluble sacrament, while reserving for themselves the right to remarry even before the death of a first wife. The custom of easy and frequent divorce among Mohammedans, where a woman had the full right to demand divorce herself, keenly offended and disquieted Hindu men. Somehow, among their group, there existed a terrible uncertainty and fear that they would not be able to hold their women under like conditions. There was another itensifying factor at work. The Mohammedan invaders were short of women, and eager to obtain them from among the conquered Hindu race. There is nothing in the Koran to forbid such unions. But to the Hindu, to whom intercaste marriage within his own fold had already become an impossibility, it was still more unthinkable to contemplate marriage with Mlechches, dirty foreigners, non-Hindus. So the first concern of the conquered Hindus was to put a stricter guard upon their womenfolk; no easy thing when opposing a victorious conqueror for whom the kidnapping of women was a common practice.

It became known that the Mohammedan religion forbids the carrying off of married women as slaves or concubines. So the Hindus, as a means of protection, resorted to marrying their daughters not only at the approach of puberty, but even as infants. Infant marriage became so common that children were sometimes promised in marriage even before, or at the time of their birth. But now that Hindu brides were becoming unattainable, the Mohammedan did not hesitate even to break the law of the Koran and began to carry off married Hindu women, whose male protectors consequently had to adopt further measures of safety. While formerly women were secluded only in the houses of the very great as a sign of distinction, the strictest seclusion was now adopted quite generally among all high castes. The women's quarters were made inaccessible, and even unrelated Hindu men were excluded from the sight of Hindu women, lest they should carry tales or spread the fame of beauty which might then be coveted. Now, when there was need for Hindu women to leave their secluded quarters, they went closely veiled so that no roving Mohammedan eye could possibly catch a glimpse of them.

To what extent Mohammedans carried on the abduction of women and the forcible conversion of Hindus is easily gauged from the fact that not more than 15 per cent. of the 70 million Mohammedans now in India are of foreign origin.

Still another powerful factor operated in favour of introducing purdah quite generally, and polygamy to a far greater extent than ever before, into Hindu society—the assertion of the world-wide tendency to imitate an upper or ruling class. It affected in the first instance those Hindus whose livelihood and official position depended directly on the conqueror, and who were in immediate contact with the Moghul court, officials, and armies. One of the Moghul rulers stated the advantages of polygamy very neatly and convincingly: a man should have four wives, a Persian to talk to, a Khersani to do the housework, a Hindu woman to nurse the children (again pre-

P.   F

eminently the mother!) and a Turkistani to whip, as a
deterring example to the other three! So Purdah,
under Moghul influence, became a protective measure
in Hindu society, while also sharing with the custom
of polygamy the great advantage of being a powerfully operating mark of distinction.

With this submission to and aping of the Moghul
conqueror, *slave mentality* took a deep and lasting
hold upon the Hindu community. Previous invaders
had in time been driven back or absorbed into Aryan
society, but from Moghul days on, by far the greater
number of India's inhabitants lived under the yoke
of subjection—the millions of untouchables under
the heel of Brahminism, the Hindu in turn under
the Moghul dominance, and all at last under the
strong grasp of the English—another factor which
inevitably tended to make for further degradation of
both men and women, for without freedom and self-
determination, human life can nowhere expand.

Because of subjection of their will during many
previous centuries, those least able to resist the negative influence of Mohammedan customs were the high-
caste Hindu women. Far from resenting their increased
seclusion, they themselves came to regard it with jealous pride to such an inordinate extent that it grew to
be an envied boast for a Hindu woman to be able to
assert that not even the eye of the sun had ever beheld
her face. Women themselves were quite content to be
shut away in crowded, airless and isolated rooms at
the back of the house, or screened in by shuttered
and trellised devices through which only faint glimpses
could be obtained of the life outside.

But in Mohammedan society conditions existed
which made it impossible for women ever to become

so utterly subjected to men as did Hindu women. These conditions contained the promise, so triumphantly demonstrated in the case of Turkey, that the Mohammedan woman would some day have a far better chance of escape into complete inner and outer freedom than her Hindu sister. The legal position of women under Islam was not only infinitely superior to that of Hindu women at the time of the Moghul conquest, but also to that of women in almost any other part of the world, particularly in Europe. In many ways the legal position of Mohammedan women a thousand years ago gave them more security and independence than Western women had until very recent times. For instance, a Mohammedan woman's earnings belonged to her absolutely, her husband having no faintest legal claim on them; whereas the California suffrage campaign of 1911 brought to light the fact that a drunken husband, who did not contribute one penny to the support of his children, could not legally be prevented from collecting and appropriating to himself his wife's wages at the end of the week.

Women under Islam had inalienable property rights. The laws brought into India by the Moghul conquerors hold good for Mohammedan women even to-day (with the exception of the Punjab, which does not follow Mohammedan law as to women's rights of inheritance). A daughter was absolutely assured of one half a son's share of an inheritance; under all conditions women received a half share. Such property belonged to women in their own right even after marriage; they were fully entitled to make contracts without any need of referring to husband or father, whose consent was not required.

This is doubly interesting when we remember that even to-day France, for instance, does not permit a woman to bank money, not even small savings, without the knowledge and express consent of her husband. At the time of marriage, a Mohammedan woman received a settlement, or dowry from her husband according to his station in life. To such a settlement she was absolutely entitled even if it were not specifically defined or contracted for at time of marriage. She had the right to claim it at any later time; in case of dispute, legal authorities decided the amount in accordance with the portion received by other women of her father's family. If this dowry was not paid, a Mohammedan woman had the right to refuse herself to her husband until payment was effected, and, until her dowry was paid over to her, a widow retained possession of all of a husband's property, though she was not permitted to sell or mortgage such property.

Dowry might be *immediate* or *deferred*; immediate dowry was paid at the time of marriage, and remained the wife's inalienable property; deferred dowry was to be paid in the event and at the time of divorce.

Of a deceased husband's property the wife received one-eighth if there were children, or one-fourth if there were none, to dispose of absolutely as she saw fit. She was also entitled to inherit from a son.

When a Mohammedan woman lived in commensality, her property rights were not affected or diminished, in contrast to Hindu joint family life, where the possessions and earnings of each member (with the exception of "gift" property) are joint property. Her husband was obliged to maintain her as long as she was faithful to him and " obeyed reasonable orders ".

The Moghul woman was likewise in a far better position than her Hindu sister in other respects. The mother was the primary legal guardian of her children, and had exclusive custody of boys up to the age of seven or nine, of daughters until the time of marriage or majority. Only misconduct could take away her guardianship, and on the death of a mother, her mother in turn became legal guardian. A child born six months after marriage was legally accepted as the husband's, and his child by a bondwoman had all the rights of legitimate offspring and the mother became free.

A father was entitled to arrange for his minor daughter a suitable marriage, but he could be enjoined, by her mother or relatives or anyone interested, not to give her to a diseased, undesirable, or unequal mate, and even prevented from so doing. Contracts entered upon for a girl's marriage by persons other than her father and mother, needed ratification by her upon attaining her majority at fifteen. After this age, marriage required her own consent, and not even a father could force her to it against her will.

Though there were several differing schools of Mohammedan law, Mohammedan women in India could be divorced, or obtain divorce, in three ways. The first was the *talak*, by which a husband could at will, even in her absence, pronounce his divorce from his wife. This form was considered " a most abominable act, hated by God . . . the most detestable of all permitted acts ". Under the *Khula*, a woman could buy her release by sacrificing some portion or the whole of her settlement. A husband might refuse Khula, but could be compelled to it by a judge. *Mubarat* was divorce by mutual desire and consent, and in this form no property passed from wife to husband.

Women might remarry three months after divorce, four months after widowhood or if pregnant, after delivery.

A wife could also sue for divorce for impotency, or if falsely accused of infidelity, or if the husband was insane or dangerously ill. But a husband's infidelity, or cruelty, or non-payment of dowry did not implicitly entitle a woman to divorce. Her rights were thus not equal to a man's in matters of divorce, nor even in property rights, though they were far higher than those of any contemporary women, with the exception of the small group still living under matriarchal forms in South India, of whom more later.

Like Brahminism, Islam also excluded women from religious teaching or positions of religious authority. But whereas Brahminism definitely forbade Hindu women even to study the scriptures, Mohammedan women quite generally studied the Koran. Many among them held high positions as musicians, poetesses, scholars, and particularly as rulers. The " most beautiful woman of India ", Nur Jahan, the wife of Jehangir, proved capable of effectively ruling the empire for her weak husband, and her name was even placed on coins and on the royal seal. She led and directed her own army from the back of an elephant until three mahouts had been killed in front of her and the elephant itself was wounded. Then, even during the orderly retreat, she cheered on her soldiers. Despite purdah, the reverence of Mohammedans for women was a far more actual, practical thing than the mother-worship of the Hindus. In the two crowning examples of Hindu and Moghul womanhood—Sita and Mumtaz Mahal—it is pleasanter to remember the Taj Mahal erected over the Mohammedan grave than the testing pyre into whose flames the blameless Sita walked ; it is more pleasant to remember how the Moghul emperor loved and revered Mumtaz Mahal, mother of fourteen children, than to think of King Rama insulting Sita for fear lest her body might have been touched by another man.

It is also of interest to remember that some Moghul rulers fought against the prevailing Hindu practice of widow-immolation. At one time they required that a widow desiring to become a *sati* must apply for permission to burn herself, which was granted only if it carried conviction as being an absolutely voluntary immolation.

Unfortunately, Hindu society was too rigid and intransigent, and Brahminism too inhibitive a force, for Mohammedanism to be able to exert any direct liberating influence upon Hindu customs. But we are inclined to attribute a special meaning to the fact that among the millions of Hindus forcibly converted to Mohammedanism practically none until modern days ever reverted to Hinduism again ; it probably did not seem an enticing prospect for men to leave a democratic, homogeneous type of society in order to return to the disadvantages of caste, or for women to return to economic dependence, unquestioning obedience, and the other restrictions placed on them within the Hindu fold ; this despite the fact that

Hindu thought and culture were both deeper and loftier than any evolved by Islam. The reason of this is that the greatest number of conversions took place from the lower castes, who had gained little benefit from the exalted metaphysical speculations of Hinduism and its tolerance of thought, while woefully limited by the rigidity and intolerance of its social customs.

But good or bad, Moghul power, even at its height, never extended over the whole of India. Hence the rigid purdah it fostered did not spread over the Dravidian South, which consequently always remained purdah-free. Even the Brahmins who had penetrated the south and won it over to Hinduism, never veiled their women there, though they led a more aloof and secluded life than did the Dravidian women. It can safely be said that in regions where Mohammedan rule did not penetrate, Indian women were spared the worst forms of their enslavement and retained far more of their ancient privileges.

But on the other hand it must not be overlooked that for centuries after the need of secluding Hindu women in conquered regions to protect them from Mohammedan aggression had disappeared, the Hindus made no move whatever to abolish purdah; on the contrary the custom was steadily gaining ground.[1]

[1] Information as to the legal position of Mohammedan women has been largely drawn from the works of Ameer Ali and A. Syed mentioned in the bibliography.

VII

CUSTOMS EXISTING AT THE TIME OF THE BRITISH CONQUEST

As the centuries passed, the Mohammedan invader in turn became a true son of the Indian soil. But the time had not yet come for him to join forces with his elder brother, the Hindu, nor for these two to gather into one fold of common interests the vast number of still older sons of the soil—the Dravidian mass of untouchables. Fallen from its ancient perception of spiritual unity into serfdom to priest-craft, Hinduism seemed to have lost its former power of absorption and unification. Division was manifest everywhere; it seemed to have become the very keynote of Indian life. Brahminical rule had at last so far succeeded in its divide-and-rule policy as to pass the point of safety for itself and for the whole of Hindustan. Aryan and Dravidian, Mohammedan and Hindu, high caste and low caste, caste and out-caste, men and women . . . all at cross purposes, all wary of each other, all afraid. The sinister shadow of organized religion stood between them and the glow of ancient knowledge.

When the Moghul ascendancy began to wane, India seethed politically with warring factions, but socially it lay inert in stagnation of customs. At this low ebb in Indian history came the shock of contact with the greed and expansion of Western powers. Holland, Portugal and France found her easy prey to acquire, and England manipulated one warring Indian faction against another in turn till she had practically the whole of India under her direct rule or tribute. No historical factor had ever brought India up against so violent an impact of alien thought or mode of life. Only a very much more exhaustive work than the present could do more than outline the infinitely complex currents set up by this impact and flowing into the life of the women. Most striking was the realization of the vast difference in customs between Europe and India. Some of those most likely to attract the interest of the English were infanticide, polygamy, polyandry, *sahamarana*, *devadasi* service, infant marriage, purdah, the joint family, and caste.

Before proceeding to delineate the changes which were to be wrought in these customs after the arrival of the English in India, it is well to first outline briefly their approximate extent and aspects, and in a further chapter to show which of them had the most far-reaching effects on the life of women.

Sahamarana had become fairly common among the Brahmins and not infrequent among the Kshatriya caste, but had not penetrated to the low-castes and untouchables. To estimate its extent for the whole of India is impossible, but data collected within a radius of 30 miles from Calcutta revealed the fact that 300 immolations took place in that area within the short space of six months. The custom had degenerated from the former voluntary dedication of widows to one of horrible compulsion; everything was done on the part of relatives, especially the husband's mother, to bring such psychic pressure to bear on the widow as would compel her to *sahamarana*. Where this proved insufficient, physical force was often resorted to, and the victim, as she struggled amid the flames in her agony, was held down by means of long bamboo poles.

Two main motives had impelled the Hindus to let this custom degenerate to such a fearful point —spiritual glamour and material gain. *Sahamarana* reveals the incredible extent to which priest-sown ideas had penetrated and the immense power of idealization and other-worldliness of that Indian mentality which, in the face of the most incredible suffering, could continue to chant the beauty of sacrifice. On its spiritual side, the Hindu woman reached in immolation the highest peak of the old Sita-Rama glamour—matehood faithful through life and after death! *Sahamarana* was indeed an ultimate test of the lofty belief in eternal soul-affinity, a terribly beautiful proof, possibly even convincing, if only it had applied to the Ramas as well in such "indissoluble" unions. But since it was only woman who followed her mate even through the gates of death, while a widower remarried within the shortest possible space of time, the dark surmise cannot be ignored that behind the popular desire and approval of seeing a widow enter the fire, behind the ghoulish application of force, was at least a partial desire to secure an undivided hold on the property of the deceased husband, upon which the widow would otherwise have had a lifelong claim to maintenance.

Widowhood. No doubt there were still many cases of voluntarily immolation, for the life of the Hindu

widow was at its best one of incessant self-denial
and service, and at its worst of unredeemed suffering.
Manu's laws had indeed been effectively enforced,
especially among Brahmins, to whom the very
thought of remarriage had become intolerable. There
is no reason to suppose that the number of widows
was proportionately smaller at the time the British
arrived in India than it is now, and statistics tell us
that even to-day there are 350,000 widows under 15
years of age, and that one out of five females is a
widow, though but one out of twenty men is a
widower. In some Brahmin communities every
third woman is a widow.

But it must by no means be concluded that all
Indian widows were condemned to a life of celibacy
and self-denial, for among the Sikhs, Mohammedans,
pastoral and military classes and low castes they had
always remarried. The Brahmin's power had not
penetrated there. Only one-third of the widows of
India belonged to castes in which strict injunctions
against remarriage were in force.

Among the widows who did not immolate themselves on the funeral pyre, yet had no right to remarry, the child widows—those girls who had to
face an entire life of deprivation, though their first
marriage ceremony had never even had the chance
to be followed by a second and by consummation
—suffered much, but usually they had at least the
advantage of remaining with their parents. She
fared worst who was widowed in the house of her
mother-in-law while still very young and before
she had born sons. Her life was often made an
intolerable hell, as she was considered guilty of her
husband's death,

The usual procedure at the death of her husband was that the widow's hair was cut and her jewellery stripped from her. Henceforward she might wear no other clothing but a plain white sari without the adornment of even the simplest border. She must sleep on the hardest surface, frequently a stone floor, eat but one meal a day of the most frugal kind, and twice a month keep a strict twenty-four hour fast, during which not even water might pass her lips. To add to the sadness of her lot, as her presence was considered unlucky and accursed, she was not permitted to join in any merrymaking or family celebration. Moreover, she was often despoiled of her share in property by near male relatives. In all cases she remained the unpaid maid-of-all-work of the family. She was lucky if her own family took her back, for in the house of her mother-in-law she remained subject to the bitterest taunts and insults. Nor did she find protection in other important respects. Cowed and wholly dependent, she was an easy sexual prey to her male relatives. Then she was faced with three alternatives, resorted to by no means rarely—the secret murder of her child, suicide, or escape to the sole possible refuge, prostitution. Others were driven to the same final position in another way ; to get away from the dreariness of their lives, they frequently went on religious pilgrimages. Sacred cities, such as Benares, retained a great number of such pilgrim widows who preferred to make a living by begging and vice rather than return to the dreaded empty home.

As long as the curse of the priesthood upon their remarriage was not lifted, the conditions described above were bound to remain the lot of Indian widows.

And it was not to the advantage of Brahmins to lift the ban : the widow was one of their most remunerative sources of income, for the widow's hand was always holding out its atoning gifts. Nor was it to the advantage of fathers harassed by the necessity of providing dowries to wish for widow-competition in their daughters' marriage-market.

But it must not be concluded that among the 30 per cent. of Indian widows never permitted to remarry, all underwent the hardships described above, other than the universally enjoined and observed practice of asceticism in their mode of life. For the widowed mother of sons remained the honoured head of the house, and they took her advice upon a surprising number of matters. Distracted by no temptations to frivolity, she often became a marvellous manager under whose hands the whole household prospered. It is a common saying all over India that neglected property needs " a widow's nursing ". And it is difficult to praise highly enough the Indian widow's gentle grace of selfless service to all around her ; she is the untiring nurse of the sick and of children, the willing and uncomplaining helper, the good caretaker of the home while others make merry. In innumerable homes, instead of being persecuted, she was cherished, and those around her tried their best to soften her lot. But their belief in Karma did not permit them to exonerate a widow from her penances, nor did the high-caste widow herself wish to escape these—she found her greatest solace in pious observances, and, under the grip of inherited thought and custom, would usually have been the one to resent most bitterly any suggestion of remarriage.

Infanticide had sprung up as the result of two practices—strict caste limitation in choice of a wife, and puberty-consummation. Both of these turned the birth of daughters into a veritable calamity in all but the most well-to-do families. When Hindus adopted infant marriage during Moghul days, a flourishing system of marriage barter had sprung up, for where the fathers of daughters were over-anxious to get them off their hands at the earliest possible moment, the fathers of sons saw their golden opportunity. The smaller the number of available bridegrooms, the more profitable it became to raise sons, and the more undesirable became girls.

Further extension and multiplication of occupations had called into existence endless sub-castes ; each new division called for additional rules, requisites, and ceremonies, and therefore offered new work to the priests. The extent to which this subdivision had been carried was exemplified strikingly by some South Indian Brahmins, one of whom is recorded as saying : " I am sure I am not guilty of exaggeration when I say that the Mudaliyars (a family and caste name) residing in Madras are divided into as many as 50 sections, no one of which can inter-marry with any other. The same obstacles to inter-marriage exist among Naydus, Pillais, and Reddis."

Such senseless restrictions naturally worked havoc in marriage, and greatly limited the choice of mates. Since in addition to this the Brahmin threatened with the most terrible curse any failure to marry a daughter before puberty, large dowries in property and jewels were inevitably forthcoming, even if this meant the economic ruin of unlucky families, where parents had neglected to exercise ' foresight '. Small wonder

that, threatened with the choice between material
ruin and damnation of soul, such timely and prudent
forethought—infanticide—was resorted to more and
more. Only the most tender and ethical of people
were willing to rear too many female infants at the
price of the certain impoverishment of the entire
family. Yet even so, it is hardly conceivable that
this custom could have become widespread among
so gentle a people as the Hindus had it not been for
one determining factor—the poisoning system of joint
family life. Women, drawn from many outside
families, all crowded together in an involuntary
group, forced to share quarters and goods, were, as
mothers, bound for their children's sake to be jealously
concerned over the use made of joint property.
Among such groups, in the heart of sister- or mother-
in-law, the intent and desire to prevent the growth
of one unwanted female infant could far more easily
rise than in the heart of its own mother. Such
infants were most frequently exposed against the
mother's desire.

Child-Marriage. It is almost inconceivable that a
custom vitiating at the core both physical and moral
forces could have been imposed and perpetuated
upon a keenly intelligent race by a designing priesthood on the pretext of divine ordinance, or that
it could for so many centuries have found such
passionate defenders, were it not that economic factors continued to operate strongly in its favour.
Since growing sons remained within the joint family,
marriage entailed no extra strain, as it was in no way
dependent upon the earning powers of the young
bridegroom. Unquestionably early marriage would
have continued in the West also, were it not that

the problem of expense entered as one of overwhelming importance. Especially among the upper classes, a man could not afford to think of marriage until his studies were finished or his livelihood established. Just the reverse was the case in India ; early marriage paid. In the first instance, since the young bridegroom lived in the joint family, his marriage need be in no way dependent on his earnings ; secondly, the little bride was always an asset, and not an outlay, as she took the place of an unpaid servant. Therefore nothing stood in the way of early marriage ; on the contrary, the little bride, in addition, brought, in most parts of India, a good-sized dowry with her, so the earlier she came into the household the better.

But between early marriage as formerly known in the West, and the abnormal form it took in India, there is a vast difference which needs further explanation. Considering that the Brahmins were the worst offenders, both in actual practice and in legislation, we cannot escape the conviction that Brahmin greed was responsible for this outrage. The younger the bride, the less the chances of her surviving for long the strain of marriage duties, and the more likely the early need for a new bride who brought another dowry ! It is astonishing to what an extent mothers-in-law and husbands had come to face the prospect of a little wife's death with callous indifference. Rarely were energetic efforts made to save her life ; the people around her let ' karma ' take its course. Why be disturbed ? It was so easy to procure another wife ! Quite generally, the place of a deceased wife was again filled immediately the funeral ceremonies of the first were decently finished, or at most, a few months later. As infanticide had proved, girl-life was of extremely low value, so that it is no monstrous accusation to draw the inference that, unconsciously at least, the knowledge of the material gain brought by repeated marriage prevented the Brahmins from making any effort to combat the evil of child-marriage. Consciously or unconsciously, a further fact must have played its part in Brahmin consideration. Each step, from the choosing of the bride to betrothal and marriage feasts, pregnancy, illness, and death, called for religious ceremonies which could be conducted only by the priest to his great benefit in money and kind : The more the merrier!

Had not these economic factors been operating in favour of the continuance of early marriage, there would have been no reason why it should not have been abandoned, once the great impetus of Moghul aggression had disappeared. As it was, there is every reason to believe that when the British reached India, infant marriage was as common as it had been at the height of the Mohammedan invasion, and that not only did it show no signs of dying out, but was still on the increase.

The worst offenders once more were the Brahmins themselves. Not only did they make it an almost universal practice among their own caste, but they tried to force it upon others as far as their power could reach. Consummation of marriage took place invariably among Brahmins a few days after the first menses of the little bride, at from nine to thirteen years of age, with the result that her poor immature body was generally subjected to the burden of pregnancy before it had the strength to carry it to a successful end. Several miscarriages and stillbirths before the birth of the first living child were usual.

Luckily the Kshatriya caste had not yet lost all its vigour and resistance, and the practice of consummation of marriage at puberty was far less common among them than among the Brahmins. Nor had the lower castes adopted the custom. The majority of the Hindu population therefore escaped the worst of its devitalizing results.

Even so, throughout India, the great majority of girls had the function of motherhood forced upon them before their bodies had fully developed or their bones had solidly set. Add to this the shocking conditions of midwifery, and the result was an abnormally high mortality of mothers and infants in child-birth, the prevalence of female disorders and children's diseases. It was estimated that 25 per cent. of Hindu women died prematurely through early marriage, and that another 25 per cent. were permanently invalided, while from 25 to 60 per cent. (the former at Delhi, the latter at Bombay) of all infants died in their first year, of whom 40 per cent. died in the first week, 60 per cent. in the first month. Immature mothers could neither bear, nurse nor rear to physical perfection the new generation, and large sections of the Hindu race were showing signs of ever-increasing devitalization and physical deterioration. This was still more apparent when the castes and sections in which child-marriage prevailed were compared with the few others which had retained the ancient custom of mating at full maturity.

That *Purdah* aggravated the evils of early marriage has already been indicated. One of the most dangerous results of this custom of seclusion was physical. High-caste women, shut away from sun, air, and exercise, fell victims in appalling numbers to the

ravages of consumption and other diseases. The
zenanas were veritable hot-houses of infections.
Early birth, weakness, disease, early death; within
this vicious circle women were confined.

As we have mentioned, purdah did not diminish
after the decline of Mohammedan aggression; on
the contrary, the tendency to veil women in imitation of those in higher stations steadily continued in
operation. As at first high-caste Hindus had imitated
the Moghul ruler, so the low-caste now continued
to imitate the high-caste. As soon as a man became
affluent enough to be able to afford a servant's wages,
that servant ran errands and made all purchases in
the bazaar. This enabled the wife to slip into purdah,
which she did with alacrity, as it conferred upon
her an incontrovertible mark of ascent in the social
scale.

But this prosperity-accession to the fold of *pur-
dahnashins* was necessarily limited. Except for this
small number, purdah never extended anywhere in
India to the low-caste groups. Economic necessity
protected them, for among actual tillers of the soil
and artisans or labourers in villages and towns, the
need of earning their living through bodily toil
effectively precluded all possibility of seclusion,
whether among Mohammedans or Hindus.

There were other groups of the population in India
whose women had never come under purdah, such as
the Dravidian and aboriginal tribes, and millions
who had originally been subjected by the Aryan
invader and then became known as untouchables.
The Sikhs, also the Parsis—fire-worshippers who
had found asylum and religious toleration in India
when escaping from persecution in Persia—never

secluded their women, nor did the Hindu women of the West coast veil themselves. Only in the north and east of India was purdah universal among the high-castes. Though a close estimate is impossible, it is doubtful if even at the height of the purdah period more than 15 per cent. of adult women were ever in seclusion. Through lack of intelligent information as well as wilful misrepresentation, a grossly exaggerated idea of the extent of purdah in India came to be generally accepted in the West, though it is hardly possible to have too vivid an idea of the resulting evils.

Polygamy, as we have already stated, had been restricted in Aryan society to royal houses until it received considerable impetus through Moghul influence. The reaction against Buddhist asceticism, which found expression in the exuberant Krishna worship, also increased the practice. But all along, economic factors tended largely to restrict it; only a small number, hardly more than 2 per cent., were rich enough to afford the luxury of supporting more than one wife. But there have been few situations in Hindu life which in the long run the Brahmin was not able to turn to advantage. The astuteness of the priests found a way to get round even this adversely operating law and to manipulate it in the reverse direction for their own advantage. It speaks volumes for the absence of spirituality, the corrupted mentality, and arbitrary power of the Brahmins that polygamy reached its ugliest phase of development among a certain small and localized section of the Brahmin caste, the Kulins of Bengal. The Kulin stood at the very top of the social ladder—highest among all the many sub-castes of the Brahmins.

Maker and arbiter of social laws, he reserved to himself the exclusive right to marry out of his restricted group. Of course, it was considered the greatest of honours to give a daughter to a Kulin Brahmin. Here the Kulin perceived his chance; he agreed to take a lesser dowry than other men, but of course insisted on his right to marry as many wives as he pleased—a highly paying business, as it was not unusual for him to marry from twenty to fifty wives, and cases of close on a hundred have been cited. At each marriage a fixed sum was paid to him. Then he left his latest bride to continue the fêted and gift-showered round of visits to his various other wives, scattered in many villages over large districts, as he rarely troubled to take them away from their father's home. But in addition to dowries and free feasting, still richer pickings of the trade could be managed by the wily Brahmin. He relied greatly on his deep knowledge of human nature, and quite often visited one wife only once or twice a year, or even less. After physically exciting his adolescent bride—a girl trained to absolute obedience to all her elders—she was left alone to her own devices, within the joint family system, teeming with male relatives of all grades, near and distant. The Kulin shrewdly calculated that it was more than likely he might receive a hurried plea to break the usual round of his peregrinations and honour some particular wife's family with his august visit at once. Great gifts were brought, for the family's honour was at stake. Villagers know how to count the months of pregnancy! The Kulin husband must be brought back at all costs for another visit in time to give semblance of legitimacy to the unborn babe. With the most exquisite indirectness and flowery language mutual bargaining then started, at the end of which the Brahmin got back tenfold what he had ' sacrificed ' by accepting a low dowry. But if the family could not satisfy his demands for consenting to "put off for their sake other most pressing business ", there remained only the deep well in the courtyard at dead of night as a last escape from disgrace.

Among the Mohammedans of India, polygamy tended to decrease after Moghul times. Their prophet Mohammed, faced by a deep-rooted evil of his day, had astutely legislated : "you may marry two, three, or four wives, but no more ; if you cannot deal with equity with all, you shall marry only one". Among orthodox Mohammedans this was being more and more commonly interpreted as an injunction against, and not in favour of, polygamy, for they reasoned rightly that it is humanly impossible for any man to treat four women with absolute impartiality, and that consequently he breaks the spirit of the law if he weds more than one. Though at first polygamy was undoubtedly commoner among the Moghul conquerors than among the Hindus, the proportion tended to become equalized with passing centuries.

Polyandry was rarely practised by members of the Aryan race in India and found no backing in its scriptures, though the *Mahabharata* contains the exceptional story of the one wife of five famous brothers. There were, however, a very few aboriginal and some Mongolian tribes which still practised it, in both the extreme north and south of India. It is interesting to note in all these cases that none of the women were ever veiled, and that they never held any position of subjection, but on the contrary enjoyed an unusual amount of freedom and independence. Among the Todas in the Nilgiris, for instance, a woman usually married all the brothers of a given family; the first-born child was allotted to the oldest brother, the second to the next, and so on until each "father" had a "son". Marriage consisted in the bride's being taken to the husbands' home, where first the eldest brother, and then each of the others in turn placed his foot on the fore part of her head; she then had to perform some household task for them, and this completed the simple ceremony. The placing of the foot on her head was not a symbol of subjugation, as is the Hindu wife's touching of her husband's feet, but merely a common and mutual form of salutation, for when younger men greeted an old woman, it was she who touched their head with her feet. Moreover, the young wife, if dissatisfied, could leave her husbands at any time and return to her parents, or find a new batch of husbands.

The Todas are a very primitive people, but polyandry may have also existed formerly among the Nairs of the Malabar coast.

Matriarchy. But the practice most alien and most interesting to ancient Aryan and modern European invader alike was that of matriarchy, of which the Nairs of the Malabar coast have been the immemorial guardians. Until very recent days no women in any part of Europe stood as high or unfettered as these women of Malabar. When the Portuguese and Dutch landed on this coast, they were actually shocked at what they considered most unbecoming freedom and occupations among women, for they found many

Nair women not only literate, but acting as teachers in schools, at a time when Europe had not yet even dreamed of schools for women. Name and descent was handed down among the Nairs through the female line, and property was completely in the women's hands. They were free to choose or reject a mate at any time. Yet marriage was, on the whole, on a lasting basis and its laws voluntarily and strictly observed. The Dravidian Nair women stood high, not only in domestic, but also in social and civic life, and held a position equal to, and economically, though not spiritually, even higher than that of the Aryan woman of Vedic times.

Devadasis. But strangely enough, while at the time of the British conquest the women of the south-west of India held the freest position of any women in the world, South India as a whole was also the home of one of the ugliest customs of the world, religious prostitution. Originally it was a holy profession, a dedication of girls to the service of the gods in spotless purity. Traces of this still survived in the recurrent practice of a seven days' fast observed by all dancing-girls before great festivals, during which fast they must remain strictly continent, and also in the symbolical marriage ceremony which was still always performed to join them to the god of a particular temple.

The duty of *devadasis* was to dance and sing once or twice a day before the image in the temple or when it was carried in procession through the streets. As gods in temples are attended as though they were living beings—ceremonially bathed, dressed, un-dressed, fed, awakened, and put to sleep—it fell to the lot of these *devadasis* to chant the appropriate hymns. Girls for ever denied motherhood crooned lullabys to stone images. It was a common custom to dedicate a girl infant to the gods in propitiation or atonement for some act, or as a bribe for some coveted favour from the gods. Certain groups, such as some weaver castes of Madras, observed a solidly established practice of dedicating all first-born girls to temple service. The extent to which the *devadasi* custom prevailed may be gauged by the fact that Madras alone had over ten thousand *devadasis* in its temples.

The custom was entirely confined to the south and was no doubt a practice left over from pre-Aryan days. It had thoroughly degenerated into an appalling form of prostitution, doubly repulsive because so intimately linked with religious worship. That the Brahmin priests had assimilated and perpetuated such a custom instead of wiping it out, is significant of the extent to which they were willing to adopt any means, not only for their own indulgence, but for binding the worshippers to their temples. For *devadasis* were at the beck and call of both priests and visitors, and brought in a goodly income to the temples. The ugliest aspect was that helpless infants were dedicated to this life of prostitution (though not of shame) and that no Hindu saw any disgrace or incongruity in this close linking of religion and sex-indulgence. Still, the oppenness of the custom was preferable to secrecy, and it was no more reprehensible than the 20,000-ducat income of Pope Sixtus drawn from brothels he himself had built, or that of some American churches derived, even centuries later, with the full knowledge of church elders, from lucrative investments in brothel real estate.

Though not attached to a temple, the nautch girl of the north of India filled a position somewhat similar to that of the *devadasi* of the south. Both were trained definitely to fill with interest and attraction men's leisure hours. The most regrettable aspect of such specialization lay not in the moral field but in the æsthetic. While in the old days dancing, singing and the playing of musical instruments had been part of the training of high-caste family women, these arts had tended constantly to drift out of the Hindu home and had at last become practically the monopoly of these pleasure girls. Consequently they had come in the end to be regarded as " not respectable ". With this unfortunate change of attitude, the Hindu home over a great part of India suffered an inestimable loss. Not only did it leave life in the zenana still more dreary, but tended to draw the men yet farther away from it. The more cultured and intelligent a man was, the more likely was he to be bored stiff by the dull vain chatter and petty preoccupations of the zenana, so that he was glad to escape and spend his leisure hours away from his eminently respectable home in the company of the stimulating dancing girls, far more for the sake of entertainment than for any sexual reasons. Yet custom and convention had grown so strong that for centuries it did not occur to these men of education to attempt to restore these lovely social graces to their own families, their ancient fruitful home.

This also meant that these arts—both in performance and enjoyment—were entirely withdrawn from growing youth. Music, dance, and song were no longer a factor of elevating significance in the education of children. Nor, in later life, could such untrained auditors take an intelligent or constructive interest in these arts. This in turn checked all further development of these noble arts themselves. The result was that they survived in their purity only in rare instances, under some special noble patronage, while on the whole a most deplorable wide-spread degeneration of music and singing took place.

The nautch and *devadasi* institutions marked the final limit of the restriction and impoverishment wrought by adverse customs upon the life of the zenana women.

VIII

WOMEN IN THE ZENANA

IN the previous chapters we have indicated the cause, extent, and reasons for stricter imposition of purdah. No doubt it would have been abolished as soon as the Mohammedan aggression and with it the protective value of purdah ceased, were it not that it found powerful support in the general age-long Hindu belief in the advisability of restricting women's freedom. Classical and later Hindu literature gives further proof of this attitude, it teems with slighting references to woman's character. "One may trust deadly poison, a river, a hurricane, the beautiful, large and fierce elephant, the tiger roaming for prey, the angel of death, a thief, a savage, a murderer; but if a man trust a woman, he will surely be reduced to wander through the streets in desolation."

The fact that purdah turned the zenana into the exclusive dwelling-place of women had far-reaching effects. It soon inculcated in their minds the deep conviction that freedom of movement outside the house would lower their standing and place them on a common level with low-castes. Not only this, but even within the house itself it made for a sharp division of family life into two sections, zenana and men's quarters. The outer rooms and verandahs became

closed territory for the women. They never visited
them except on rare and furtive excursions, and when
fully assured that no men were about. Servants only
took care of these quarters. This had the unfortunate
result of withdrawing all housewifely interest and
pride from these rooms, though it was in them that
the family's guests were received. Verandahs, gar-
dens, the outsides of houses and the adjoining portions
of the street consequently and inevitably assumed a
neglected appearance—spotted walls, dust in every
cranny, rubbish-heaps and litter of all sorts in court-
yards and by the side of the doors became the common
order of the day. Servants did not hesitate to fling
our garbage and refuse into the street as the easiest
method of disposal. The joy in beautiful surroundings insensibly disappeared from the daily world in
which men lived. Nor did the women preserve a
practical sense of beauty within their own quarters.
Zenanas were usually overcrowded, poorly lit and
ventilated, and swarmed with small children—still
more difficult conditions under which to renew and
cherish the beauty of outer things, of walls, furniture,
or the joy of colour. Moreover, the fact that these
rooms were never the home of social cheer, in which
men took part, inevitably made for neglect. In
consequence the women's rooms soon became the
barest and ugliest in the whole house, with rolled-up
bedding tucked into any odd corner, and clothing hung
over racks in full view. Under such crowded segregation, shut away from all cultural life, with no
stimulation from outside, how could women have
retained that sense of beauty which certainly had been
keenly alive in former ages ? It disappeared so wholly
from the home environment that women grew in-

sensible to all ugliness or untidiness of surroundings.
Only on the rare occasions of great religious festivals
did the ancient custom of drawing geometrical designs
in coloured powders before door-sills still persist to
add an unusual touch of transient beauty. Otherwise
the sense of beauty survived in only one form in the
lives of women. A particular factor conditioned this.
The segregation of sexes both within and without the
home inevitably brought about an over-emphasis on
sex interest both in children and adult women within
the zenana ; it made for prurience among adolescents
and over-stimulation in wives. Taught from earliest
days that to please their husbands was their main aim
in life, women under these conditions transferred what
would have been a normal interest in home decoration
entirely upon bodily adornment. The possession of
beautiful saris, and more particularly of jewellery,
became and still is, a veritable obsession with Indian
women. Their quantity, value, and workmanship
was estimated very closely and compared with much
secret and open jealousy and heart-burning. A little
bride's main consolation was to find that the jewellery
she brought compared favourably with that possessed
by the women of her new household ; or if, to her
shame, it fell below their standard, she attempted rest-
lessly to increase and better her treasures. It has
been estimated that the interest on capital unpro-
ductively invested in women's ornaments covers the
full amount which the peasants have to pay in land
taxes. I have had an endless amount of pity showered
on me by Indian women for my lack of ornaments,
and the idea that I could treasure some ornament
purely for the sake of its beauty of form and colour,
apart from its money value, has been received with

scorn. Only the lifting of purdah and the release of
women will restore to them a sense of balance in this
matter, renew their interest in home beauty, and
awaken in them a desire to adorn their mind at least
as much as their body.

The drawbacks of the zenana went further. Purdah abolished all possibility of high-caste women's
participating in the social life of the community.
Visits, feasts, discussions, musical parties, all these
took place in the men's quarters. Only the houses
of the very great were so constructed that a screened
or latticed gallery enabled women to observe unseen
the festivities in the central hall. By far the greater
number of them never participated in such social
events in any other way than by retaining the ' privilege ' of working behind the scenes for endless hours,
sometimes for days, to prepare the innumerable
delicious dishes and dainties to be served to the feasting men—dishes which custom forbade them even to
taste until the men had had their fill. This exclusion
from stimulating discussions and diversions completed the evil effects of the prohibition to study the
scriptures. At the discussions of men, women could
have kept in touch with the life of the community;
the scriptures—which contained not only religious
and philosophical matter, but also poetry, arithmetic
and rhetoric—would have given training to their
minds. Deprived of both, their mental life became
inevitably stultified. Men succeeded so amazingly in
their efforts that they were able to inculcate deeply
into the minds of women the conviction that to desire
knowledge was not dignified nor virtuous. They
became incapable of aspiring even to learn to read
and write. Most women would have been heartily

ashamed of an accusation that they were hankering after these very elementals of knowledge, and hotly resented it. This went to the extent of making many Brahmin women honestly believe that their knowing how to read would bring evil and sickness upon the heads of their husbands, most dreaded of possibilities. For long ages, religion taught that absolute self-abnegation alone could bring women near to the ideal type of womanhood.

There is no doubt that such teaching at its best succeeded in producing an exquisitely selfless, softly gracious, tender type of womanhood, but a type fearfully inhibited and negative on the whole. At its worst, such unquestioning contentment and limitation led not only to mental, but to moral stagnation as well. The lives of women were filled by monotonous routine, by sensual and frivolous preoccupations. Where women of all ages were compelled to live daily in inescapable and uninterrupted intimacy, under at least an outer show of absolute obedience to husband and mother-in-law, it was inevitable that dislikes, pettiness, jealousies, and endless squabbles should germinate and mature. The extent to which even high-caste women could not escape degeneration of thought and feelings is clearly indicated by the form of expression their quarrels tended to take. Whenever they dared to vent their emotions against their equals or inferiors, their shrill scolding was full of vile language and obscene abuse. Still more amazing and revealing was the coarse ribaldry in which these delicate creatures delighted. Little children who grew up in the midst of such stifling, warping conditions, witnessed these scenes, drank in their meaning, and in turn lustily handed on their spirit. No doubt all zenana generations have heard, as I have, twelve-year-old boys in a transport of rage scream at an old servant the ultimate insult, " I'll sleep with your wife ! " and be rewarded by appreciative smiles all around—a terrible revelation of knowledge harmfully acquired by observing children forced into the too close intimacy of adult ant-heap life.

Children were bound to suffer in other ways from the mental starvation of their mothers. In a desire to quiet the babel within the zenana, what more natural than to soothe infants with opium, or frighten them into obedience by harrowing tales of monsters and demons lurking to grab them around the corner ? And what of the indiscriminate praise and scolding meted out in an endless stream ?

So imprisoned and restricted within the zenana, it is not surprising that the vital urge towards expression in women had to pour itself out through such twisted and warped channels ; the marvel is that despite all the ugliness and frustration, great beauty of aspiration and tenderness of feeling sprang up ever anew within the Hindu home. To complete the concise picture of the home background against which Indian women lived and moved, it is essential to realize that from the earliest days the joint family system has prevailed in most parts of India, though chiefly among the upper castes, where possession of property and of a large family house enabled this custom to retain its hold. Among the lower castes the trend towards more and more minute division of land, the need to disperse in search of work long ago led to the virtual disappearance of the joint family ; another reason for the much greater amount of liberty always enjoyed by low-caste women. Its persistence among the only classes whose men were in possession of knowledge and culture is significant; the mentality induced, fostered, and perpetuated by life within the joint family system makes for inordinate regard for authority and submission to power, and is the chief factor in the continuance of the slave mentality (a term first applied by Indians themselves in self-criticism) which had taken its primary hold on the Hindu mind with the advent of the Moghul conqueror.

In the joint family, father, brothers, their sons and all male descendants remain under the same roof. Girls taken in marriage are added to this group from the outside, while sisters and daughters of the family in their turn leave it to be absorbed as wives into other families. All property, except a bride's 'six-fold property' (mostly wedding gifts and ornaments) is joint property held under the unrestricted control and at the absolute disposition of the oldest male member of the family. To him, moreover, unquestioning obedience and respect are due, and are automatically rendered. Living in such a large group involves enormous self-discipline on the part of all younger men; whatever their personal likes, dislikes, or particular interests may be, they must be modified and made subservient to the demands and general interests of the entire family. Every strong individual desire or aspiration, which might subvert the peace or general welfare of the whole group, is ruthlessly suppressed and inhibited. This makes for so strong a clan feeling that a man, forced for some years to live apart at a distance, when asked about his family, will always mention the ancestral village home, never his wife or present dwelling; to him first and second cousins are all " brothers ". Within the joint family,

each individual interest or concern is everybody's
business, and all individual earnings are everybody's
property. It allows of no privacy, no holding aloof.

Like so much else in Hindu society, the joint family
became in time a petrified survival which no one dared
to touch. For a younger member to leave it, would
have brought down severe social criticism and disgrace. In ancient days the joint family offered decided
advantages ; it made for concerted and more effective
effort in procuring food, caring for cattle and lands,
or in defence. But in later ages, when the Kshatriya
was no longer called upon to be a warrior or administrator, and most Brahmins were no longer officiating
priests, but all had to turn to new occupations, the
old system developed terrible drawbacks which far
outweighed its remaining advantages. True, it still
made for the lessening of the cost of living in food,
housing, servants' wages, and clothes. There was no
rent to pay, younger members could wear outgrown
clothes, women and children were satisfied to eat
food left over by men. It still kept intact the family
fortune, and ensured that the most distant and weak-
est relation was taken care of, so that actual want was
unthinkable for any.

But the terrible drawbacks of the joint family
system became especially clear with the splitting up
of occupations. Where the income no longer entirely
depended on landed property, but on professional
earnings, the savings effected through joint living
could no longer offset the drain caused by the presence
of large numbers of non-earning members. Capital
showed an alarming tendency to dwindle. The worst
aspect of the system lay in the crushing imposition of
conformity, the killing of all initiative and incentive

to individual effort during the critical formative period
of youth, the utter lack of training to responsibility;
in the premium it put on idleness, in the disheartening
exploitation of able and earning members by the
parasitic weak, and more than all in the unrestricted
property power consigned to one single hand which
not infrequently encouraged crass mismanagement.

Such was the family background for high-caste
women. Where growing male generations were so
restricted, women—under still further limiting laws
operating upon them alone—were bound to suffer
most within the joint family system.

After the crystallization of woman's position in
the home during the Moghul period, it remained
practically static for hundreds of years. So, when the
British came, it was as it had been centuries before,
still persists up to the present time, and as I myself
came to know it intimately in orthodox and backward
purdah sections of India. Woman's position seemed
the final proof of the existence of an " Unchanging
East ". In the joint family, the mother, or in her
absence the wife of the oldest male member, holds the
post of honour. Though she herself as a young bride
started in abject submission, when old, she is often
virtual ruler of the entire household. Even grown
sons will rarely go against her will or express wish in
any matter. She is the one final granite stronghold
of orthodoxy and preserver of outworn customs, and
for a little daughter-in-law to defy her is almost unthinkable. Every female member is bound to implicit
obedience to all her regulations, directions, or orders.
These extend not only to household matters, but even
to the daughter-in-law's intimate relations with her
own husband and children. According to the innate

bent of her nature, this oldest woman is either a true
" ma ", an actively kind and benevolent provident
mother to every being in her household from the
eldest son's wife down to the youngest bride, to children, servants, beggars, and even to animals ; or else
she is a formidable meddler and absolute tyrant, all
the more insupportable because of her untrained mind
and limited horizon, under whose iron rule every
younger woman cringes without redress. If she is
the mother of the oldest men in the family, she retains
her position of authority at the head of the household
even after her husband is dead. But once this
mother-in-law in a family has died, and the eldest
son's wife has succeeded to the envied position, she
in turn, if she becomes a widow, is superseded, by the
wife of the next eldest son. Woe to her if her rule
has been harsh ; in the unenviable and undefended
lot of a widow, she is then paid back tenfold in her
own coin. Just such an instance has come under my
own personal observation. A certain small boy's life
had been made almost unbearable through the perse-
cutions and privations inflicted on him by his oldest
sister-in-law. He escaped at last owing to the need
of being sent away for schooling. When he finally
returned after many years, he found her, her husband
having meanwhile died, reduced in station to a pitiable
degree. She even had to save food from her own
barely sufficient ration, in order to be able to give to
a beggar the daily dole which all widows so ardently
desire to offer as part of their manifold penitential
rites. Broken in ' spirit, humbled beyond belief,
timidly hungry for the kindness which was withheld,
weighted down by the sense of guilt that is upon
every widow's head, she now centred all her affection

upon her former victim, who in his turn could both generously and genuinely sympathize with her afflictions as distance had enabled him to escape both the mental and physical hold of caste and family spirit.

Least important and least worthy of consideration in the complex joint family life is the newborn female infant. Not that she is generally treated harshly; Hindus are naturally kind and gentle, and she is sure to get some share of affection from various sources. But she is too unremunerative a prospect to be able to command a welcome. She will be an unmitigated expense from beginning to end, will never contribute to the home by work of her own, will leave it for good between 12 and 15 years of age. Worst of all, when she does go, she will take with her in the shape of dowry a good slice out of the family fortune. The knowledge of all this is bound to affect the attitude of various members of the vast family in different ways; should she with several other sisters, be born of a sonless woman, they all will bear the brunt of vented spite and scorn. The mother, however, knowing how soon she will lose her daughter for good, often lavishes upon her an immoderate amount of indulgence. Yet even so, from her very first years the sensitive girl cannot fail to be painfully aware how much less welcome and cherished she is than her fortunate brother, how very little she counts. Training she receives practically none; about the only definite information imparted to her is that she is destined to be a wife—(lucky if she is fair-skinned and beautiful, so that someone may take her without asking for too great a dowry)—and that then she must be a Sita to him, he her deity, her prime duty in life being to please him and not annoy his mother.

At an age when girls in the West play eagerly and under little restraint in unconscious joy of free bodily movement, when their minds begin to expand and drink in wider knowledge of the outer world, the little Indian girl is suddenly shut away from all play and all further sight of outsiders, especially men. She gets no more exercise, little fresh air and sunshine, and usually at the age of 12 has all the airs and manners of a full-grown sedate woman. So, unfree and unsure of herself, without emotional discipline or resistance of mind, with body weakened and immature, she is taken into some strange household as its youngest bride. There she is the central object of curiosity; her garments, ornaments, behaviour are minutely examined, compared, criticized. She must be absolutely obedient to all, instantly willing to render any service demanded by any older person. She may not speak unless spoken to, may not wear what she pleases, may not buy, choose, or order anything on her own initiative. Her sisters-in-law spy upon her every action and she is sharply reproved for any shortcoming. In poor families she is made to work harder than a servant would be. In an affluent family, some single uninteresting task is assigned to her, such as picking over rice, drudgery with no educative quality whatever. The strict discipline of obedience is suddenly substituted for the lax indifference or indulgence of the parental home, and is her only training and education.

But probably most far-reaching in its ultimate results is the form which a young bride's relation to her husband is bound to take in a joint household where her every move is the concern of everyone else, where she sometimes has not even a room to herself,

yet where the main interest of all centres around her
sex life and capacity for bearing sons.

I am not now speaking of marriage with excessive
age differences, nor of the ghastly cases of consummation with girls on the border of infancy, but
of those of girls of 12 to 15 years of age where the
difference in age between husband and wife is less
than 10 years. Detailed accounts of their experiences
I have heard from the lips of Indian women themselves. Generally the first weeks and months had
been passed by these brides in the husband's home in
passionate homesickness, an intense feeling of for-
lornness, bewildered shyness, and agonizing self-
consciousness. The child-wife never opened her
mouth save to answer a direct question, and then
twisted in discomfort if it had to be more than a
mere yes or no. She was the first to rise in the morning, took the dust of her husband's feet, then waited
to serve as she was bidden. When she sat in company
with the other women during the day, and the footstep
or voice of her husband sounded in some adjoining
verandah or apartment, she had at once to retire into
an inner room, and was sharply reprimanded if she
lingered for a moment. Never was she permitted to
see her husband in the daytime. Her meals she could
take only after everyone else in the household had
been served ; then she ate whatever was left. If
unexpected guests came in, not infrequently there was
nothing left. Yet she never dreamt of complaining.
Though she had been taught to look forward to the
special duty of cooking daily with her own hands some
at least of her husband's food, her mother-in-law
jealously retained that privilege for herself, and thus
denied her that most valued comfort of serving. Not

until the last member of the household had retired
might she herself go to bed, no matter how tired or
indisposed she might be.   Only then did she come
face to face with that stranger, her husband.   Spell-
bound shyness, awed respect and sex consciousness
prevented her from being able to talk to him more
freely than to any of the others of the household.
Moreover, having risen at dawn, she was by bedtime
usually too tired and sleepy for anything more than
submission to the inevitable sex act, an act into which
her mind and soul hardly entered.   For many months,
husband and wife remained totally ignorant of each
other's thoughts and feelings ;   then she found there
were but few of his thoughts that she could share at
any time, as his life outside the home was a sealed book
to her.   Yet in her loneliness and intimidation, the
comfort and relaxation of sheer physical proximity to
this one being in her strange surroundings brought it
about that she began to cleave to her husband more
than to anyone in the new household.   Though she
did not realize it, her husband came to take the place
of a father in the little bride's feelings.   As the insurmountable barrier of exaggerated respect and obedience had, in the past, put an unnatural distance between herself and her own father, she was apt to
find this substitute-father more comforting, or at
least more approachable, than her own parent had
been.

But this comfort was hers only at the weary end of
day.   Even when her husband fell ill with fever, his
mother would not permit her to come to his bedside.
Worse still, she received black looks, as though she
were guilty of having brought about this illness.

But the most trying and intimidating fact during

the first months in her mother-in-law's house was that never for one minute could she escape the oppression of being under a ceaseless watch, never had a quiet hour to herself, never any privacy. Her monthly periods even were a matter of intense curiosity and discussion in the zenana, their recurrence both a taunt and an accusation. Then came at last the weary months of pregnancy, the infinite lassitude of carrying a new sapping life in her weak body. Finally the agony of childbirth, shut up in a dingy airless room, with every woman of the household holding aloof from her as from an unclean thing, no matter how much her heart cried out for comfort. An old dirty low-caste untrained midwife handled her roughly, and there was scorn and utter lack of sympathy even in that despised creature's voice when she informed the little mother that the new-born child was a daughter. The little mother felt that she had committed an unforgivable sin, and her mother-in-law's cutting scorn confirmed this openly. She also had to suffer the superior airs assumed by those whose first-born had been a boy, the humiliating taunts of more fortunate sisters-in-law. After that came the endless fretting of the infant in her weary arms, till at times the little mother's nerves and patience were so frayed that she screamed at the mite and shook it till its head almost fell off, only to cover it afterwards with sobbing kisses of frantic repentance.

Not until she had herself born a son did life grow bearable. The coming of her first son was like a great warm glow; it won her immediate consideration and automatically gave her the right to hold up her head somewhat and find a voice. Pride in her son became the main consolation of her life; the rearing

of this son and attendance upon the slightest wish or
need of her husband her supreme duty. But hardly
more than a child herself, how was she fit to rear her
son? Ignorant and superstition-ridden, how could
her mother-in-law direct her wisely? They fed him
irregularly and unwisely, put him to bed and woke
him up at all hours, over-indulged him in every way,
and then, when he ailed, they resorted to charms;
endless religious observances and ceremonials, gifts
to Brahmins and beggars of every sort—those were the
methods by which they brought up this whimpering,
devitalized fragment of humanity, sprung from an
under-developed mother.

But more important even than the physical dangers
and devitalization from generation to generation was
the directing of emotional forces into abnormal channels, a result following inevitably from child marriage,
seclusion, and the crowded herding into joint families.
Nothing could be more fruitful or revealing to Indians
themselves than the attempt to study these conditions
with newly opened eyes and to apply to them the
tests and interpretations of modern psychology. In
the first instance, two things were bound to happen.
The greater a girl's innate but undeveloped capacity
for individual choice, volition, and action—all
tendencies sharply deprecated from her earliest
days by those who surrounded her—the deeper the
sublimination of these qualities and the more intensely
did she finally throw herself into forms of expression
of exactly opposite characteristics: unquestioning
obedience, total abnegation of self-will, tireless service,
lack of initiative. The greater her frustrated urge to
outer freedom and independence, the fuller her escape
into spiritual submission. So, the more finely en-

dowed she was, the more was she bound to turn into the very image of the ideal wife desired for ages by Hindu men—a Sita !

Thus far, all well and good. Such intensely intro-verted women would have been ideal mates for strongly extraverted men. But the majority of Indian men are themselves not normally extraverted men ; on the contrary, they are far more deeply intro-verted than those of any other race. Life in the joint family system, agelong political subjection, and the fact that Indian men are sons of such unfree mothers as these, have deeply and inescapably marked the men themselves. The very subjugation they have success-fully forced on their womenfolk has recoiled upon themselves.

The repressed Indian bride, her sex life roused and called into function prematurely, her mental faculties starved and stunted, her emotional life over-stimulated, is hardly and rarely able to find in the utter stranger to whom she is given in physical marriage long before emotional or mental approach is possible her perfect complement and counterpart, or to obtain through him a normal release and functioning of the whole of her nature. The very fact that she is likely to seek a father-substitute in him mitigates against normal matehood. Added to this is the excessive emphasis placed on her bearing a son, and this son's tremendous easing significance in her life ; in consequence the Indian mother is bound to pour out upon her son an abnormal amount of love, and to expect from him emotional fulfilment ; an amplitude of life which should by rights come to her through matehood only, and not in motherhood. A hundred symptoms of this are noticeable even outwardly ; adolescent sons are, in exuberance of mutual affection and dependence, not infrequently fed by their mothers, hand to mouth, as if they were still babies; I have seen a highly educated Hindu mother give her dry breast by the hour to her five-year-old son to still his fretful clamouring; and it is not unusual for mothers to continue to nurse their sons for two and even three years on end. Thus the Hindu mother makes demands upon her son and renders services to him which for ever warp his sense of proportion and frustrate his earliest attempts at a normal expansion and extension of affections towards the outer world, frustrate his *socialization*. She shackles her son with unbreakable chains and leaves him mother-complexed beyond hope of release by conscious later efforts of his own. His instinctive infantile rebellion against her excessive demands or excessive showering of love upon him, against her exclusive emotional possessiveness, this wholesome rebellion is suppressed even long before he reaches adolescence. It becomes sublimated into its opposite—intense mother-goddess worship, that baleful ideal held before growing Hindu youth for ages past. Little do even the most educated Indians —blinded by the glamour of mystical interpretation —dream that this shining exaltation of motherhood, this worship of womanhood in the abstract, upon which they pride themselves inordinately, hides unplumbed subconscious depths of uncertainty, hatred, and fear. Little do they realize that this exaggerated worship of the *mother* is the very cause of their deep-seated contempt for *woman*; of their unconquerable distrust of, yet hungry dependence upon, them; of the frustration of their desire to find fulfilment in matehood because they seek in the wife a mother instead of a mate; of men's ultimate attempt to free themselves for ever from all desires of the body.

It is time that Hindu men should start to analyse and re-examine in the light of modern psychology the attitude of their priests and themselves towards women. A sojourner amongst them—knowing how restricted the womenfolk even of Western-educated men often are—is likely to grow weary of listening to the unconvincing exposition of their self-deluding idealization—which is in reality merely excuse and compensation—or the enthusiastic reiteration of how much more than any other race the Hindu reveres womankind. Equally fruitless is the uncritical assurance of outside sympathizers that this is really the case. It is despite, and not because of, Hindu men's conscious attitude towards womanhood, that Hindu women, at their best, really rank among the world's most gracious, dignified, and winning examples of their sex. In their keeping lie slumbering radiant powers of unfathomed promise, for Hindu women possess qualities deepened and purified by agelong suffering and service.

Never has man dug a deeper pit for himself than did the Hindu when he worshipped goddesses and degraded woman, when he adored the mother and slighted the wife. His own hope of release from this self-forged frustration lies in purging the poison from the holy sources of life; in respecting sex, not in the abstract, but in the concrete form of the wife. Religious and philosophical speculation must give way to true spirituality translated into action in daily life; escape from desire translated into perfect attainment of the pure goal of desire; unreal mother and *devi-*

worship must make room for real and living respect of the female mate.

Only by setting their women free and opening wide to them the door to absolute self-determination in all forms of expression and development, by restoring to them their Vedic status—the unrestricted use and training of all bodily, mental, and spiritual faculties both in the home and in society, will Indian men be able to achieve their own personal emancipation. Only free adult girls will be able to become true mates and balanced mothers, break through the vicious circle of misdirected emotional and psychic strength, and in addition, restore the wasted physical forces of the Hindu race. Only sons reared by such fully and freely living mothers will have the inner independence and assurance needed to lead a normal healthy life of social constructiveness. The road to this is blocked by no outside force, political or otherwise, but by barriers erected by Hindu men themselves. These must first crumble or be torn down ; the joint family system must go, caste in its narrow sense must go, priest-rule must go, illiteracy, untouchability, all artificial inequalities, must go. This will release the dormant force of woman and turn it into a powerful agent of social reconstruction and nation-building. Then only can Indian men hope to win, or if won, for ever retain, a true national consciousness and national freedom.

It remains for us to examine when and to what extent the light of such regeneration dawned on the Indian horizon, what were its sources, to what extent the coming of the British helped and hindered, and what other new forces are at work in this " Unchanging East ".

IX

ENGLAND'S PART IN REFORM CONCERNING INDIAN WOMEN

UNLESS we bear it clearly in mind that none of the customs which attracted the attention of the British conqueror were universal in India, and that some were very limited in extent, their delineation in the preceding chapters may leave the impression that all strength, beauty, and hope had been wiped out of the lives of the women of India, all free expression checked. Yet how was it that, even under these customs and laws, such a woman as the Rani of Jhansi could win immortal fame through her leadership of men in dauntless resistance to the foreign invader? Or that the Begums of Bhopal, behind their purdah, remained famous as wise and strong rulers, or that a Mahratta queen of Indore in the eighteenth century could still distinguish herself as a supreme administrator, build a City Beautiful, and raise the entire status of her people?

Whence came their strength? How was it that even quite ordinary women in the shelter and seclusion of the zenana frequently acquired a rare efficiency, a quiet self-assurance and a balanced strength and judgment which easily outweighed that of their men to whom the outside world was open? How was it that

Hindu society—so harsh in its express laws for women —yet kept enshrined in a niche of undying adoration exceptional beings who had broken these laws? That Radha, for instance, the wife of another man and therefore an adulteress, could have been worshipped as Krishna's lover by a people who laid supreme stress on the physical chastity of women, or that the memory of such a woman as Mirabai, the Gujerati songstress, was deeply cherished, though every action of hers had been a violation of man-made laws? As a wife she had abandoned her husband, as a queen rejected the wealth and pomp of a throne to wander in beggar's garb in search of yogis, to sit at their feet in the dust of the road, to drink in their knowledge of the only lasting truth, and then to break forth in her songs of love divine; she had aspired and chanted two centuries ago as had the Vedic priestesses in the dawn of her race.

How was it that over and over again, out of the very midst of caste, joint family, purdah and child-marriage restrictions, there arose women whose lives once more revealed all the beautiful traits of character and brilliance of mind that had graced Vedic and epic days?

One reason was that though the cleavage, dating from Brahminical times, between thinking and living was ever growing wider instead of lessening, yet the ancient traditions of independence and heroic virtue, once so vividly illustrated by the Kshatriya caste, had been kept alive. For though the Hindu priesthood had won the power to partition society into the most confining cubby-hole system ever evolved in any human society, it had no power to pre-shape souls to fit. Each new generation brought a goodly crop of square pegs whom no amount of trimming from earliest infancy onward could make to fit round holes. The more closely prohibitions and restrictions were drawn, the more joint family and caste denied all initiative to individual expression, the greater grew the resentment and ferment in the hearts of gifted youth. This was doubly significant when we consider that square pegs continued to be born in the very midst of the priestly-caste itself; for the Brahmins were not a celibate priesthood, and therefore did not draw the bulk of their membership from specially predisposed types. As with Western ministers' sons, Brahmin children were the most likely to develop bitter antipathies to Brahmin restrictions. Brahmin pegs of tough hard wood were the hardest to whittle down. For the corrupting craving for organized power was after all not an inheritable or congenital characteristic, yet every Brahmin born, no matter what the bend of his nature, was by right of birth entitled to be in turn possessor and preserver of the accumulated knowledge and spiritual insight of the race. Therefore, as to these exceptional spirits Brahminical learning was accessible from earliest childhood, they had unusual chances to discover in the depths of the scriptures proof that in ancient days existed freedom of living and a pure faith. This gave them reason and justification for rejecting the later accumulation of priestly restrictions and class domination. Such men were the least likely to feel respect for social laws which they knew the astuteness of their own kind had manufactured. Not infrequently these very Brahmins, superior to and scornful of all prohibitions to the contrary, still taught the ancient knowledge to their wives and daughters, just as Yajnavalkya had done in ancient days. Such Brahmins also were very often the teachers in great Kshatriya families, or, turning wanderers, went through village after village telling and re-telling the marvellous epic stories, so high in spiritual and cultural values, which kept alive the ancient glow.

Though priestcraft had succeeded in regulating and restricting to the minutest detail the *freedom of living*, it could not restrict the *freedom of thought*, for that freedom was inherent in the very structure of Indian philosophy and religion from its earliest days. Its all-embracing evolutionary quality gave full and equal scope and *raison d'être* to all speculation, all -*isms*, monist, dualist, agnostic or even atheist; the roof of Hinduism spread out equably over all. Consequently, though social forms of life had been fettered and the great unthinking mass of Indians lived on in unquestioning obedience to priestly mandate and caste-rules, independently thinking people were ever tempted and perfectly free to explore the many avenues of speculative thought. Unlike the Christian Church, Hinduism had never made free thought a crime.

Yet the Brahmin priests could by no means have been unaware of the danger of freedom of thought to established social forms or ritualism. But they were too astute and far-seeing philosophers to attempt the futile task of crushing liberty of thought. Everyone was left unhindered—so long as he did not try to transfer his freedom of thinking into an attempt at forms of action which might threaten social convention, that structure upon which rested the welfare of the priests. Though that point of danger was reached over and over again by thousands upon thousands of individuals, a *safety-valve* had been evolved, had become part of Hindu thought, and worked for thousands of years—the diversion of dynamic energy away from worldly agitation into spiritual search. This safety-valve had been adorned with the greatest attractions ; it led to a state of life in absolute freedom from caste rules, material worries or concerns, surrounded by the halo of popular admiration and reverence, rewarded by the acquisition of supreme merit both on earth and hereafter. Though the general rule had laid down that human life must pass through all four stages, that therefore married life must precede " renunciation ", yet exceptionally those who felt an unusual spiritual urge—in other words, those who were inordinately restless and divinely discontented—were allowed to enter the path of spiritual search at any age, even during adolescence. Such personalities, too strong or radiant to be safely kept within the caste structure, were therefore through age-old spiritual compulsion gently urged to leave the social fold, long before their inner ferment could clear into mature judgment or any plan of socially subversive action. Having cut the links with everyday life by becoming " seekers of truth "—*swamis, sanyasis, yogis*—their main aim thenceforward was the inward conquest of all desire, the abjuring of all preoccupation with worldly concerns. This was the process, the precaution by which potential social reformers had their sting painlessly drawn, their forces socially frustrated—so that the structure of priestly supremacy and economic exploitation remained safe.

It was no rare thing for women of unusual calibre to become *sanyasinis* on reaching the age when those of their kind in other countries bent all their mature

energies on reforming the home and any conditions
under which their sex and children suffered. For
unless such women were in the favoured position of
being the oldest woman in the joint family, they had
no scope for the expression of special talents ; all
they could do was to let themselves slowly be crushed
inwardly, or find escape in renunciation.

Sometimes, however, a woman so gifted found herself not only oldest woman of the household, but
also in a position of worldly honour and power, such
as that of a queen. This " ma " was continually
called upon to extravert, to act for her dependent sons
and all the other women. Thus her training as
absolute head of a vast domestic establishment, her
habit of directing and controlling its many various
and intriguing personalities, and particularly her
never-broken power over her sons, gave her an
immense advantage when it came to transferring
these talents to the business of ruler, to social housekeeping. Then hardly a woman on earth commanded
greater possibilities for good or evil. In such a
case, even priest rule was not strong enough to stand
in the way of her self-fulfilment within her own
group. If she cared to make actual use of her powers
instead of remaining a figurehead, nothing could
prevent her from leading an army or reforming a
town or building hospitals, if she so chose.

Moreover, among the high-caste masses, all those
vital enough to be stirred by restlessness, yet without
sufficient strength and independence to hold out
individually against the terrible pressure of their
surroundings, invariably transferred to such rare
insurgent spirits all the adoration of their own frustrated beings. This aspect of Hindu society is of

tremendous significance; this is why Indian youth can be so easily captured and swayed. As single individuals they have no ghost of a chance to succeed in rebelling against the iron structure of caste and joint family, but if some outside factor enters and acts on the accumulated welter of their repressions, youths surge forward in mass movements like flood-water when the gates are opened. They will follow a rare personality, a leader, with all the fervour and abandon of the " seeker after truth ", for whom no more rules exist and whom no power of priest or family or material interest can any longer hold back. Such was the lure of Buddha, such the character of his following; in varying degrees, all free and great personalities, be they rulers, saints, or merely singers, have always retained in India more than anywhere else, this power of insurgent thought and action, this ability to capture an adoring, escape-hungry following.

The size of such a following was in exact proportion to the strength of the leader's personality and the extent to which his striving made appeal to their suppressed and sublimated desires and embodied their spiritualized aims. At its core, the Hindu goal of life has never been material possession, but spiritual perfection. That was the reason why Buddha, sword-less, could sweep through India like a sea, but why on the other hand Britannia, with all the might of her physical supremacy, could capture India's imagination for but a fraction of one of Brahma's seconds, and could not hold it, for she had gone to India with no spiritual aim. This also was the reason why, in time, when the glamour of newness and the shock of re-newed political subjection had worn off, the foreign Government was to be faced, in the person of Gandhi, with puzzling problems in a shape wholly alien to all Western experience.

England's principal aim in coming to India had been material gain, not the desire to sweep India, as Buddha once had done, clean of all the cankers gnawing at her vitals. At the beginning—and first impressions have a way of persisting in race-memory—she brought not peace, but the sword. If, instead of the *imperialist spirit*, carried by merchants and soldiers, sustained by organized force, subduing India by intrigue and war, the *Christian spirit*, carried, not in word only but in deed, by some great unselfish and truly superior being or Government, could have peacefully penetrated India from the West, some Francis of Assisi with a heart of gold overflowing with pity for the downtrodden—women and untouchables —without condemnation, we might once again have witnessed such phenomena as those of Buddhist times. Then we could point to them with pride as proof of a great accomplishment, an incontrovertible support for the white claim to superiority. But though our churches proselytise in the East, no Western nation has itself, as a unit, or in its form of government, as yet been Christian. The superiority exhibited by all white powers, when dealing with other races throughout the world, has always been merely the astuteness of the acquisitive Judas, never the tenderness of the beneficent Christ. England took, and meant to hold, India for her own and not India's benefit. The other European nations whom she ousted had tried to do the same; such selfishness is not a trait peculiar to any one nation, but is the very core of all imperialism.

This being the case, it was unlikely that India could hope for social betterment at the hands of the new conqueror unless any change involved was definitely to the advantage of, or at least did not endanger, imperial interests. There was the possibility that ingrained social evils, whose eradication might endanger England's hold on India if she took the initiative thereto, would be permitted to flourish without a hint of interference, that humanly desirable reforms, distasteful to the great majority that constitutes the orthodox, would be officially discouraged as threatening the *Pax Britannica*. Should this latter prove to be the case, it must inevitably mean the strengthening of all the orthodox forces in India, particularly that of the Brahmin. This, and the discouragement arising from subjection to alien rule, would also strengthen the forces of reaction and degeneration along every line for a considerable time.

Before making a short survey both of the history of reform and of the forms these checks on progress took, and in view of the fact that a superficial knowledge of life in India leads many Westerners sincerely to hold the opinion that Indians are inferior and unfit to rule themselves, it may be interesting to refer to outside testimony. It is that of an observer who had the chance of studying the aptitudes of Indians and the conditions prevailing in their country at a period before priestly rule and foreign subjection—Moghul and British—had had their chance to crush Indian initiative. Megasthenes, the Greek ambassador to the court of the Hindu king Chandra Gupta, wrote of India :

" The inhabitants, having abundant means of subsistence, exceed in consequence the ordinary stature and are distinguished by their proud bearing. They are also found to be well skilled in the arts . . . they almost

always gather in two harvests annually; and even
should one of the sowings prove more or less abortive,
they are always sure of the other crop. It is accordingly
affirmed that famine has never visited India and that
there has never been any general scarcity in the supply
of nourishing food. [Sixty millions to-day have but
one daily meal!] . . . But further there are usages
observed by the Indians which contribute to prevent the
occurrence of famine among them; for whereas amongst
other nations it is usual, in the contests of war, to ravage
the soil, and thus to reduce it to an uncultivated waste,
among the Indians, on the contrary, by whom husband-
men are regarded as a class that is sacred and inviolable,
the tillers of the soil, even when battle is raging in their
neighbourhood, are undisturbed by any sense of danger,
since the combatants allow them to remain quite unmo-
lested. Neither do they ravage a land with fire nor cut
down its trees. . . . The Indians do not raise monuments to the dead, but consider the virtues which men
have displayed in life and the songs in which their praises
are celebrated, sufficient to preserve their memory. . . .
They live frugally and observe very good order. Theft
is of very rare occurrence. The simplicity of their laws
and their contracts is proved by the fact that they seldom
appeal to law. They have no suits about pledges or
deposits and confide in each other. They neither put
money out at usury nor know how to borrow. . . .
Truth and virtue they hold alike in esteem . . . they
have a high regard for beauty. . . .

" Of the great officers of State, some have charge of
the market, others of the city, others of the soldiers,
while some superintend the canals and measure the land,
some collect the taxes, and some construct roads and set
up pillars to show the by-roads and the distances.

" Those who have charge of the city are divided into
six bodies of five each. The first body looks after
industrial art. The second attends to the entertainment

of strangers, taking care of them, well or ill, and in the event of their dying, burying them and forwarding their property to their relatives. The third inquires of births and deaths, so that these among both high and low may not escape the cognisance of Government. The fourth deals with trade and commerce, and has charge of weights and measures. The fifth supervises the sale of manufactured articles which are sold by public notice, and the sixth collects the tithe on such articles. There is, beside the city magistrates, a third body, which directs military affairs. . . ."

History can bring a thousand other proofs of the ability of Indians not only to rule themselves, but to produce, at their best, states of exceptionally high culture and general public welfare. So far we have found that three main factors had furthered the fall from the high state of living pictured by Megasthenes —subjection to priest-craft; misdirected emotional and sex-energy through child-marriage and seclusion of women; creation of slave mentality by long subjection to the Moghuls.

What now was going to be the effect of the new subjection? How could the Indian races win their way to a new state of greatness? Could the white invader help through his form of government? Or did the new hope for India lie in the powers of re-generation slumbering within Indian thought itself? Or was there a third factor operating, not so immediate or clearly traceable?

Though the scope of the book will admit of only a faint outline of this, it is the writer's considered opinion that England, *as a Government*, through its official policy, has done more harm than good to the cause of Indian women. But English influence, by way of inspiration flowing from its books, its history, and the contact between individuals of both races, has given an inestimably valuable impetus to Indian striving, has imparted the violent impact needed to shock India out of her somnolence. Her great moral reawakening is no doubt due to contact with Western thought, to the growing awareness of national differences, to acquaintance with and sensitiveness to criticism from other lands and people. Increasingly swift means of communication; the spread of specific and general information through world-wide news agencies, due to Western initiative; industrial and scientific development—all this gave India a chance to undertake an undreamed-of stocktaking within her own four walls, a chance of re-education in this new " international university course of comparative achievement and morals ".

From the first contact with England, and particularly from the introduction of an English system of education, a curriculum modelled on the needs of Englishmen in England and not of Indians in their own homes, there resulted at first an intense interest in Western forms of culture on the part of educated Indians. Indian youth grew up for some generations with practically no knowledge of their own history save as it was seen through English glasses, and without any acquaintance with the ancient knowledge and culture of their race. The universal tendency to imitate a ruler, that ruler's ignorance or contempt for Indian culture and tradition, combined to ingrain in the Indian mind a scorn for all things Indian, an intense feeling of inferiority, and an eager desire to emulate the foreign ruler in everything. The more perfectly this was done, the larger and jucier the plums of office which the conqueror distributed to such imitators.

Then came reaction. These Westernized Indians began to realize that Government was not with them in their hopes and attempts to change social conditions in India. Government seemed mainly concerned with material progress, in whose immediate profits the West could reap its share. Doubt began to assail these Indians as to whether the Government had the best interests of India at heart. This, and their increasing knowledge of conditions in Western society, many of them very disquieting even to the most advanced Indians, made them pause to question whether the adoption of Western culture in all its phases was after all desirable. They started to clamour for reform of ancient evils on the one hand, and a return to the pure traditions of India's own past on the other. They claimed that progress could be achieved only if based on the lines of their own racial culture. It is these rare spirits, these square pegs, who, though spurred on by foreign contact, were yet forced to independent action without foreign support. Drawing around them an enthusiastic following, they gave to Indian reform its first great impetus and direction, instead of retiring, as formerly, as hermits to the forests. Had they found fearless backing on the part of Government, the worst of Indian evils would long ago be things of the past instead of troubling the present.

But Government did not move, nor did the Indian leaders themselves find effective means of carrying on the fight or putting pressure upon the Government until at last an Indian Assembly came into being. Only then was there a means of concerted action for reformers from all parts of India, an opportunity for realizing that at almost every turn the Government was failing to lend its support. The orthodox gloated over this, and felt far securer than ever in their position. But while the foreign Government thus played into their hands, they, for their part, did not fail to turn to advantage the tide of disillusionment over Western rule. While social reformers pointed back to Vedic sources, the vast mass of orthodox leaders pointed to the far more convenient later sources as a sacred authority in support of such customs as child-marriage or purdah. Growing resentment against political subjection and Western criticism also for a time tended to strengthen all the forces of reaction.

As for the part of Government in all these conflicting streams, there is no doubt that Indians would have initiated legislation earlier and brought pressure to bear in favour of desirable reforms far more quickly if left to fight out without interference the issues between reactionary and radical forces. Under normal conditions, social reform would have been among the first concerns of any autonomous Government. But already Moghul supremacy, instead of bettering Indian progress had harmed it, for it weakened Hindu resistance, killed initiative, called into being slave mentality, and strengthened reactionary tendencies. A new ruler as alien as were the British was still less likely to be in a position to initiate reform. Their only hope of safely establishing their hold was by keeping on the right side of the majority among the Indian population, which meant rallying to itself the support of the orthodox. Not only did they not dare to initiate reforms which would antagonize this most powerful group, but for the same reason feared to support indigenous reformers who strove for change. To allay the fears roused by missionary efforts at Christianizing, the British Government, which could only exist so long as it united its interest with those of the orthodox, had given the solemn promise of absolute religious non-interference—a thing of deadly import for the interests of India and Indian reform. For since the Brahmin had managed to interweave religious feeling and sanction into almost every aspect of Indian life, had, for instance, linked the ideas of puberty and marriage so inseparably as to give child marriage the force of religious law, the Government's hands were tied. Its promise of non-interference had allied it solidly with all the forces of reaction.

That is why, as we shall see, reformers were met with such disheartening dissuasion in their efforts when at last they were in a position to bring forward plans for reform in the Legislative Assembly. But on the other hand, there was one definite thing to be said for the Government. First of all, many English officials were, as individuals, wholeheartedly in favour of reform; but as parts of the administrative machinery, they knew only too well how futile it would be to permit reform bills to pass unless it were possible to promise and ensure their enforcement. Over and over again, suggested laws could have been passed had Government members in the Assembly thrown their votes into the scale in their favour instead of voting against such measures or abstaining from voting at all. But they knew that they would then be faced with the unenviable and very likely impossible task of enforcement and that such laws might easily turn into a mockery, existing on paper only. For instance, the native State of Baroda, far ahead of

British India in all matters of reform and education, had bravely passed a law against infant marriage as early as 1904. But the orthodox had made just such a mockery of it as the British feared to see repeated. Infringements of this law in Baroda were punished by money fines so low that parents merrily went on marrying their girls under the proscribed age limits, and paid the fine as an almost negligible part of the usual marriage expenses. How much can be said in favour of the attitude of Government may be illustrated by the comment of a well-informed liberal Indian Assembly member concerning enforcement of marriage reform. The most radical change could be made immediately, he averred, *if* the Government was prepared to place a policeman within every orthodox home; but not otherwise!

To go back to the beginning of this problem of native versus Government reform. The practice which more than any other was bound to attract the notice of the new-comer from the West was that of burning widows on the funeral pyre of their husbands. A vague and widespread notion exists that to the British Government is due the credit for putting down this frightful custom, and even fairly well-informed people labour under this misapprehension for lack of exact information. The Portuguese conqueror, Affonso de Albuquerque, was so horrified at the practice that he immediately enforced its abolition when capturing Goa. He found no bitter opposition. But empire-solidifying expediency stayed the hand of the British. The facts are these: as Government took no steps at all, a group of missionaries and Bengalis in 1801 first collected data around Calcutta, and brought their report to the notice of Government with a plea for action. But nothing was done for a whole ten years later; and then the Government took a fatal step. Instead of issuing an unequivocal prohibition of further immolation, English officials were ordered to attend such funeral ceremonies, not to prevent the burning of widows, but merely to ensure that no visible physical compulsion was placed upon the victim! Such action, of course, was quite powerless to prevent the far more potent mental and spiritual pressure brought to bear upon widows to urge them to immolation; but what was still worse, the presence of English officials at such ceremonies actually gave an appearance of official sanction to the burning of widows. This not only enormously hampered the efforts of reformers, but actually brought about an increase and strengthening of the frightful practice.

Realizing the hopelessness of the English official attitude, the great Bengali reformer, Ram Mohan Roy, bent all his efforts to directing a widespread Indian agitation in favour of abolition of *sahamarana*. But the orthodox, feeling their hand immeasurably strengthened by the British condonation of the custom, put up a bitter fight. While in Goa the orthodox had accepted abolition almost without protest, in Bengal they went so far as to found a journal, *Chandrika*, for the sole purpose of defending immolation and to combat Ram Mohan Roy's efforts. Indian reformers asked indignantly why, where Portugal had dared, the great British ruler had not also come forward to put down his foot. Their taunt was, and is, that England has never hesitated to defy orthodox opinion and to enforce unpopular edicts when their results benefited English interests alone (such as, for instance, the doubling of the salt tax or the excise duty on cloth

P. K

from Indian factories in favour of Manchester), but that she is ever slow to put down evils whose eradication might hurt British interests and benefit India alone. There is a certain amount of undeniable truth in the accusation.

Not until 1829, a whole generation after its attention was officially drawn to the abuse, did the Government itself take action and declare *sahamarana* illegal. Meanwhile an additional 70,000 widows had died the fire-death, whose torture earlier Governmental action could easily have prevented. But it must also not be overlooked that in the Indian native States, where Britain had no right to interfere in such matters, *sahamarana* was not abolished until after 1857, another full generation later than in British India; nor is there any reason to believe that, if left to itself, British India would have acted much sooner than did the native States, though undoubtedly British pressure upon Indian princes has always been effective, and might have been used beneficially in this instance.

It is to be regretted that England, by not enforcing the abolition of widow immolation when first appealed to, missed a wonderful chance of demonstrating beyond cavil, though possibly at the risk of material loss to her own interests, the truth of her claim that she was governing for India's benefit. But, by the irony of fate, it is doubtful whether the sum total of suffering among the widows of India was really much reduced by the abolition of *sahamarana*. For yet another generation no law was passed giving these widows a legal right to remarriage. Instead of the sharp but short agony of death, they now entered upon a life of endless deprivation. For despite the law passed at last by the British, the number of widow remarriages among the high castes, especially among Brahmins, remained infinitesimal. The religious horror of such remarriage, and the social stigma placed upon any family which allowed one of its widows to remarry, acted so strongly against it as to nullify completely even the lure of economic gain. By Hindu law, a widow lost all her maintenance rights if she remarried, and this would have made her relatives the beneficiaries through second marriage; yet even this inducement was not sufficient to overcome the prejudice. If we recall that the opportunity of getting hold of a widow's share of maintenance had played its part in inducing general approval and even enforcement of immolation, an action enjoying religious sanction, and then see that in this instance this same desire for gain no longer operates when it defies such sanction, we may realize what a terrible power priestly interpretation of religious duty had gained upon the Hindu mind. Governmental dilatoriness and timidity temporarily increased the widow's sufferings, but it is Hindu orthodoxy which kept it in being. But desire for reform arose in many parts of India. Powerful leaders called ardent reform societies into existence. As early as 1855 the great scholar Vidyasagara spoke and wrote eloquently in favour of remarriage for widows, basing all his claims on ancient pure traditions and uncorrupted scriptures. Ram Mohan Roy, who had fought *Sahamarana*, also adovcated remarriage. He drew around him a very advanced group, the Brahmo Samaj, which discarded caste, Purdah, child-marriage, and restrictions on widows. For several generations it was in the forefront of all reform in India. Its inherent weakness lay in the fact that its religious appeal was eclectic, and further, that it tended

to imitate Christian ritual in its meetings, too alien an
innovation to attract great following. Far more important from the Indian standpoint was a group which
arose in northern India. Its founder, like Ram Mohan
Roy, had also sprung from the Brahmin caste, one of
those insurgent spirits whose vast possibilities for
influence have already been pointed out. This Swami
Dhayanand was a profound Sanskrit scholar, a per-
suasive speaker and dynamic personality. He founded
the Arya Samaj Society, which now counts many
millions of adherents. He based all his claims and
efforts at reform not on Western example, but on an
appeal for a return to ancient Indian truth. He proceeded to prove that most degenerate customs were
later impositions and corruptions, finding no sanction
whatever in the most sacred Hindu scriptures, the
Vedas. The Arya Samaj, with a new intense pride in
things Indian, recoiling sharply from western domination, pledged itself to the purification of Hindu
society—to the abolition of caste, or untouchability,
of child-marriage, to widow remarriage, and to the
furtherance of an Indian type of education for boys
and girls alike. As its call was not to forsake Hindu
ideals, but to re-establish the old pure faith, as it
renewed and strengthened Indian pride and confidence,
it gave relief from the torturing feeling of inferiority,
and could capture Hindu hearts without reserve. The
influence of the Arya Samaj was immense, and is
still continuing unabated. While it had a strongly
nationalistic and political tinge, other reform movements began, pledged purely to social betterment, such
as the Servants of India Society. This too was called
into being and largely supported by Brahmin insur-
gents, established its centres over all India, and

extended its efforts on behalf of women as well as men. The intensity and genuineness of its desire for reform and to serve the needs of India can hardly be better illustrated than by the rules to which its members voluntarily subscribe. They take the vow of virtual poverty; no one may accept or use more money for himself than is absolutely necessary for maintenance, Rs. 40 a month. It is in such indigenous reform that the hope of India rests. Except for the initial impetus given, no outside force can ever equal it in promise. These organizations have not had sufficient Government support. The Arya Samaj, for instance, is at cross purposes with the official world.

But on the other hand it must be stated that where the Government was able to act without defying Hindu law and orthodoxy, which would have meant antagonizing the vast majority, where it had no fear of jeopardizing British interests, it did not hesitate to make use of its power to put down existing evils. This was instanced in such matters as thuggee and infanticide. As Government was able to place the latter offence within the scope of the criminal code, it took an unequivocal stand against it. But nothing was done to remove the causes of this evil—child-marriage and polygamy—and there is no doubt that the practice, to a considerable extent, was merely driven underground. It was so easy, after an unwanted infant could no longer be openly exposed, to deprive it of necessary care and feeding without fear of detection or possibility of proof. Even present-day census figures indicate that the custom is still resorted to by certain groups in some parts of India. Nor is it likely to disappear completely until marriage is no longer made compulsory by religious edict, dowries are no longer ruinous, and female life is valued as highly as male—all matters solely in the hands of Indians.

As for the other customs mentioned in an earlier chapter, Government, bound by its pledge of religious non-interference, could not but condone what missionaries condemned. It was for Indian initiative to abolish such evils. Unquestionably, Western influence gave the impetus to such reforms as that of the abolition of the institution of *devadasis*. But what is of greatest interest is, firstly, that it was not attacked until Indians themselves had a voice in legislation, and could attack it in their newly constituted assemblies, assemblies established only because of the ever more insistent demand for Indianization ; secondly, that the desire for reform was voiced first in that section of India, Madras, where an open conflict for power had broken out between the Brahmin caste and the lower castes, and where the Brahmins were steadily losing ground. It is also to be noted that not until Indian participation in legislation and administration had begun and Brahmin ascendency in that province weakened, could an attempt be made to bring temple funds under public control. This is a further proof that the more completely administration is autonomous, the greater are the opportunities for bitterly needed social reforms. Only Indians dare tackle such reforms as these which affect powerful temple institutions. Cochin and Travancore have already legally abolished *devadasis*, and the complete disappearance of the practice is within sight.

As for that extreme form of abuse, Kulin polygamy, it is also passing, for its bitterest critics have arisen within its own fold. One of these, a personal friend of my own, a Kulin Brahmin, has long ago discarded his sacred thread, taken his one wife out of purdah, and scathingly attacked his group—to great personal loss—both in the spoken and the printed word.

The very restricted practice of polyandry remains still untouched, as the primitive and numerically small group of people whom it affects seem quite contented under it.

One hopes and is inclined to think that when Government gave the fateful pledge of non-interference, the English did not realize the extent and abominable cruelty of the custom of child-marriage, for otherwise non-interference would be a matter for undying accusation against any ' civilized ' power. It may be said, however, that where Indians themselves were so astonishingly slow to wake up to the need of reform, one need hardly wonder that the foreign Government did not greatly concern itself over the fate of India's child brides. It was unusually difficult for a foreign Government to see into the sheltered privacy of the Indian home and to realize where surgery was most needed.

There is good reason to believe that the majority of Indian men themselves were unaware of the full extent of the vitiating power inherent in the system of child-marriage. There are four outstanding explanations for this : hopeless spiritual subjection ; separation of living quarters ; polygamy ; widespread ignorance. Of the abject cringing to priestly rule enough has already been said, but the second aspect, separate quarters, deserves further consideration. Habit and apathy are tremendous fetters and have great power to blind. Just as a physician is popularly accused of not observing sickness in his own family,

so no doubt the Hindu also became chronically inob-
servant of details of women's life.   His was more a
lack of realization of, than indifference to, suffering ;
for under ordinary conditions, the average Hindu does
not voluntarily or consciously inflict pain.   No doubt,
a great share of the guilt of cruelty towards child
brides lies at the door of joint family and separation
of living quarters.   The little bride, a stranger in a
vast household, fares badly if it comes to a battle of
interests or sympathies.   The husband's mother, in
her inordinate fondness for her son, has little patience
with an ailing wife ; she will stifle any complaint
which might work against his interests.   But the
husband himself labours under the disadvantage which
the separation of living quarters imposes ; he hardly
ever sees his little bride except at night and in dim
light ; she is too shy and reticent to think of troubling
him with her complaints unless they grow unbearable.
So as a general rule it is very likely that her ailing and
unhappiness actually escape his observation, the more
so since it must be remembered that the orthodox
Hindu has little chance of observing other women,
and is therefore not so readily struck by comparison
in appearances.   The third, polygamy, remains a
serious factor, and will continue such until it is legally
abolished.   For though very few Hindus have actually
more than one wife, they know that the door is always
wide open for men and hermetically sealed for women.
A Hindu mother, remembering her own lack of girlhood and her physical suffering, frequently attempts
to delay the consummation of her little betrothed
daughter's marriage.   But the threat to substitute
another in the daughter's place unless she is sent at
once upon demand, invariably brings the mother to

immediate acquiescence. As the law is against the mother, she dares not refuse against the express wish of the bridegroom's family, no matter how immature her daughter or how desirable it would be for her to enjoy but one or two additional years of growth. For if the son-in-law should make good his threat and take another wife, her daughter would retain— by virtue of the absolutely binding betrothal ceremony —the status of wife even though the physical marriage would never be consummated. This would mean that she might never remarry, and must virtually lead the desolate life of widowhood. Be a man 15 or 50 years of age, the law is on his side if he consummates his marriage with a girl of 10.

But if polygamy were legally abolished, since betrothal is absolutely binding on Hindus, no bridegroom's family would be able to force the too early surrender for consummation of a little bride against her mother's wishes. But for thousands of years hardly a voice was raised in favour of the abolition of polygamy, nor did Government see fit to interfere.

Legally, neither Indian men nor the foreign Government have ever taken any step against polygamy. One reason for this is that it would in many cases work an undeserved hardship upon men. Where immature youths were continually forced into uncongenial marriages against their will, it seemed fair that they should still have a possibility of future choice of their own. But this hardship would have operated only for a generation or so ; it would in itself have spurred men on to hasten the abolition of all forms of compulsion and particularly of child-marriage.

Another reason operating against abolition lay in

man's very instinct to polygamy, an instinct which yet frequently recoiled from seeking satisfaction in prostitution. Where Western men kept mistresses besides their wives, the Indian considered it fairer to marry them. It must not be overlooked that such plural wives in India are in a far better position than are the "extra women" of Western men; the latter have always laboured under the heaviest social ostracism, while the former have a legal status, respected social standing, and economic security for life, and the inestimable boon of the right to legitimate offspring. But only 2 per cent. of Indian women were thus benefited by the custom of polygamy; the rest of them, especially child brides, were harmed by its ever-present potentiality for evil.

The fourth and last prop of the custom of early marriage—ignorance—was the most far-reaching and the most difficult to combat, because it was so many-sided. The zenana life, lack of education, lack of information and stability, all went to its making, all contributed to a colossal failure to realize the evil and extent of this custom. An absurd reticence had sprung up among Hindu men concerning their families; it was considered the worst possible form for a man to inquire concerning the women in another zenana. "How is your house?" was all that a man ever dared to ask about another man's family. Where even a father or an older brother was not permitted to see the face of a younger son's wife, it is easily imagined how little one man knew about the family of another, one caste about the intimate life of another, or one province about the next. In the world of men, a conspiracy of silence seemed to envelop the question of zenana life. Probably each man accepted sickness and death among his womenfolk as a matter of karma, with little to be said or thought about it, and certainly not as a matter to be discussed with his neighbours. A queer mixture of guilt and reverence concerning family affairs seemed to brood over the minds of men, keeping their tongues tied and their minds wary of probing or questioning. When first brought into contact with Western customs, Indian men tended to be somewhat envious of and attracted by the Westerner's chance of premarital romance, but they were far more repelled by the knowledge of the practice of divorce. So, realizing comparatively little of the ills of child-marriage, but reading much of the heart-ache and heart-break of Western love, and its light treatment of marital responsibility, India settled back doubly content to rest quietly in the assurance of the priests that all was as well as could be within the sacred Hindu family, which nothing could disrupt.

Yet, though the Government took no initiative, individual Englishmen and European missionaries expressed their condemnation of child-marriage. As time went on, the spread of Western science, no doubt, contributed to a realization of its enervating effects. Medical science, based on a thorough knowledge of anatomy and of physiological processes, proclaimed that only mature bodies can perpetuate a healthy race. Observant Indian thinkers became aware of an increasing physical deterioration, mental timidity and moral instability among their people, and traced it to its source. Within the Brahmin caste itself—those worst offenders—the first redeemers arose. Almost a hundred years ago these Brahmin square pegs no longer showed any inclination to bury themselves and their discontent in "renunciation", but bent all their efforts upon fighting the priest-caste and forcing a hesitating and unwilling Government, step by step, to put its seal upon each small gain in reform.

The outline of child-marriage reform, in short, is this. In 1860 agitation resulted in the passing of the *Age of Consent Law*; operating under the Indian Penal Code, ten years was made the age below which it was rape to cohabit with a girl. This was at a time when Brahmins quite commonly married their children as infants, and a bride was taken into the husband's family before puberty.

In 1872 Keshup Chandra Sen, a powerful and fearless Bengali reformer, succeeded in getting a special act passed which provided the first and only escape for those desirous of marrying beyond the orthodox pale. This *Native Marriage Act* permitted girls of 14 and boys of 18 to enter into marriage without the need of religious sanction; but if either was under 21, the consent of the parents was required. This act made interracial, intercommunal, or inter-caste marriages possible.

In 1886 an agitation on the Bombay side led by Malabari, urged reform regarding early marriage, but the State refused to interfere. Government gave the following reasons, "in the competition between legislation on the one hand and caste or custom on the other, . . . the Legislature should not place itself in direct antagonism to social opinion"—a stand which a foreign Government could not sustain and still continue to exist, save when avoiding the problem of social reform!

In 1888 it was still legal to consummate marriage

when the bride was 10. Up till then, not a single case of rape had been brought into court. Such cases must have occurred, but were never reported. In that year another Indian reformer, Madhava Rao, proposed, as the only practical preventative, that Brahmins who married girls under 10, even though only by a betrothal ceremony, should be fined. The World's Women's Christian Temperance Union at Calcutta simultaneously demanded that the age for cohabitation be raised to 13 or 14 years. In the same year, at the other end of India, a large group of Rajputs had already agreed to fix the marriage age at 14 for girls and 18 for boys. But not till 1892 was the *Age of Consent Law* amended to fix the age for consummation at 12.

From that time on Indians all over India continued to agitate for a still further raising of the age limit. In 1904 the native state of Baroda took the lead and passed its *Infant Marriage Prevention Law*, fixing the marriage age at 12 and 16 respectively. But as has been mentioned, its mere imposition of a fine resulted in no very effective check.

Realizing the futility of leaving any such loophole, further agitation was directed towards setting a minimum age below which any marriage should automatically be void and illegal. As this would involve the illegitimacy of children, it could safely be left to interested relatives to expose offenders for the sake of the retention of property. Sir Hari Singh Gour agitated for years to bring about reform ; he desired the marriageable age to be fixed at 14 for girls, 16 for boys. His proposals were opposed and repeatedly blocked by Government members in the legislative councils. Two new Bills were blocked in

1912. In 1925 these reformers at last succeeded in passing the *Age of Consent Law* to fix the marriageable age at 13.

It was disheartening for Indian reformers that they never had the generous support of the Government behind them. "Time and again, this Government stands in the way of progress in Hindu Society," such a man as Srinivasa Iyengar exclaimed.

In 1927, again in face of official opposition, Harbilas Sarda introduced the *Hindu Child Marriage Restraint Bill*. Having realized that all other forms of legislation were futile and could be evaded and flaunted by the orthodox, his Bill aimed directly at fixing the minimum age for girls at 14, and also sought to decree all marriage under that age invalid. The Legislative Assembly appointed a select committee to deliberate over this bill and to introduce whatever changes might be necessary "to make the measure acceptable to the House". Whether *pro* or *con*, people in all corners of India took up their stand. Reformers opposed any change in the bill, the orthodox wished to have none of it.

But meanwhile Miss Mayo's book had appeared, causing an unprecedented storm of resentment in India. General Indian opinion proclaimed that Imperial interests had instigated its writing. Moreover, Nationalist feeling was already strong and all radical opinion was aligned against the foreign Government. So, naturally, it was to the Government's interest at this juncture to rally the support of the orthodox people of India around itself, and carefully to refrain from any action which would antagonize this reactionary group. For this reason, and possibly to sustain Miss Mayo's indictment and to gain time, the Government appointed the *Age of Consent Committee* to tour all India and discover how the 1925 law had worked. This proposal met with stubborn protest from the elected members of the Legislative Assembly. They claimed that since a Bill for further reform was even then under consideration, it was unnecessary and a useless expense of Indian money, to gather more information. The Legislative Assembly refused to vote funds to cover the expenses of this Government-appointed commission. But the Government granted the necessary funds over the head of the Assembly.

Some of the reformers claim that this was fatal to the Bill then pending, because the Commission's tour all over India, collecting opinion from every source, everywhere stirred up orthodox interest and discussion, and, together with the delay involved, gave the orthodox time and impetus to muster all their forces and bring all their influence to bear upon their representatives. The committee presented its report in 1929. Voting on the Sarda Bill had been postponed till its appearance. It was then passed in a very amended form, with its fangs drawn. It no longer made marriage under 14 flatly invalid, but merely provided for the punishment of infringers. A man of 18–21 who marries a girl under 14 may be fined up to Rs. 1,000, but may not be imprisoned in default of payment; a man over 21 similarly offending must pay or go to prison, the maximum penalty being one month in prison or Rs. 1,000 fine.

This leaves the door open, without incurring grave risk, for offenders between the age of 18 and 21. But the bill, after being passed, was not to be effective for another six months. During that time, a regular orgy of child marriages took place all over India ; " thousands and tens of thousands " of parents made haste to complete the ceremonies before the law had power to interfere. While this had the sinister effect of showing how many of the orthodox still clung to the old customs, it had also a very cheering side : it was proof that they considered that the law would be an effective check. In other words, as Hindus on the whole are very law-abiding, it meant that even the majority of the orthodox felt that, the law once in operation, they would have to conform. This being so, there is reason to believe that such a law could have more easily, and with equal effect, been passed and brought into operation when the question of marriage reform was first brought up—if only Government, instead of opposing, had thrown its weight on the side of such India-initiated striving.

Whatever may have been the motives of the Government in appointing the *Age of Consent Committee*, and despite its arbitrariness in overruling the Legislative Assembly, the report prepared and submitted by that body is of immense value and importance. It is the first and only instance of so thorough-going an investigation into the effects of any ancient Indian custom, and it has provided everyone, orthodox as well as reformer, with incontrovertible statistics and information. Not only that, but it has proved, even to the most enlightened Indians themselves, how much such thorough-going investigation is needed, for even they had failed to realize the full force of the evil. Mr. Jayakar (member of the R.T.C.) expressed the view that the Age of Consent evidence is " a relentless showing-up of cruelty and selfishness ". Shah Nawaz stated that he had been under the impression that the evil of early marriage, early consummation, and early maternity was not so great as it had been made out to be, but he now realized that things were far worse even than described in the report.

Strengthened by all these facts and this exact knowledge, reformers will be able to proceed with more certainty and determination. But what is most important, the women of India are now finally awake to the need of reform. Their outstanding organizations have unanimously supported the Sarda Bill and opposed its alteration. Now that it has been passed in a weakened form, they are forming vigilance committees to prevent, or bring to light, any breaches of the law, and thus make it in practice what it was first intended, and they desire it, to be.

The fact that the Government has been "terribly shy of introducing any social legislation", as Bahadur Sapru expressed it, and that "a foreign Government has retarded the intellectual and social progress of the country by its very dilatory methods and by its slow and cautious measures" as Lajpat Rai, member of the Arya Samaj Reform Society, put it, has intensified in the minds of Indian liberals and reformers the desire for full control of legislative and administrative tools and machinery. No doubt an autonomous Government would be free to take greater risks and initiative. Indeed, reformers will need every bit of additional power available in any form, for the struggle against their own reactionaries will be a hard and long one. Stubborn and vigilant effort will be needed to enforce already existing laws, and fierce determination to put through further reform. For even now, in February, 1932, news comes that orthodox forces have been able to defeat a Bill which attempted to secure for a widow an independent share in her husband's property, in place of her present precarious maintenance rights which keep her still dependent on the good or evil will of her nearest male relatives. News also comes that a Bill has just been shelved till the autumn session, a meek little Bill granting the right to divorce merely for those Hindu wives whose husbands are insane, leprous or impotent. Its introduction caused a bitter storm of protest on the part of orthodox men who still, quaintly enough, continue to express abhorrence at the thought of widow or wife remarriage, while in the same breath they calmly continue to arrogate to themselves the right to remarriage and polygamy. But it is very significant that a Moslem member came forward with the suggestion that the bill be circulated with a view to enabling women to express their views—a startlingly fresh departure for Indian men on the Assembly floor. It shows to what extent the recognition of the importance of women as a social factor has percolated through Indian brains.

It remains now for Indian liberals to prove how far they are willing and able to accord to women the unhampered right, not only to voice, as they are doing now, but also to enforce the woman's view on such questions as concern her more deeply than anyone else. Whatever be the attitude of Government in its precarious and unenviable position, the majority of English people, as individuals, rejoice over every gain and wholeheartedly back up the aims and aspirations of Indian women.

X

WOMEN'S PART IN EDUCATION

" EDUCATE a woman and you put a knife into the hands of a monkey," is a popular Brahmin saying. But it looks as if the days of Brahmin proverbs and Brahmin ascendancy were both on the wane. " Educate a girl, and you educate an entire family " ; this saying of a great Western liberal, though much less catchy, has yet become the slogan of Indian liberals. To-day, the monkey seems to be on the point of getting in an effective retort at its male tormentor. The Indian girl, once educated, is likely not only to see to the education of her whole family, but to put new life into her community as well.

How efficiently the knife can be used is best seen in the two native States of Cochin and Travancore, both of which, owing to women's agitation, have lately abolished the *devadasi* system. Travancore, under a splendid woman ruler, though still only eighteen per cent. of literates among women are listed in the last census figures, has raised its proportion in the short intervening time to 50 per cent., according to Dr. Muthulakshmi Reddi. Its women have more rights to-day than those of many a European State. They have full and equal votes with men, and no bar exists to keep them out of any public office. Recently five women have been nominated to the Legislative Assembly of the State, and one woman has held the post of Minister of Public Health. Travancore had been the first Indian State to grant the franchise to women. But taking the last general census figures (instead of the latest local figure) we find that the average proportion of female literacy for the rest of India is very low, only 2 per cent. as against 18 per cent. in Travancore. Not only this, but while in the whole of India one girl was educated to seven boys, Travancore even then had the astonishingly high figure of 18 per cent. of girls to 28 per cent. of boys. In view of the amazingly progressive condition of Travancore, the realization grows more strong that it is lack of women's education more than all else that is holding India in chains. An educated womanhood could far more easily fight its way to freedom from bondage to priestly injunctions and ancient customs. The question arises, Why is a country with so high a traditional culture lagging on the whole so far behind in present-day women's education? Statistics tell us that among the Hindus, only one girl is educated to eight boys, while among Mohammedans conditions are still worse, for only one girl is educated to eleven boys. Is this wholly due to priestly restrictions and the crushing power of custom, or does closer examination reveal another important factor?

The first thing which strikes an investigator is this, that native States, such as Baroda, Mysore, Travancore, and a few others introduced compulsory education years ago, and have done away with the tuition system, but not a single British province has yet followed their example. Travancore is spending

25 per cent. of its total revenue on education—it is the biggest item on its budget—but British India is spending only 7·2 per cent. on education. The question immediately arises, Why is British India lagging behind? What is England's part in the education of Indian girls? Is it that here, too, as we have found to be the case in social reform, the foreign ruler may be unable, in intention or capacity, effectively to further the best interests of Indian education?

Just as the ordinary person in the West with a mild interest in India accepts unquestioningly the current impression that England has abolished widow immolation, so also he sincerely believes that England has brought such education as there is to Indian girls. Sir Thomas Munro said in 1813 :

> " If a good system of agriculture, unrivalled manufacturing skill, a capacity to produce whatever can contribute to either convenience or luxury, schools established in every village for teaching reading and writing and arithmetic, the general practice of hospitality and charity towards each other, . . . are signs which denote a civilized people, then the Hindus are not inferior to the nations of Europe, and if civilization is to be an article of trade between England and India, I am convinced that England will gain by the import of cargo."

How then does it come about that to-day, just one hundred years later, there remains but one school for every five villages in India? May it not be because political subjection of itself—be alien rule good or evil—is bound to bring about degeneration? Just as we have found Hindu purdah and infant-marriage to be the direct results, in the evil forms they have taken, of political subjection to the Moghuls, may not subjection to British rule have to a great extent called forth the very defects of character and institutions which, it is now claimed, make Indians unfit to rule themselves? This frequent suggestion is made here merely because of its bearing on the education of Indian girls in particular, and the general retrogression in cultural, though not in material values, which has taken place in India during the past centuries.

What are the facts? From ancient days onward India always possessed a highly developed system of education in its Brahmanic Sanskrit Schools. Of Brahmanic education the Rev. F. E. Kedy wrote that it was at least not inferior to the education of Europe before the Revival of Learning. But elementary education was provided also for the two lower groups of castes in a form which effectively supplied the special needs of Kshatriyas and Vaishyas. A popular, indigenous and satisfactory kind of instruction was imparted to all the trading and agricultural classes. Its only drawback was that it excluded women, the lowest class—the Sudras, and the untouchables. This system, evolved during the Brahminical period, continued despite Buddhism and the Moghul invasion, until the British came. During the Buddhist period, the schools were thrown open to all castes and creeds, girls and boys alike, and a high level of general literacy prevailed. The Brahminical Revival once more excluded Sudras and women from the schools in some sections and classes of India. But the Brahmin priesthood was never able to enforce its restrictions universally. So, while one school took care of boys in every village, in some parts, there still existed schools for girls also. Among the Sikhs, for instance, who overthrew the Brahmin yoke nearly six hundred years ago, no prejudice obtained against women's education. The same was true among the Punjabis, and in most parts of the south, where Brahmin rule had only slightly penetrated. In Delhi alone, for instance, prior to the imposition of the British system, six public schools for girls were kept by Punjabi women teachers, many of whom were often wives of Brahmin square pegs. Dr. Leitner wrote of these groups that

"much reading of the elementary religious books, sewing, embroidery, cooking with extreme care for the household, great neatness, tenderness in trouble, and gentle meditation in family disputes, constitute the chief features of female home rule and education in the better classes, who regard their female relatives with a respect and a religious affection of which we have not even the outward profession in Europe".

But when the British took over the administration, the old system became completely disorganized and disappeared, for it no longer answered the new needs, nor received the governmental support without which no system of education can flourish for long. When the alien Government initiated their educational policy in India, they restricted their efforts entirely to the male population, just as the Brahmins had done. "No funds were allotted for the girls' education." This meant that girls could profit by it only if their parents were willing to send them to the schools meant for boys, an almost unthinkable condition for India in those days. Dr. Leitner, the authority quoted above, traces the decline of women's education after the British occupation and gives the main reasons. First among them came this fact, that the foreigner opened his schools in public places and arranged for a system of inspection by men. Purdah groups objected to sending their girls to be taught along with boys and exposed to view. Moreover, even if this objection could have been overcome, closed conveyances would have been needed to take the girls to and from school, an expense for which no arrangements were made. This alone sufficed for generations to keep high-caste girls away from such schools. Moreover, all but the most radical were suspicious of the foreign learning. What the ortho-dox saw of the life and habits of white women in India was too radically opposed to their own ideas of what woman should be and do, to make them eager to give their girls Western education.

But the one factor which operated most heavily against popular education of both girls and boys was the fateful decision of Macaulay in 1834 that English should be used as the medium of instruction, and that vernaculars were " a waste of time ". The difficulty implied in the change from one language to another, and the utter uselessness of the foreign language to the common people, to all but those few who were training for service under the foreign ruler, raised an insurmountable barrier. The introduction of the British system brought about an enormous decrease of indigenous schools, reducing the former number of one school for every village until it became one to five.

It would have been in the best interest of India at that time, if the Government could have patronized the existing Brahminical system and remoulded it to include all the countless millions of low castes, outcastes and women. But the British could hardly have done other than they did. It was absolutely imperative for the handful of British administrators in the vast sea of Indians, to save their own energy and effort in every possible way. They could not carry on their self-imposed task of administration without an army of English-speaking clerks. The system of education they introduced was admirably calculated to produce these. "We must at present do our best to form a class who may be interpreters between us and the millions we govern; a class of persons Indian in blood and colour, but English in tastes, in opinions, in morals and in intellect." But that such a course was more to the interest of India than of England or even equally so, cannot be maintained. Besides bringing about the decrease in popular education already mentioned, it had another immediate deleterious effect; it stressed the money-making side of education as opposed to its cultural interest. Pupils entered these schools mainly as the only open door to lucrative service under the Government. But for each one who now proceeded with it, four others did without the education by which their fathers had formerly benefited.

Where boys fared thus, girls fared worse. It was useless to praise the English system, or to blame the stupidity of Indian customs, or the stubborn orthodoxy of parents who kept their girls at home and refused the benefits of education. To ensure sound progress, each country must be given step by step the kind of education suited to the needs of its majorities in the manner acceptable to it. This the foreign Government was unable to do. It had neither the time, the knowledge, nor the men to spare. Faced by their own needs, and with England and its imperial interests at heart, how could this little group of enterprising, courageous Britishers, busy over their tre-

mendous task of empire-consolidation, have considered
the particular needs of Indian women?   Understaffed
and overworried, how could it be expected that an
alien administrator—whose women even in his own
home country were still likewise labouring under
educational disadvantages—should have the vision
or the ability to evolve and put in working order a
system of schooling really suitable for girls whose
mode of life was so utterly alien, so hidden from him?

Therefore, instead of bringing about an expansion, the first effect of British rule in India was actually
retrogression in the field of women's education.
The initiative in modern education for women, says
Dr. Reddi, was taken, not by the British Government,
but

> "by missionary societies, helped by Raja Ram Mohan
> Roy, the Indian reformer, and individual Englishmen,
> such as Mr. Hare.   It was, however, in 1849 that a
> member of the Bengal Government, the Hon. Mr.
> Bethune, founded a school for Hindu girls in Calcutta
> and induced Lord Dalhousie to lay a duty on the Bengal
> Council for providing funds for girls' as well as boys'
> education".

In Bombay also, some English professors lent
wholehearted encouragement to the efforts of a
group of Hindus who took up the question of women's
education, opened schools, set to work to prepare
textbooks, and even started a journal advocating
the education of women.   Individual effort partly
compensated for Government failure.   "For many
years", Arthur Mayhew says, "the Government
educational efforts among women were tentative and
hesitating.   Bentinck and Macaulay contemplated no

attack on the ignorance of half the population of India and more than half of its vital forces."

It was thus a diminutive minority which had occasion to send its girls to school in these early days; these were drawn from the most radical group and from those closest in touch with the foreign administration. Thus we find the anomaly that in 1881 actually more Indian girls studied English than their own mother tongues. This led for a time to an artificial state of things. It was considered a mark of distinction among the majority of this small group to ape the foreign ruling class in all respects, and to train their girls as much as possible like English girls. The higher and more intensely Western the education they received, the less did they know or value their own ancient culture, and the more did they come to treat it with indifference and disdain. This created a deep gulf between them and the rest of their countrywomen. These very women, who should by virtue of their higher education have turned their trained energies to social and educational work, wasted their time in imitating the empty social life of the majority of white officials' wives in India. This retarded educational progress for at least another generation.

But luckily, the girls who had received this first de-Indianizing education were not all daughters of office-seekers under Government, but often of our square pegs, the social reformers. Their aim was not merely material advantage. These were the people who were capable of appreciating fully the real benefits of English culture, though in a manner somewhat disconcerting and upsetting to British Governmental interests. For they found in English thought, life, and literature a wealth of ideas placing liberty above all else and upholding the rights of individuals, the will of the people. Three main reactions followed from their English-patterned education; they were made politically conscious as never before; they recognized the evils of their own society more clearly by contrast with an alien society free from Indian forms; they readily took to the English sport of criticizing authority in power and calling it to account.

These Western-educated square pegs early realized that what India needed was not the top-heavy denationalizing education which turned out thousands of English-speaking clerks, but elementary, vernacular, Indian-modelled schools available to all castes, to girls as well as boys. They also realized that, for a long time to come, special provisions must be made for purdah groups to meet their objections.

These Indian women, more even than the men, realized that educational methods must be fundamentally overhauled and remodelled. Neither the old and discarded Brahminical system nor that of the British would do. A curriculum must be prepared, textbooks must be created, whose subject-matter should be primarily Indian and intimately related to the daily life of children in primary grades. The greatest stress at this period must be laid on primary, and not higher education, for reformers could not count on getting hold of girls for more than the few years preceding their early marriage. The system of Government education in India, modelled exactly upon what an English or Scottish boy needed at home, was little likely to benefit an Indian girl. It did her no good to read of hares and bluebells and

Santa Claus, of Hastings, of English months which correspond to no Indian ones—all things which she acquired parrot fashion to forget again as rapidly, as they had no intimate vivid relationship to the life she knew in home or village. It was desirable that she should be taught such subjects as would best fit her to cope with her own future intimate family and motherhood problems. It was far more important that she should learn something of hygiene and sanitation, of the care of children, the value of food, a little sewing, etc., than that she should be able to read English books. In reading, it was far more important for her to have such mental food as would enable her to apply it immediately to quicken and enrich the intimate life of those about her, for her to be able to read aloud in the vernacular from Indian books or papers what would interest the zenana group at home. Could this come about, it was indeed true that one girl's education might mean the educating of an entire family—and how much more numerous a family than the European commentator had dreamed of !

But how to put these ideas into effect ? Dissenting opinion had as yet no means of enforcing its voice in administrative policy, had no Governmental channels for effecting any modification of the existing educational policy.

The only hope lay in setting up independent schools, a course which was then adopted in many parts of India. The Arya Samaj of Northern India had soon established more schools for boys and girls than any one of the many missionary societies ; the Brahmo Samaj had established an excellent school for girls in Calcutta ; in Poona the seed had been planted which was in time to blossom into the first Indian Women's University.

But this was indeed uphill work, for where a population contributes through heavy taxation its share toward the support of governmental schools, it is no easy task to find the money to maintain a duplicate system. Indian reformers especially desired that schools should be free, since abject poverty would prevent great numbers, even among the middle classes, from sending girls to school under a tuition-fee system. Many a school was established and struggled on for years, till it found itself faced by insuperable difficulties. As such schools made a greater appeal to the public and inspired more confidence than Government schools, attendance usually expanded far more rapidly than funds and accommodation. Their founders had to choose between turning away pupils, and appealing for Government grants to enable them to expand. But the latter course was possible only for schools willing to conform their curriculum and examinations to Government requirements, and for those which charged fees to pupils. This problem seriously restricted and delayed the evolution and rapid spreading of a wholesome, suitable, indigenous system of education, for many bravely started schools, after a long and hopeless struggle to keep alive in independence, had to give up their most treasured principles, conform, and accept Government grants.

I know, for instance, that the head of the most important such school in Calcutta resisted valiantly as long as possible, and then gave in with heavy heart. Her greatest sorrow was that poor girls, too poor to pay the tuition fee demanded by Government, had to be turned off in consequence of the acceptance of the grant. An effort was made to compensate for this by establishing scholarships, but these could not fulfil the need or nullify the damage.

This conflict in aims and interest between the Governmental and indigenous educational policies is one of the main causes for the clamour which arose for Indianization.

The ever-growing conviction among those Indians who took an intense interest in Indian development was, therefore, that what India needed was neither missionary nor Government schools, but a truly indigenous system. Many Western observers and critics are coming to the same conclusion. For the top-heavy English system had to an ever-increasing degree turned out college graduates whom even Governmental needs, which had first called them into being, could no longer absorb. These largely town-bred youths were unfit for, nor would they have considered, village teaching. Unabsorbed and unemployed, they made up that seething, combustible mass of malcontents which later took to political discussion and extreme action as to water in a parched desert. So, in the long run, this educational system, called forth by English imperial needs, was to result in imperial frustration.

An American observer some years ago expressed the opinion that the best thing for India would be to close its top-heavy colleges for some years, and to expend the money and effort thus saved on primary education.

Certain it is that reformers among Indian women echo this conviction of the need to bring education not only into the villages, but into the very heart of purdah homes. A later chapter will show how they have proceeded to carry this into effect. The Indianization of the legislative and administrative bodies promises to further this greatly. For an Indian administration will see its way to making grants of Government money to indigenous educational institutions without any longer requiring them to conform to Government school standards. In time, Government schools themselves will undergo complete transformation.

This, in fact, is what we are witnessing to-day. Now that women have obtained a voice in municipal affairs, they are definitely exerting all their efforts to bring pressure to bear towards modifying the Governmental system of education and making it answer the deeper needs of India.

In the native States there was no need to fight against an already established retarding system, or to attempt the difficult task of financing a separate alternative system. This, without need to go into further details, explains why education has made far more progress in some native States than in British India. All effort could go directly towards new upbuilding and development. Not only so, but native States could set aside a far greater proportion of their revenue for education than the Government, burdened by an appalling army budget for the defence of imperial interests, has seen fit to do in British India. Government spends 31·4 per cent. of the revenue on defence, and only 7·2 per cent. on education, as against Travancore's 25 per cent. for education. This partly explains also the enormous discrepancy in the following figures, though the existence of the matriarchal system in the two first-named States must also be taken into consideration as a particularly favourable factor.

Literates among Women over Five Years of Age

	Per cent.
Travancore State	17·3
Cochin State	11·5
Baroda State	4·7
British India	2·0

It likewise lends interest to the fact that the Central Provinces have the low proportion of 0·43 per cent. of female literacy, and that Delhi itself, the seat of the alien Government, has only 2·9 per cent., though Bangalore, in the native State of Mysore, has 9·1 per cent.

Other figures drawn from the Educational Commissioner's latest report further indicate the trend of educational interest in India. At present, in British India, for lack of other facilities, girls are often reluctantly sent to Governmental institutions, but the moment indigenous schools are made available in any section, these girls are withdrawn from the Government schools. Yet the movement for educating girls has grown so strong that even in Government schools girl pupils have increased between 1920 and 1930 by 30 per cent. as against 16 per cent. between 1910 and 1920. In the United Provinces alone, the enrolment of girls from the backward Mohammedan community increased between 1920 and 1930 by 53 per cent., from the far more highly educated Hindu group by 28 per cent. Then comes the surprising figure of 379 per cent. increase for girls from the depressed classes, and of only 9 per cent. for Indian Christians.

P.   M

These figures are a telling indication of the need for education for girls. Much work needs to be done, and it must begin with an entire rewriting of all textbooks, the remoulding of curricula, and the infusion into them of Indian literature, Indian arts, and Indian problems. Under the Government system, all textbooks were concerned with English instead of Indian problems. It is this factor which has detached Indian youth and led them to take an exaggerated interest in political movements, instead of a sound interest in indigenous social concerns. We need only remember the influence which social problem-plays, for instance, have had in the West, to realize what opportunities have been neglected in India. If Indian textbooks, from the lowest primary forms upward, are made to embody references to Indian customs, such, let us say, as a condemnation of the ruinous custom of huge marriage expenditure and dowries, the excessive economic waste of women's ornaments, the extortion of the native moneylending system, and by contrast the safety of postal savings-banks, etc., enormous social gain may result. Those things would sink into the child's mind and bear direct fruit.

These are changes which Indian hands and brains are fittest to undertake ; the sooner financial support can be procured for such work, the better for India. In fact, step by step with the increasing Indianization of the administration, interest in educational changes has also increased. Since in many provinces Indians have been appointed ministers of education and made responsible to the Assemblies instead of directly to Government, education has received a tremendous impetus, though their departments are still hampered by inability to secure enough of the Government-controlled funds.

Tardily, Government itself is also waking up to realities. Not until a Committee of eminent educationalists under Sir Philip Hartog made an extended study, did it seem to realize that India could not progress educationally, as far as girls were concerned, without women teachers, and that a mere two Government training colleges for these for the whole of British India were hardly enough. The five existing missionary colleges Hindu and Musulman girls will not attend. But even so, it is owing to the agitation of Indian women, aided by Lady Irwin, that the most promising educational move has lately been undertaken ; it is proposed that a Central Home Science Institute be established at Delhi which graduates and matriculates from all parts of India may attend, to be specially trained as Domestic Science Teachers. They are then to return to their own States and Provinces, there to translate and teach in their own vernaculars the knowledge acquired. Hygiene, cooking, needlework, laundry work, first aid, dietetics—all the arts essential for the improvement of the home are to be taught. It will be the first institution of its kind in India, and it is bitterly needed, as the present lack of teachers in these branches is the greatest drawback to reform. One very important problem has presented itself during the deliberations over the working plans for this Central Home Science Institute —the choice of language in which instruction is to be imparted. As no single Indian language could be understood by all the pupils, coming from every part of India, English was naturally suggested, for since only matriculates and graduates will attend, it would be the one common language bond already existing. But the resentment at the retardation which the introduction of English into the schools has caused to primary education, is deep and lasting. Bitter opposition was expressed by several speakers to the adoption of English. Miss Feroz-ud-din was

> " sure that no nation could ever rise to the pinnacle of greatness and glory unless it received its education through its mother tongue . . . was not convinced that the graduates who would learn in English would be able to teach in the vernacular, as she had noticed that English-speaking girls could not speak even a few words in Urdu. She forcefully refuted the suggestion that English was a universal language and stated that against one woman who knew English there were 99 who did not. She declared that if there were 300 languages already in existence in India, that was no argument why there should be 301 ".

Then Rajkumari Amrit Kaur wanted to know

> " to which Indian language out of the 300 existing, Miss Feroz-ud-din was referring. She herself attributed their gathering in that Hall purely to their knowledge of English, and mentioned that Miss Feroz-ud-din herself had made her speech in that language. She explained that the idea underlying the scheme was not to eliminate Indian languages, but to train teachers as early as possible, which it was impracticable, at the moment, to do in any other language ".

Miss Khemchand pointed out that " while she did not want to make the English language the *lingua franca* of India, the fact remained that India could not do without English ".

This discussion, which took place in the leading Indian women's organization, vividly illuminates one of the most constructive contributions which England has made to India—despite all drawbacks, the introduction of English has given it the only medium of intercommunication so far practicable. While it has harmed and retarded primary education, it has enabled the intelligentsia of all India to share, interchange, and consolidate their views, their knowledge, and their plans of work. It has been urged that Hindi should be made the *lingua franca* of India, but this would hardly ever have the same pregnant possibilities that English offers of keeping the Indian intelligentsia in touch not only with each other, but also with the outside world.

To show to what an extent educational problems are now occupying the thoughts of eminently capable Indian women leaders in educational reform, and the means of suggestion and criticism they employ, I shall append here, without further comment, various extracts from the latest available report of the All-India Women's Conference held in Lahore in 1931. They embody the actual voice of Indian womanhood of to-day. [Italics are mine throughout.]

" We have found that the Conference has become a great power in the land and has been the link—the indissoluble tie—between the creeds, castes and communities that inhabit this great and ancient land.

" *We, women,* through the Conference, *have realized that all our differences of caste, creed and race should sink in our attempt* to achieve a common purpose in our efforts *to better the conditions of our sisters.*

" We have awakened from a long rest, from too long a sleep, to a realization of our actual needs. Awakened womanhood is determined to undo the wrongs of ages, to bring back our lost civilization, in short to bring about the real Indian renaissance and the regeneration of India.

"Women representing all communities and races in India, having gathered together in 25 constituent Conferences in order to express their opinion on education in general in India to-day, and on the education of girls and women in particular, and from these Conferences having elected representatives to exchange views at the above All-India Women's Conferences, hereinafter record the result of their serious study of these problems, and express as Resolutions their convictions, based on their practical experience and intuition, regarding the broad general lines on which they believe that it is imperative for the good of their children and the future welfare of the Nation that Reforms in education should be carried out.

"Women are grateful for the immense service already rendered to the Indian people by the various educational authorities, official and non-official, in India. *The present system*, however, *was thought out primarily*, they believe, *in the interests of boys*, and was formulated by men. *The time has now come for women to review and reform this system.*

"This Conference defines Education as training which will enable the child or the individual to develop his or her latent capacities to the fullest extent for the service of humanity. It must therefore include elements for physical, mental, emotional, civic and spiritual development. *The course of study* arranged for this purpose *must be so flexible as to allow of adaptation to the conditions of the individual, the locality and the community.*

"At every stage of education the spirit of social service should be inculcated.

"Moral training, based on spiritual ideals, should be made compulsory for all schools and colleges.

"In all education of girls, teaching of the ideals of motherhood, and in making the home beautiful and attractive, should be kept uppermost.

" Agriculture should be included in the curriculum as a compulsory subject in schools in rural areas and as an optional subject in all other schools and colleges.

" A complete course of physical training should be made compulsory in all boys' and girls' schools and should include as much cheerful recreation out of doors as possible ; Eurhythmics and Girl-Guiding on Indian lines should be included.

" Systematic medical inspection should be made compulsory in all schools and colleges ; and, in the case of girls, the inspection should be carried out by medical women. Where possible school clinics should be started and arrangements made to deal with cases of malnutrition.

" Girls' schools should be inspected both by women having general and also by those having technical qualifications.

" The second line of work suggested was that each Constituent Conference should take up the question of school buildings and play-grounds in its own neighbourhood. There seemed to be a consensus of opinion that most girls' schools were badly housed, and had no play-grounds, but as they were usually situated in hired buildings these conditions could be improved.

" The suggestion was that the Standing Committee Members should report next year as to how many schools they had been able to get moved into clean, airy, healthy buildings and surroundings . . . this would be a most valuable and important piece of practical work.

" *Proper facilities* should be provided in purdah educational institutions *for girls who observe purdah*.

" This Conference approves of cinema films being used for educational purposes, in schools generally and in rural schools in particular.

" The Conference in its memorandum has emphasized the necessity of reforming and enlarging the conception of Education in Universities, Training Colleges and

Schools. It views with interest the progress that has been made and joins with the constituent Conferences in reiterating the importance of the inclusion in the curricula of the study of—

(*a*) Sociology, Home and Domestic Science in all its branches.

(*b*) Fine Arts (Music, Painting, etc.).

(*c*) Specifically Indian Culture, including the Vernaculars and Sanskrit, Arabic and Persian.

(*d*) Physical culture.

" This Conference is of the opinion that—

(*a*) priority should be given to the claims of girls' education in every scheme of educational expansion,

(*b*) it protests against the omission of girls from schemes of compulsory education,

(*c*) it urges that *compulsory education should be enforced* wherever it has been established, and that public co-operation should be secured *to ensure the regular attendance of pupils until their twelfth year*, because it realizes that educated mothers are a sure guarantee of the education of the coming generation and an essential factor in the advance of a nation."

" This Conference is strongly in favour of compulsory primary education for girls as well as for boys ; it recommends all Local Governments and Local Bodies to take immediate steps to introduce compulsory education in urban, suburban and rural districts in such a way that at all district headquarters and towns the scheme shall be in full working order within five years and shall be universal within twenty years. This Conference is of the opinion that this *compulsory education should be made free* in all schools provided by public authorities *to all those unable to pay for it*."

" *Our Conference has repeatedly asked for a better provision for the education of girls in the annual budget of the Depart-*

*ment of Public Instruction, but the response to this demand has
not been very encouraging so far.* Everyone agrees with it in
*theory, but in practice we are very nearly where we were before.
Let us exert ourselves to the utmost to get sufficient financial
support from Government* as well as from the public for
fitting girls for all departments of life.

" A closer examination will reveal the fact that *the slow
growth and development of women's education* even in those
provinces where conditions have been favourable, *has
been mainly due to the lack of funds* to finance the new and
revised scheme. Expenditure on women's institutions
in percentage of the expenditure on the men's institutions
is 14·4 in 1927 in British India.

" Now Madras and Punjab are the only provinces that
possess a woman Deputy Directress—an officer who is
charged with the duty of starting new schools in school-
less centres, of opening training centres for women
teachers wherever there is need, of modifying syllabuses
for the girls' schools and of advising the Director on
matters relating to girls' education.

" THE MADRAS POLICY.—The scheme consists of a
ten-year programme of expansion, and includes the
opening of a hundred middle schools for girls, eighty
rural training classes for Hindu women, ten rural training
classes for Muhammadan women and the provision of
stipends." (This is the province with the strongest anti-
Brahmin movement, and most advanced in education.)

" Miss Khemchand pointed out that *the responsibility*
[for enforcing girls' education] *fell on the shoulders of
women,* and the necessity of forcing men to accede to
their reasonable demands, *as if they did not do it, the men
who were the only persons in charge of District Boards, Municipalities and educational institutions, would never do it of
themselves.* As a result of the efforts of the Conference,
not only had the syndicate of Patna University appointed
lady members on the Secondary Board of Education,
Board of Studies for Music and Geography, etc. etc., but

the laudable efforts of Mrs. Das of Patna had resulted in a number of ladies having been elected as members of the various District Boards and Municipalities. One lady had even stood for the Membership of the Legislative Council. In regard to the Ajmer Constituency, the efforts of the Council had resulted in regular medical inspection of school boys and girls, and a special committee of the Rajputana and Central India School Board had been appointed to inquire into the question of curriculum for girls' schools. One woman has been nominated to act on the committee by the Government of Madras, to advise the Government and the Director of Public Instruction on matters relating to women.

" As the result of our propaganda, signs of activity for the amelioration of the general condition of women are visible all over the country. More and more institutions, industrial schools, free training classes for imparting instruction in domestic arts to poor women, boarding-houses for women and women's co-operative societies are springing up day by day. Education of women generally is receiving the greatest attention from our workers. Village-visiting sub-committees, school-visiting, slum-visiting, mill-visiting, and jail-visiting sub-committees are coming into existence. Play-grounds are being provided for women, welfare-centres and maternity homes are being started and maintained wherever possible by our members."

" *There is ample evidence to show that there is a keen demand both on the part of the parents and the public for the education of their girls.* Even in the so-called purdah province, the few existing schools have been over-crowded and admissions for new pupils have been refused.

" This Conference reiterates the importance of tackling the problem of Adult Education in every way possible and urges the Government, Municipal Councils, Local Bodies and Women's Associations to organize classes and centres for the promotion of literacy and general education among adult women, and suggests the establishment of cinemas, moving libraries and publication of suitable books and magazines in the vernaculars. . . . Rajkumari Amrit Kaur . . . said she had been approached by older women requesting that they too should be granted some facilities for education and she firmly believed that their claim was a just one. . . . She considered it the duty of everyone to afford the adult women of the poorer classes facilities for learning home crafts, etc., which might bring them in small incomes.

" This Conference reiterates the importance of educating girls of all communities in the same schools in order to promote mutual understanding and a common cultural unity.

" *The Rani of Mandi* condemned the system of educational institutions requiring children to fill up forms stating their castes and creeds. She *appealed to everybody not to tell their children whether they were Brahmins or untouchables, Syeds or low castes. Everybody should treat everybody else alike, and if any caste questions were ever put, their children were to be taught to say that they were ' Indians '.*"

" This Conference requests its delegates to visit the schools in their locality ; to investigate cases of differential treatment of Depressed Class children and to report to the authorities concerned. It urges that Provincial Governments and the Governments of Indian States be requested to enforce the laws already existing for the admission of Depressed Class children to schools.

" . . . the lives of saints, spiritual teachers and religious personalities should be included in the daily lessons of the pupils without any of the myths, legends, rituals and ceremonies, which have ever been the fruitful causes of quarrels, religious fights, bloodshed among the people of diverse creeds on earth, so that *the fundamental unity of all the great religions may be brought home to our girls and boys.*

" CALL FOR UNITY.—India is pulsating with a new life and a great awakening has come upon its men and women. Our duty, *the women's duty at this crisis, is not to curb the growing nationalism,* not to check the flowing tide, *but to direct it and guide it through useful channels.* At the same time, we should revolt against all forms of violence, injustice and unnecessary and uncalled-for interference with the basic human rights. Let us not forget that in the nation-building process women have ever been playing a great and glorious part as citizens, wives and mothers. We are born to create and not to destroy, to love and not to hate ; therefore let us create life, love and beauty and promote peace and harmony among peoples and nations. This Conference itself has demonstrated in full the union of all communities, creeds, races in India on a common platform of service to the nation. Let this feeling of friendliness and comradeship, that is a marked feature of the Conference, be developed into love—that perfect, pure and simple love—the mother's love that would be enduring and that would embrace, within its fold, all humanity."

This was spoken during the fifth Congress of the All-India Women's Conference—an organization which has captured the interest and aligned the forces of women to an amazing degree. In one single year 33 constituencies sprang into active life in different sections scattered all over India.

In view of the fact that these organized Indian women now have the power of the vote to bring effective pressure to bear upon officials, the foregoing analysis of educational needs and their proposed plans of work are most encouraging. The education of Indian girls can be in no safer hands than those of the Indian mothers. The light of Vedic freedom and high living is indeed glimmering again on the Indian horizon, when a woman of a royal house stands out in public with the demand that distinctions of caste be done away with—a resolution which received the unanimous support of the whole group of assembled women. It is equally thrilling to have another woman, Dr. Muthulakshmi Reddi, one of the staunchest leaders, declare in favour of giving in Indian schools ethical teaching of a kind which would make children familiar with and appreciative of the best in all religions. This is a very advanced step, yet it derives directly from India's ancient tradition of religious tolerance. India has always led the world, and likewise promises to lead it in the future, in religious toleration. Hindu-Mohammedan religious friction is a very recent product of political turmoil; Europe, with the frightful misery of its religious wars, should be the last to dare reproach India for religious intolerance. In view of this, it is doubly satisfying and a matter of tremendous promise and significance that Indian women have taken this public opportunity of declaring in favour, no longer of religious tolerance only, but of mutually appreciative religious sympathy.

It would seem as if, where Brahmin priesthood has disgraced and degraded its spiritual mission, Indian womanhood has risen to lead India back to her ancient unity. Indian womanhood has now taken the *bonti* in both hands—that sharp curved knife which serves every conceivable household purpose from slicing vegetables to cutting a navel cord. It is a tool so efficient that it can do almost everything but talk. But now that the days of absolute obedience and submission are gone, the " monkey " behind the *bonti* has started to talk—woe to the Brahmins!

If some twist of magic irony should suddenly make

the age-old threat come true, and the husband should die whose wife learns to read and write—soon there would be so vast a pall of smoke over the fair face of India from Brahmin funeral pyres as would prevent even alien bombing aeroplanes from coming to the rescue of Hindu orthodoxy.

XI

SOME 'HELPLESS' WOMEN OF INDIA

EVEN the briefest account of the women who, in India, have done remarkable work in reform and education, would of itself fill a great book. But to mention a few may serve to let the West appreciate to what extent women of the future promise to have the power to further development in India. Such women will take from Western systems and apply in India whatever may be genuinely helpful, while continuing to treasure and guard the valuable content of their own traditions. No outsider, no matter how understanding and sympathetic, will ever be able to equal these Indian women in insight into the real needs of the growing generation, or in wisdom of choice when trying to find what will answer such needs.

Let me start with one with whose work and life I have been privileged to come into close contact, Lady Abala Bose. She is the daughter of a reformer, a member of the Brahmo Samaj, and not only has never been in Purdah, but had the rare privilege of being given regular physical exercise in childhood—no doubt the source of her unflagging physical energy.

She took a four-year course in medicine in Madras, being the first women of her section to take up such studies. At twenty-two she married a young Bengali Professor of Physics of Calcutta University, a man who had voluntarily taken it upon his shoulders to liquidate a debt of his father's of Rs. 40,000, though under no legal obligation to do so. For years they both sacrificed many a comfort until this load was off their shoulders. But even afterwards, Abala Bose continued to supervise personally every detail of the expanding household, taking that intimate, motherly, unobtrusive interest in the welfare of every creature under her roof which is so characteristic of Indian housewives. Every morning by seven she had already bathed and breakfasted. Breakfast-time was also the visiting hour for friends and relatives, and as often as not for people who came to consult with her on outside matters. Breakfast cleared away, Abala Bose sat on talking with these visitors, but her hands were not idle—she herself prepared every bit of the vegetables and fruits needed for that day. She pared them, cut them into cubes and slices, washed each ready pile once, and then let the pieces drop into shining brass bowls full of clear water, so that the cook had nothing more to do than make them into delicious curries or other dishes. Thus, even in this modernized household, the absolute purity of food was as rigidly controlled and ensured as it is in orthodox families where the housewife, no matter how high her rank, first bathes, and then dons a special clean linen sari to prepare and cook the food with care as scrupulous as if performing a religious ceremony. Not only that, but Abala Bose herself makes all the purchases for the household, driving to the New Market for that purpose, closely examining all she buys, and driving good bargains, for no one better than she knows the value of money and what great things even a little of it can accomplish in impoverished India. For her house and family she purchases and uses largely Indian materials, and is fully alive to their beauty. She keeps the accounts, writes out the laundry list for the dhobie, engages and supervises the *durzi* (tailor) in his mending and making of new clothes, sees that the entire house is kept spotless despite listless servants, bandages cut fingers, entertains guests, arranges the usual dinner for about six people or a special feast for sixty, with the same unruffled, unhurried, competent ease and despatch. At each and every turn she looks to the minutest details of her absent minded husband's comforts, his clothes, his food, his appointments. Nothing is ever forgotten, nothing only half done. At every meal she sees to it that he has only just what is good for him; knowing his impatience and carelessness, every little thing is made ready for him as if for a baby. None of these personal details are left to servants. The orange pulp on the plate before him has not a trace of skin or seed, the shelter of the mosquito curtain not a single imprisoned tormentor, as a result of her care. Every evening at dusk, no matter how absorbed or unwilling he may be, she persuades, cajoles, or purloins her husband from his preoccupations, to take the ride in the open air so necessary to his health and work. Before or after their return and dinner, there are endless letters to write, more visitors to talk to, and the family to settle to sleep.

This sounds a daily programme sufficient to fill a woman's whole time. But it is cited merely to illustrate one phase of a Hindu housewife's attitude toward life. Be it under compulsion or free from it—at no

stage, no matter how high her station or how Westernized her training and education, will she neglect, or
relegate to other hands or brains, the care and welfare
of her home.

But this scrupulous and quiet fulfilment of endless
domestic duties is but one half of Abala Bose's life.
The other half is smoothly woven into the web of her
daily occupations, so that no friction results between
the two.

She is profoundly interested in the bettering of
woman's status all along the line, and sets a thousand
wheels in motion through her dynamic energy, starting with her nearest relatives and reaching outward
thence. Her nephew was induced to sponsor the
first bill for Woman's Suffrage in the 1921 Legislative
Council of Bengal; she herself was one of the signa-
tories to the All-India Woman's Delegation to the
Hon. E. S. Montagu, Secretary of State for India, in
1917, which demanded woman suffrage and education.
Abala Bose has also travelled extensively in Europe
and America, and has had full opportunity of com-
paring and selecting. She has come out of this as
intense a patriot as she started out to be in early life.
But her patriotism and interest in education are not
theoretical; they are pre-eminently practical—as
practical as is her housekeeping.

She is the founder of the *Nari Siksha Samiti*, or
Women's Education League, an organization intended
to further women's education in every possible way;
the consultations, meetings, and work involved by it
are endless, and start while Abala Bose sits preparing
her vegetables in the coolness of seven o'clock. One
of her objects was to bring education to purdah
women, instead of waiting till they should break free

and come out to seek information of their own accord. She knew that the mother-in-law behind the purdah is the most formidable obstacle to progress, and has power to keep all women under her within the purdah, all girls away from school. Win her over, and half the battle is won, the younger generation is liberated ; so through Abala Bose's efforts a whole chain of purdah schools has been started, not only in Calcutta, but extending wider and wider through dozens of villages. Then came another realization, the need of relieving widows, and their value as teaching material. One of India's greatest difficulties, arising naturally out of the old conditions, was that so few women teachers were, or still are, available. It was most desirable, for the satisfactory training of girls, to displace the old-time Brahmin pundit by women teachers. Abala Bose, after endless effort, started her Widows' Home, in which two objects might simultaneously be achieved—women could be taught industrial handicrafts to free them from their dependence and to fill their lives with interest ; they could also be trained as teachers to carry on the work of the purdah schools, both in the towns and villages. This Widows' Home has for years received daily care and direction, encouragement and supervision from Abala Bose herself, in whose heart and brain deeper and greater plans and hopes are continually blossoming. One widow had come to the Home, quite unlettered, but showing from the first all the marks of an unusual intellect. In next to no time she could read and write, and soon was even able to be sent out as a pioneer for village work, for the purpose of establishing adult centres and juvenile schools. The intention was to impart the rudiments of literacy, but above all, through talks, illustrations, and examples, to teach the elements of hygiene, sanitation, food values, child care, and handicrafts. To ensure the successful establishment and progress of such village centres, it was important to win over the local big-wigs, above all the pundits. Abala Bose's Brahmin widow, only a short time ago, not uncultured, but illiterate and without hope in life, dared to face these village elders in meetings to argue matters out. She bore herself with quiet dignity in her widow's austere garb, and repeatedly won in the battle of wits against the village pundits. Abala Bose is ever on the look-out for such unusually promising women, and if once they are discovered, she brings all her influence to bear to get them trained, abroad if necessary, for ever wider and more responsible work.

But this is not all. Abala Bose's family helped to found the great Brahmo Girls' School, and her own share of property has gone towards its upkeep. In this school an effort is made to evolve a practical blend of Western and Eastern educational methods and aims. Particular stress is laid on inducing girls to take physical exercise, and to eradicate the traditional and home-ingrained dislike of high-caste people for manual work. There is not a day on which Abala Bose, when in Calcutta, does not attend to some of the affairs of this school herself; she is the unfailing supporter of its new experiments, and adviser of its teachers. No wonder that her day, too busy for the usual noonday rest of the tropics, rarely ends before eleven o'clock. Yet never, in all the years I have known her, do I remember having seen her flustered.

Abala Bose has no child, but her unremitting care for a scientist husband, curiously dependent and absent-minded in small things, and for a drove of nephews and nieces, has given her that same training in extraversion which we find to be so marked a characteristic of Indian head-of-the-household women. I have cited her case at length (without her permission, but knowing she will forgive me) as an embodiment of that quiet reserve of strength which exists still untapped in millions of Indian women, and bears within itself such untold promise when once it shall be released for social service, as hers has been.

It is because of this intimate beholding, this actual experiencing, that I hold the deep conviction that the education of India's girlhood and womanhood is safest in, and will be most fruitfully directed by, Indian hands.

To illustrate how effective can be such Indian-initiated and managed reform, let me cite the case of another enthusiastic Bengali worker. Saroj Nalini Dutt was one of the women who came under the influence of Abala Bose's purdah school and village-reform ideas. She also was a high caste, married, had travelled, and had received a thorough education in Calcutta. She also realized that the mother-in-law of joint families, if orthodox, is the real obstacle to progress, and that reform must be brought to bear intimately on the home life of secluded women. The few schools established by Government are not attended by, and therefore of no use to, orthodox Indian girls.

Saroj Nalini Dutt, wife of a Government official, went with her husband for a few years' stay at a time —for Government officials are shifted frequently—to various places in Bengal. Wherever she went, she used all the effects of her high enthusiasm and winsome personality to establish community centres calculated to quicken the entire life of each village. In these centres, both children and adults were taught the elements of reading and writing, classes were held for women, to train them in industrial handicrafts; first-aid courses were given, midwives trained, simple hygiene and food values taught. Women were urged to take an interest in hospital work, and given all the rudiments of civic training. A special effort was made, and that successfully, to reach purdah women. These centres definitely refused to discriminate between caste, class, or religion; not only so, but a valuable attempt was made to draw the various groups together on a common social basis, and the social arts, such as music, singing and the drama—so long despised as practically the monopoly of prostitutes—were once more encouraged. As almost all the workers in these village centres were from high castes, many of them Brahmins, they had the power to make these despised arts once more acceptable. While missionaries, because of their very foreignness, and their converts, because mostly drawn from low castes, were always met with guarded reserve or even veiled antagonism, and their innovations with uneasy suspicion, these high-caste women on the other hand, were met with a respect and confidence which greatly facilitated the acceptance of reform. While Hindus are always wary of the missionaries because they know and distrust their proselytizing motives, they knew that in this case these high-caste workers came to them with no selfish intention. This is another of the many reasons why indigenous reform promises infinitely more, and why Government funds turned over to such groups, accomplish infinitely more than Western efforts. What two or three highly paid

Westerners would absorb, while giving less effective service, will keep going a hundred Indian workers who can reach the people as can no one else. With what gratifying rapidity such reforms can spread is best seen from the figures of *The Central Association*, formed to correlate the work of all those *Mahila Samitis*, or centres, which Saroj Nalini Dutt had established throughout Bengal. In one year these *Mahilas* had increased from 7 to 50, in the second year to 100, in the third to 158, and in the fourth to 240, all organized and managed exclusively by women, though male lecturers are called in, whenever funds permit, to give talks and lantern lectures on special subjects. This organization has established an *Industrial Training School* at Calcutta which already has 500 students, and has sent out over 400 trained women for village work. How earnest and radical are the devotees to this new crusade for social reform can best be gauged by the fact that some effort has been made to succour even prostitutes. In one instance at least, a Brahmin woman has set a glorious example by actually being trained for midwifery, that most despised of professions. Especially satisfying is the fact that widows, once so hopelessly cut off from active interests, are finding in all these forms of work the marvellous release and satisfaction which valued and useful social service can give. During this transition period we must almost be glad that the prejudice against remarriage is still strong, for it ensures the availability of social workers from this source for a long time to come.

Speaking of widows, we will cite one special case to show how much high courage and selfless striving lies hidden in this field. One of these women, trained in the *Poona Widows' Home*, was inspired by the idea of helping to build it up into a great institution. Though its founder was already working for the establishment of the Women's University, this Poona centre was still a very humble thing and incredibly hampered both by lack of funds and trained teachers. This particular widow, though knowing hardly a word of English, decided to visit the United States for a double purpose, to acquire a working knowledge of Western educational methods, and to collect funds. Quite without money, she landed in San Francisco about twenty years ago, having earned her passage as travelling aid to an Indian and his family. She overcame her mighty difficulties, accomplished her object, and has long been a valuable worker back in her own group.

A most interesting, many-faceted figure was the famous Pandita Ramabai, particularly significant once more as being the daughter of one of our Brahmin square pegs. Despite popular disapproval and even ostracism, her father, a Sanskrit scholar profound enough to have pierced through the sham of his own priestly caste, himself instructed Ramabai in Sanskrit lore. She became the very image of Gargi, that woman scholar who had successfully argued with Yajnavalkya, one of the greatest sages of antiquity. Together with her father, Ramabai visited many of the most sacred temple sites, saw through their corruption, but profited by the learning stored there. She met the greatest pundits and became famous for the profundity of her knowledge and the powers of her dialectic. She could repeat nearly 20,000 stanzas of the *Puranas* by heart, and often replied in arguments in the form of poems composed on the spot. In

Calcutta, she came in touch with the important early reformers of the Brahmo Samaj, such as Keshup Chandra Sen, who were congenial to her views. But though she interested such liberal groups intensely, it was a very small group which really appreciated her, and pointed to such a woman with pride. The vast mass of the orthodox bitterly opposed her activities, the more so because she repeatedly worsted in public arguments the local shining lights, those pundits who had set out to humiliate her, for to every objection they could raise in favour of old customs, she could quote a stanza from some still more ancient and more sacred scripture to refute them.

After the death of her parents she was without family ties. As she had remained unmarried beyond the age laid down for Brahmin girls and was at war with all the customs of her caste, marriage offered a special problem. No Brahmin within the pale would have her, few others were her equals. Of her own choice she at last married a Sudra, a member of the lowest and still despised caste, but a man who had obtained a good education. This congenial marriage was cut short by the husband's death, but served still further to embitter the orthodox against her and make her feel more than ever at war with society.

At last she found her way back to the Bombay Presidency and came in touch with men of such eminence and power as Tilak and Judge Ranade. In the latter's house, she was surrounded by congenial spirits, and started her work by organizing the *Arya Mahila Samaj*, a society opposed to child-marriage and seeking to raise the status of women through education. Here both men and women sat at her feet in weekly meetings, at which she put forward her radical views in inspiring talks. She, who knew the Sanskrit scriptures as did few, pointed to the state of freedom existing for women in ancient days, and denounced the later degeneration. India will perish unless women are raised again, she shouted from the house-tops, for "ignorant, unpatriotic, selfish and unculti-vated, they drag men down with them". She pointed out how deplorable was the existing state of things. By 1881, out of 99,700,000 women and girls directly under British rule, after more than a century of that rule, only 200,000 had yet been taught to read or write, and these could "not all be reckoned as educated, for the school-going period of a girl is generally between 7 and 9 years of age".

Her influence and personality soon began to tell, so that it was she who, as the chosen representative of the women's cause, gave evidence before the Edu-cation Commission of S. W. Hunter, and uttered the bitter indictment that "in 99 cases out of 100 the educated men of this country are opposed to female education".

The continuous opposition she had encountered throughout her life, and her realization of the seeming hopelessness of women's position, aroused in her bitter resentment against the Hindu priest class. She despaired of all possibility of women's escaping from its fetters. When in addition she had occasion to contrast the callous indifference and exploitation of the Brahmin priesthood in the case of widow-pilgrims to sacred shrines, with the work of mercy and loving-kindness of the Sisters of St. Mary the Virgin among prostitutes in London, she fled from her perplexities and sense of frustration into the escape of conversion to Christianity. This gave her at last a sense of

personal release and peace, but it broke the strength
of her power for reform in India. For when she
returned, she had to contend against not only the
orthodox, but even the radical Hindu group.
From then on, they met her efforts with the guarded
suspicion which is always shown to white missionaries.
Her work aroused opposition because of her continued
proselytizing tendencies.

At Bombay she started the *Sarada Sadan* (Home of
Wisdom) for training girls and women, especially
widows, but, because of this religious opposition,
what might otherwise have grown under her hand
into a wonderful institution, failed to flourish. Then
her work with widows and her former experiences at
sacred temples drew this remarkable woman to a new
experiment. She disguised herself in the garb of a
religious ascetic and visited the sacred cities of Northern India for a closer investigation into the fate of
pilgrim widows. She saw " hundreds . . . I might
say thousands of widows, young and old, come to
these places every year and fall into the snares of the
priests . . . when the poor women get a little older
. . . they are turned out to take care of themselves as
best they can . . . oh, the sin and misery and heartless
cruelty of men to women ! "

Pandita Ramabai's last experiment was in the Central Provinces and Central India, ravaged by famine
in 1896. She opened a rescue home at Mukti, and
took in girls who were famine victims, cut off from
their families. At one time she had nearly 2,000
such starvelings under her care, ranging from babies
to women of 30 years of age. All were without the
elements of education ; she organized a school in
which, as soon as possible, the pupils of the higher

classes became teachers of the lower. Often hardly knowing where the next day's food for her charges would come from, she struggled on with undaunted courage till the day of her death. The Ramabai Mukti Mission still continues to shelter hundreds of deserted widows.

But though Pandita Ramabai's work had been limited because of the antagonism aroused by her conversion, yet her influence upon other personalities had been telling. Judge Ranade's wife, in whose house Pandita Ramabai had begun her social activity, was one of those who had been fired by her enthusiasm. Mrs. Ranade's case is again of particular interest, for while Ramabai's Brahmin father had educated his daughter despite caste injunction to the contrary, here was a girl who, married at eleven to a man of thirty-two, was fully taught by her husband despite bitter opposition from the rest of the household, especially the women. These women of the family-in-law made her suffer intensely. But hers was a marriage embodying all the beauty of ancient Hindu tradition in a lifelong unbroken companionship between husband and wife. Judge Ranade steadily encouraged his young wife, sustained her step by step till she found the strength to defy all conventions and start work of her own. Fifty years ago this woman stood up to read in public an address to the Governor of Bombay, petitioning for a girls' high school for Poona. It was an act so unusual in those days that it required splendid courage. Once launched on the path of reform, Mrs. Ranade was indefatigable. She started to teach illiterate women and widows, and later expanded her work into the *Seva Sadan*, a society devoted to " education, mutual helpfulness and national service ". This organization, wholly Indian as it was, met with less prejudice than Pandita Ramabai's, expanded rapidly, and soon had over a thousand married women attending classes for primary instruction. The society had an ever-increasing influence, and took active steps to promote maternity and infant welfare, while its founder continued to lead in all agitation for compulsory education, women's suffrage, and other reforms. To Mrs. Ranade is due to a large extent the credit for winning, as early as 1922, women's suffrage in Bombay Presidency.

A very different type of woman is Sarojini Naidu, India's poetess. In her live again not only the ancient Vedic singers, but the inspiring women leaders of heroic days. At the call of her country she turned from her singing to the public platform, and has since then swayed millions through the emotional power of her speech. She has headed many deputations of Indian women, such as that to the Hon. F. E. Montagu, then Secretary of State for India, to plead for women's rights. She was at one time President of the Madras Provincial Congress, and had the greatest unofficial honour of India bestowed upon her by being made President of the Indian National Congress. She served for long periods on its organizing and subject committees, took part in the Conference of the International Women's Suffrage Alliance at Geneva, has been the valued adviser of the greatest men of India such as Gandhi, has suffered imprisonment for the national cause, has lectured on India to thousands of eager listeners in the United States, and last but not least, was one of India's representatives at the Round Table Conference in London, following this up, by way of relaxation, with a strenuous trip to Africa on behalf of her troubled countrymen there. She has gone like a meteor in flaming splendour from success to success, and knows the West and all its faults and merits as intimately as she knows her India. She shrugs her shoulders with a sardonic smile when she hears the modern legend that Indians do not know what is good for them, and are not fit to govern themselves. She has told the men of her own race just what she thinks of the ancient outwork trash of customs, she has told the foreign Government just what she knows it can never hope to achieve for her people, and has (bless her heart!) told the present writer how absurdly futile and tiresome it is for Westerners to persist in writing about India!

If we marvels, the proud hundred per cent. literate women of the West, could keep pace with this down-trodden woman of India, our unemployed would not equal the untouchables of India in numbers, nor our prostitutes exceed in proportion the *devadasis*. Had we retained our missionaries for work at home, we might perhaps be able to point to-day to 15 per cent. of real Christians in the West, instead of having, after more than two centuries of proselytizing, converted merely 1½ per cent. of Indians.

We might go on endlessly to multiply examples of the blossoming into power and promise of the forces that lie dormant in Indian womanhood, mention women rulers such as her of Travancore, who has appointed a woman Health Minister, has abolished the *devadasi* evil, and whose state has anticipated British India in educational progress; mention individual work such as that of Dr. Muthulakshmi Reddi, a successful physician, whose active life and service has been crowned by her election as Deputy

President of the Madras Legislative Council and latest President of the All-India Women's Conference; or that of a woman Municipal Commissioner of Indore; or the director of the Baroda Women's Hospital, the first Indian woman doctor to be head of a hospital; or that heroine of steely persistence, Mrs. Hansa Mehta, boycott leader; or the soft-voiced determination of Bègum Shah Nawaz, who declared to the world at the Round Table Conference that, whatever the men might do, India's women stood united; or such a woman as Kamala Devi, the powerful organizer of women's associations.

Every passing year will see a twofold increase in the number of Indian women to arise and draw after them an enthusiastic following, women whose greatest pride is always that they are rooted in the high traditions of their ancient land.

XII

SISTER NIVEDITA AND MAIDEN-AUNT MAYO

DESPITE all the claims of missionaries to the contrary, the Hindu woman who refuses to adopt Christianity has at least one inestimable advantage—she gets a reasonable amount of sleep! Her child could not possibly finish before dawn the all-inclusive Christian evening prayer: " . . . bless ma—bap, bless my paternal grandfather, my maternal aunt, my eldest brother's wife, my youngest brother's eldest wife, my mishima, my pishima, my didi, dada, etcetera. . . ." Towards the raw grey dawn, the mother would be forced to reprove her in a weary voice, " Why, Lotus-bud, how *can* you forget your kind English godfather, your blonde sister, and your honourable auntie! "

For the munificence of Western providence remembered that to them that have, more shall be given, and it has seen fit to provide the Hindu woman with a few more relatives, white ones this time; a benevolent red-faced uncle, an adoring elder sister, and a carping maiden aunt, none of whom may possibly be slighted or passed over.

When her kindly godfather, the white Sirkar, first made the Hindu woman aware of the supreme desirability of Christian civilization and the utter worthlessness of all things Indian, she, trained for ages to a touching obedience, did her level best to mend her ways and gain an approving smile from his blue eyes. If her father or husband was wealthy enough—having himself had the incomparable boon of a Cambridge or Oxford education—it was likely that she would be taken for a thrilling trip or for schooling to Paris and London. In this case her metamorphosis came with the greatest ease. She soon blossomed out, could discuss spicy French novels herself in the best Oxford drawl and contribute her very own poems to the latest women's magazines. When she returned to Calcutta, she could dazzle and startle her world, drive unveiled through the streets in an open victoria, gently push forward into full view the shining tip of high-heeled French slipper on silk-clad foot, and twiddle a brilliant sunshade over her lovely head. In the evening, she could entertain friends and family by tinkling " Home, Sweet Home," on her piano, wear her sari, as nearly as assiduous pinning would permit, just like Western decolleté dress, hold her wineglass or cigarette between her gleaming finger-tips in just the proper way, display the latest bracelets from Cartier's, and bemoan the fact that Calcutta was not cool enough to permit of her wearing cloaks from the Rue de la Paix.

Brahmin orthodoxy had raged against such indecent behaviour ; but from the very ranks of Brahminism —that hearth of the keenest analytical thought—there rose as we have seen, those who saw deep and far enough. They had perceived the danger of both the old orthodox restrictions and the new Western impositions. Dayanand in the North, Rama Krishna in Bengal, Vidiasagara in Madras, and a score of others had come forth to declare that the quickest way forward lay in the farthest return backward; they pointed to the freedom and greatness of Vedic days, and adjured the people to do away with every obstacle in the path to a revival of old days and thought.

Then a new shock of amazement and joy had convulsed India—an Oriental power had dared defy the omnipotent material supremacy of the West; Japan actually defeated Russia.

Still more stirring—from that West had come people, white people, who revealed the unsuspected beauty and greatness of India's own culture and her ancient treasures; Max Müller of her literature, Havell of her art, Blavatsky and Annie Besant of her religions, Margaret Noble of the inner life of her homes. India had raised her incredulous head and strained to listen further.

Miss Noble had been a radical educationalist in her own England, became influenced and inspired there by the dynamic Swami Vivekananda, and determined to devote her life to work in the interests of India. Nurtured in a free country, where she was an exponent of the most advanced and liberal ideas, she failed, on her way to India, to follow the usual Britisher's custom of discarding simultaneously woollen clothing and British principles the moment Suez was passed. She retained in India, for India, the quaint notion that the old ideas of liberty and self-determination might equally apply to a ' coloured ' race; that love, faith, and freedom are the only lasting basis for human well-being—that no nation is good enough to govern another, and that even good government is no valid substitute for self-government.

As " Sister Nivedita ", Margaret Noble settled down in the heart of the Calcutta slums to share the life of simple Indians; she discarded Western dress, adopted Bengali speech, ate Indian food, and generally went to the extreme of viewing everything Indian through the rosiest of spectacles. Even child-marriage, forced widowhood, and purdah, received from her an appreciative pat on the back. For it had come to her as a powerful realization that at this period India's worst enemy was the utter hopelessness of her subjection, her slave mentality; her greatest need a revival of faith in herself, of pride and self-esteem. Tireless as teacher and social worker, prolific in contributing to the most popular journals, a powerful and inflaming speaker, Sister Nivedita kindled the torch of national love and aspiration in thousands of youthful Indian hearts—doubly effectively because she belonged to the very race which, as bureaucrats, were in the habit of treating Indians and all things Indian as dirt under their feet.

A bitterest critic of English behaviour and English rule, Sister Nivedita—the Englishwoman whose *Web of Indian Life* has found thousands of voracious readers—was instrumental to a great degree in giving back to India her lost pride and a passionate hope in a renewed, glorious, independent destiny of her own. This found its first outward and abortive expression in the 1905 revolt in Bengal. Under this impetus, many Indian women who had been educated in the West, or educated on the Western pattern in India, stopped turning over the pages of the latest issue of *Punch*, driving to tea-parties, or dancing in the hill stations in imitation of Western society dolls, they stepped out of their French-heeled slippers, draped the sari once more in the simple old modest way, and closed the lid of the tuneless mildewed piano. They

tied the bunch of household keys again to one corner
of their sari and tucked the other tight round their
waist, ready for real work. They started to open
schools, visited purdah ladies to talk to them about
hygiene and sanitation, took an interest in hospitals,
cared for the poor, aided flood and famine victims—
and saw to it that the drinking-water at home was
boiled !

In all this they were inspired and sustained by
Sister Nivedita's example, even long after she herself
—broken in health through flood and famine relief
work, passionately admired and mourned—had died
in the arms of Lady Bose.

Two generations later, Sister Nivedita's work and
ideals had blossomed to the point where Hindus dared
anew—for the first time in almost a thousand years
of subjection—dream of being masters in their entire
house, to rebuild and set it in order according to their
own taste and judgment. Suddenly there appeared
from the land of the free and the home of the brave
a brand-new, and to Hindu women inconceivable,
kind of relation—a woman who never had married !
—Katherine Mayo. She told them in the most un-
mistakable terms what despicable vermin they were,
how unspeakably degraded were all Hindu ways, how
utterly unfit they were to dream of taking care of
themselves, and how lucky to be in the care of such a
kindly blue-eyed uncle.

Englishwoman — American ; Sister Nivedita —
Maiden-aunt Mayo ; what supreme Western actresses
to cross the tragic Indian stage ! Sister Nivedita's
memory will for ever be cherished in India, Maiden-
aunt Mayo's for ever loathed ! Yet in ultimate analysis,
the work of both is of inestimable and possibly equal

value to India. Then why the difference?—Because
in Margaret Noble's heart there glowed true Christian
love, in Katherine Mayo's hand there gleamed the
sword of puritan righteousness and intolerance.
Of Miss Mayo's part more later; but let us mention
here, between these two extremes, the many other
Western shuttles which have been flying back and
forth across the face of the Indian tapestry, each carrying its own particular colour of thread—the presence
in India of thousands of other Western women which
helped to make or mar it. First, because most
numerous, and least effective in their primary aim,
came all the various kinds of Christian missionaries.
All attempts at christianizing have been woefully
unfruitful; after centuries of vast effort, converts
comprise merely 1½ per cent. of India's population.
Several reasons account for this. The most prominent
is the innate contradiction which exists between trying
to hold a country by force and simultaneously win her
over to a religion of love. The West cannot success-
fully hope to be ruler and prophet at once. The
denominational contradictions and antagonisms of the
Christian groups in India itself likewise fail to inspire
enthusiasm in Indian hearts; nor does it escape
observation that the Christian missionary is seldom
free from the white ruler's loathed attitude of race
superiority. The teaching of brotherly love and
humility from such lips is likely to be met with a
polite but sceptical smile. Last, but by no means
least, comes the fact that Hinduism, though in its
crystallized forms incredibly intolerant of any infringement of caste rules within its own group, has yet
always been amazingly tolerant of all other religions;
—there is nothing to prevent Hindus from appre-

ciating and even incorporating into their own belief
the spirit of Christianity, nor do they feel it must
imply giving up allegiance to Hinduism. Educated
Indians, quite generally, readily accord to the figure
of Christ a place as one of the great teachers of mankind, but that is as far as they care to go, or as Christianity will ever be able to go in India. For, when
Christ himself has failed to make the West really
Christian, his pseudo-followers can hardly hope to
succeed in the East.

On the side of education and medical work, however, the Christian missions have done immensely
valuable service. Also, the presence and example of
such socially active women could not fail to be a
stimulating factor in the stagnation to which women
of high caste were condemned. It is best to let a
Hindu woman express how she and her sisters appreciate the work of missionaries. Dr. Muthulakshmi
Reddi, addressing the All-India Women's Conference,
said :

> " I feel I would be failing in my duty if I did not offer
> a word of tribute to the several missionary educational
> organizations who have been the pioneers in every
> province in the cause of female education. The woman
> population of this country have been placed under a deep
> debt of gratitude to the several missionary agencies for
> their valuable contribution to the educational uplift of
> the Indian women. I honestly think that they have done
> more for women's education in this country than the
> Government itself. Of course, at present, India can
> boast of several other religious bodies such as Brahmo
> Samaj, the Rama Krishna Mission, Arya Samaj, Sananta
> Dharma, Theosophists, Parsis, Islamia, doing work in
> the field of women's education, but in the past the Chris-
> tian missionaries were the only agencies in that field, as

is seen from the history of their institutions which are spread throughout the length and breadth of India, even including Burma, under the selfless and devoted management of Christian workers, both men and women. Had it not been for these noble bands of Christian women teachers, who are the product of the missionary training schools, even this much advancement in the education of the Indian women would not have been possible ; even at this day in every province, we find the missionary women teachers working hard in a spirit of love and faith, in out-of-the-way villages where the Hindu and Muslim women dare not penetrate. Even now, they form the strength of the teaching profession."

Let the same great Indian woman leader, Dr. Reddi, also express her country's acknowledgment of the share which other white women have had in different kinds of work, such as

" the supply of adequate medical aid to our women and children and . . . the organization and development of maternity and child-welfare work in India. Even in this field, European Missionaries were the pioneers in organizing medical relief and in establishing hospitals and dispensaries for women and children in India. The first medical woman, named Miss Clara Swain, came from America in the year 1864. Then in the year 1881 the Queen of Punna sent a message enclosed in a locket through Miss Bielby, a missionary lady doctor, to Queen Victoria, telling how the women of India suffered when they were sick. The good Empress Victoria, having been moved by the helpless condition of Indian women and children, instructed the Viceroy's wife, the Countess of Dufferin, who was coming to India, to organize immediate medical relief for the Indian women. Accordingly the Countess of Dufferin, soon after her arrival in India, issued an appeal for funds to open hospitals for women and children and to give medical education to the women of India. Thus the Countess Dufferin Fund Organization came into existence.

" Subsequently, the wives of the successive Viceroys having interested themselves in the health and well-being of the Indian women and children, the Lady Chelmsford League for organizing maternity and child-welfare in India, the Victoria Memorial Fund for the training of the indigenous dais in the elements of modern midwifery, the Lady Hardinge Medical College for Women, the Lady Reading Health School have been established and are doing excellent work, for which we cannot be sufficiently thankful to those good ladies ; but still it is a deplorable fact that even now medical aid to women is limited to cities and municipalities, while the women in the districts and villages suffer and die unrelieved, and their condition is more or less the same as it was when the Queen of Punna sent the locket with the message to the Queen-Empress ".

But the work of foreign women in India was important also in lines other than that of missions or medicine. For instance, Annie Besant's championing of Indian aims and religion also helped greatly in the new awakening of India, a fact signally acknowledged by the nation when she, a European, was given the honour of becoming the first woman president of the Indian National Congress.

Among Englishwomen of brains, training, and high position, there were also a good number who took particular interest in and supported the establishment of schools, art-schools and teachers' colleges. On the other hand, we cannot but regret the presence in India of a great number of wives of white officials, officers, and merchants whose only concern seemed to be the erection of walls around themselves and their

little cliques high enough to permit no Indian sound
to penetrate and disturb the hot peace of these little
artificial British islands in a dark sea. Practically
their only work consisted in giving daily orders in a
cool tone of superiority to low-caste servants, whom
they treated as belonging to an altogether different
species of being ; their only source of knowledge of
things Indian lay in this contact. To grant, much less
to seek, social contacts outside their small white group
never occurred to them. The lower the station of
these Englishwomen in England, the more superior
and supercilious their tone in India.

Indians watched from a distance, observed the
endless intrigues and flirtations of the hill-stations,
and wondered—was it a sign of race superiority for
these white women to hold aloof in disdainful leisure
from the vast life of the country round them—a country which provided them with ease and luxury far
beyond any their own home could have offered ?—
to idle in a country with so crying a need for workers ?

Indians calculated that the Indian money which
went to keep one of these white women would suffice
to open a dozen village schools, yet she never even
cared to ask if any schools existed. Indians, watching
such a white woman, began to fear that her parasitic
attitude towards life was the very outcome of her
freedom and education, and the orthodox pointed to
her as the most telling argument against giving their
own women a greater measure of liberty.

But no matter how conflicting the influences, Indian
women benefited on the whole by contact with Western women. A great new stimulus lay in the opportunity for immediate and personal comparison. The
more the Indian woman came to know of the West,

the more she observed the unfettered life of white women, the more she asked whether the rigid limitations imposed on herself were after all quite so divinely ordered as the Brahmin priesthood had made her believe. So, from the first brave though bigoted missionary woman to the last harsh social critic, Western woman has played her part in the life of her Indian sister, often in ways quite undetermined by her own willing.

Some of the ripples from the big splash made by the last white critic I myself had occasion to observe. During the autumn of 1927 I studied in the company of Indian friends some outstanding monuments of Indian architecture, sculpture and painting. We went to the stupendous rock-cut temples and monasteries of Elephanta, Ajanta, and Ellora. I marvelled at the strength, dignity and persistence of the Indian culture that spoke from these ancient walls and that met my eyes in a vitally living counterpart on roads, fields, and in the villages round about. For simple peasant women still walked from river to hut with inimitable stately grace, carrying on their heads waterpots of the same ancient perfect shape, still wore ornaments on head, arms, and ankles identical with those that so delighted me when pictured in the frescoes nearly two thousand years old. And though these women were totally unlettered, they yet bore the ineffable stamp of that ancient culture ; they read no books, yet were familiar by word of mouth with dozens of the most inspiring tales from the Hindu epics, and their manner and gentle speech conveyed a gracious and unaffected hospitality.

By contrast, there flashed through my mind the memory of ghastly hours in Western tubes, the rude jostling, the blatant voices, and the flutter and crackle of vile sensationalist dailies—general literacy combined with the voracious reading of utter trash! I realized more vividly than ever before how wide a gulf may exist between book-learning or literacy, and culture, and I turned with renewed pleasure and sympathy to my simple Hindu village hosts.

In an uplifted mood I finally went back to Bombay, to wake up with a jolt. A surf of boiling discussion broke around me regarding a book that had just appeared, Miss Mayo's *Mother India*. I regretted to find my Indian friends so hurt and incensed, for my main feeling was merely one of great pity for the writer. She had come to this ancient land only to wallow in its gutters, and had never felt the thrill of adoration for its gleaming hill-tops. I recalled the " muck-raking " days during which I myself first went to America from Europe. Their disclosures of American iniquities were revolting. In my intense sympathy for the underdog it was natural for me to take on an indignant militant attitude towards all the filth-preserving, mind- and body-emaciating agencies of social injustice. But this did not blind me to the fact that these negative aspects were not the true America, the lasting, freeing factor in world progress.

Miss Mayo had come to a country so great in the annals of history, so complex in its social web, with a set of preconceived notions like a dog on a special scent. She, a journalist, had not hesitated to rush in where Government feared to tread and scholars longed to learn. India, to her, meant merely the inside of hospitals and slums, luridly accentuated.

It was interesting to note the reactions to her book of dwellers in the country she had attacked. I had

a discussion with Dr. X., a Hindu physician, member
of a liberal religious sect, and an untiring advocate of
social reform. Dr. X. had immediately bought two
copies of the book, circulated them constantly, allowed
each reader only a few days, and kept on urging others
to buy and read it also. He felt confident that the
book might incite them to working with a will to
eradicate the evils exposed.

"It is all true, all her accusations; we reformers
have been shouting these imprecations and exposures
from the housetops for several generations. Miss
Mayo says nothing new."

"It is just because you Indian reformers have been
patiently working year after year," I replied, well
remembering the endless hours of ungrudging unpaid
service that this doctor took from his much-needed
rest and sleep to devote to reform, "that I feel it so
ungenerous and heartless on the part of a Western
tourist to write as she has written, and as if no one
here had ever lifted a finger to change things. I am
ashamed that a white woman should have hit so hard
and so blindly."

"I know how you feel," he said with quick sympathy for my distress, "but never mind. It is a good
thing it was done. Our people as a whole have
hardly responded to our plea for co-operation in
eradicating long-standing evils. They have been too
indolent. They have found it far less trouble to
themselves to sit back and criticize us reformers for
officious self-seeking than to help us. Now criticism
has been directed against the whole nation from the
outside, and they feel the smart of national pride.
They are stung as we have never been able to sting
them. The worse the criticism from the outside, the

more they may be shamed into action." The bitterness of years of frustration and fighting sounded in his words.

A week or two later I paid a call upon a veteran painter. The old gatekeeper recognized me and motioned me to go right up, taking it for granted that I was expected. But I had not telephoned beforehand. Upstairs I passed a new servant, and asked him to go ahead and announce me, for from the large verandah—the painter's usual worksroom—came several voices, and I feared to interrupt. But the servant must have said merely " a memsahib," for when I stepped out on the verandah, the old master took his hookah stem from his lips and boomed, " Oh, it is you ! I wondered what memsahib could have wormed her way up here ; I thought it was another missionary or tourist female prying around for information to distort. We've had enough of them ! Come and sit down. Haven't seen you for a year. What have you been doing ? "

With glowing enthusiasm I mentioned my recent trip to Ajanta, and my joy in copying some of the frescoes. To my utter surprise I touched no chord. Gruffly he brushed the subject aside.

" I've never been there, and I don't care to go. We've had too much Ajanta ! We've had too much of everything that is old. It's time the young painters stopped painting gods and epic heroes. It's new life we want ; paintings of to-day, not imitations of the old. What good does Ajanta do us ? We have to open our eyes to the life of the street, the village scene, the beauty of the cobbler round the corner."

He himself was just then, between sentences and

puffs at his inseparable hookah from which rose per-
fumed smoke, working at a delicate water-colour of a
slim girl dancer with braid flying and feet barely touching the ground, amid a circle of watchers such as
might be seen daily in any bazaar.

I was a little hurt at his indifferent reception of my
news. Ajanta had been a deep experience, a spiritual
discovery, which in itself would always link me to
India with a feeling of joy and warmth. But here
was one of the first Indian painters to break away from
Western influence and to return to full Indian expression, making light of it. Yet in his early work
he too had imitated the old Moghul and Rajput schools
—by means of thus leaning on old Indian masters he
had himself broken with Western-taught and West-
imitating art.

My very enthusiasm for Ajanta was apparently
pricking this old iconoclast into opposition. He
feared that my enthusiasm, though flattering to his
national pride, might weigh enough with students to
turn into an obstructive element. He wanted nothing
to interfere with or retard the healthy modern tendency
towards breaking free from all fetters, whether European or ancient Indian.

" What's the use talking of what we have done in
the past; what, I ask you, have we done in the present? What have we done that will compare with
monumental work such as that of Rubens, da Vinci,
and those fellows? . . ."

Never had I heard the old master speak like this,
in apparent self-depreciation hitting ruthlessly at the
principal modern art endeavour of India. Yet something thrilled in me in response, for I realized what lay
behind this startling self-criticism: an assured sense

of latent power, and faith in the renascent art of India already so rich in promising buds ! An intense pride showed through ; it implied : you Westerners need point out to us neither our ancient glory nor our present shortcomings ; we are well aware of them ; but we have the power to build anew and solidly at our own pace and in our own good time, and from our own strength. Foreign criticism has led us astray, foreign teaching has wasted our time and effort, and even foreign enthusiasm may do harm.

The painter then showed me some pastel portraits he had done that year. Pastels are for India an untried medium. He also showed me a painting of charming fresco-like quality, in tempera used over a coating of simple Ganges mud. Indicative of the new current in India, this old master makes new experiments without end.

I felt in some strange way both glad and sad : glad to see this eager confident exploration of new ways and means in art, this great inner assurance that presages a new period for India ; sad to realize that Westerners have managed to lose the confidence of India, that even well-intentioned Western interest has already become non-essential. But I was also glad to know that side by side with these new pioneers walked Indian women, the first to turn to art since ancient days.

Then one young nephew asked me some question about *Mother India*, that burning topic on every tongue. The old painter burst in hotly :

" Why don't *you*, who have lived here amongst us in our homes, as one of us, *why* don't you write an answer to say you never saw any such things—that it is all vile slander ! " His tone was challenging.

" But some of the accusations *are* true ! " I threw
back at him eagerly. I had for days past taken every
opportunity to question all sorts of people among my
friends concerning the alleged facts in the book, and
to elicit definite challenges or acknowledgments. For
I had been astounded by many of its claims. How
was it that I, who had lived so intimately and for so
many years in Indian homes, rich and poor, Hindu
and Mohammedan, had seen no trace of the majority
of ugly facts the author cited ? Some of the state-
ments, such as that of the sexual degeneracy of the
Bengalis, I knew beyond doubt to be so exaggerated
as hardly to deserve a passing thought.

But I was only too glad to grasp at the chance of
discussion with this group of eminent intellectuals ;
there were five or six present. I began to put some
definite questions with the honest desire to know the
truth. My choice unfortunately fell on the Kali
temple ; instead of a direct answer, someone retorted
with a reference to Upton Sinclair's horrible Chicago
stockyard revelations. I found at once that imper-
sonal discussion was impossible, and moreover that
not one of the persons present had as yet read the book.
Their acquaintance with it was merely based on hearsay, from large excerpts and heated discussions raging
in papers and periodicals. I argued that, in order to
discuss such a book or combat it effectively, a close
study of it was absolutely essential. But no—they
would not spend good money to buy it and so further
enrich the defamer.

Such heat of feeling and lack of cool reasoning was
surprising. It was unpleasant to find even intellectuals succumbing to a wave of mob antagonism and
surging race-hatred. I reiterated that I could not

decry the book wholesale, as it did contain some grave truths, and pressed my point that they should read it before attempting to form final opinions or enter into discussions.

" All right," the painter finally agreed, " I will give a certain amount of time to it. I am quite willing to do that, though I won't read the book. If you really want to know, come any day at any time and I will give an hour and a half or even two to answer your list of questions." This offer, though well meant, coupled as it was with a refusal to read the book, seemed so unpromising that I kept silence and never availed myself of it.

As we parted, there was tension in the air and a marked coolness on his side. He had expected me to be an unreserved partisan of India, while I was more concerned with disinterring the truth than with taking sides. Was I, I mourned to myself while descending the wide stairs of the old house, was I, because I refused unreservedly to denounce such a book, to be classed as an alien and a sister of the Miss Mayos ? Was there never any escape from race-feeling, even among friends ?

On the train from Bombay to Calcutta I shared a compartment with an English missionary just returned from a year's leave. Her face was beaming each time we drew up at a station, and she pressed to the window for the sheer pleasure of watching the Indian travellers stream past. She turned to me with genuine emotion.

" I feel as if I were *coming home*. I have worked here for over thirty years. It is more my home now than England. I love these people."

Of course we spoke of Miss Mayo's book.

" I do not approve of her sort of exposition, and it

P.   P

is going to hurt our work," she said. Then, suddenly leaning forward to me eagerly, " But, you know, every word of it is true ! "

Greatly surprised at this statement, which seemed at variance with her eager joy at her homecoming, I probed further, only to learn that she had merely heard the book discussed by English friends in Bombay, but had not read it herself !

The first people in Calcutta with whom the subject again came up were Sir Jagadis and Lady Bose. Their attitude was an easy, slightly bitter and scornfully smiling dismissal of it as something beneath their notice. Read it ? They would not waste their time and money, nor soil their hands with it ! They knew the West too well to pay attention to this particular woman's mental kink.

Some time later, I had occasion to discuss the book with the British Political Agent of one province. He is considered a terror (though just), in his relations with Indians. I had been told of one instance where he gave a petty raja one week's grace to eliminate his European mistresses and cut down his flotilla of motor-cars from twenty to four if he did not wish to follow hot-foot in the steps of a recently degraded and dethroned prince. This Political Agent unhesitatingly stigmatized the book as " grossly unfair, filthy, vile ".

About this time the son of the *mahant* of a famous Hindu temple begged me for the loan of my copy. " My father has read it ; the raja gave it to him. He says it is all true, or most of it." The father is a man quite indifferent to social work, of unsavoury reputation, popularly accused of temple misappropriation and dissolute life. The son is a pure idealist eager for reform. After reading the book, he de-

nounced it as distorted. I wondered which Indian
eyes saw truer, diseased ones or clean?

I also discussed the book with educated Hindu
women. I had made a list—and a surprisingly long
list it was—of all the allegations in it which were
quite new to me, such as atrocious torture of mothers
in childbirth, etc. Concerning these, I especially
questioned one woman whose moral and mental outlook I highly esteem, whose honest fearlessness has
been tested in endless labour and sacrifice for social
reform—the veteran Lady Bose. She herself had
started a widow's home and opened nearly thirty
purdah schools. All her life had been spent in the
interest of women's education and in the effort to
raise their status in every way. She did not rant or
inveigh; hers was a brave and shamed readiness to
admit blame wherever it was deserved. Too busy
with actual reform work to care to spend time in
reading the book, she evinced astonishment rather
than indignation at the mass of distorted or extremely
rarely documented allegations. With genuine surprise she would exclaim: "Where *could* Miss Mayo
have heard this? Why, I never heard of it! Where
in heaven's name could she have unearthed that? I
have never known anyone even to mention such a
custom, no, not even in the days of the past!" Then
she would stop, ponder, and add thoughtfully, "May-
be it is or was true somewhere, at some time, in India,
but certainly not to our knowledge." The part of
Miss Mayo's book that my Bengali friends most
bitterly resented, and which is the most unfair, was
her accusation of deliberate and conscious sexual
excess. Sexual excess indeed exists, if abnormally
early mating may be called so, but it is neither de-

liberate, conscious, nor profligate. Miss Mayo totally overlooked the fact that in the castes (such as some Brahmin castes of Bengal) which enforce on parents early marriage of their children by compulsion and the threat of ostracism, the boy is quite as much a victim as the girl. Young boys in joint families have absolutely no choice, nor any way of protecting themselves. That they are weakened through too early marriage is no fault of theirs. Only after the power of the priests, and with it, the stranglehold of caste, has been broken, will it be possible for any outside observer to draw just conclusions. I am personally convinced that at that time the Indian will be able to hold up his head in any company of men.

Even from my own observation, though necessarily limited as it is at present, because child-marriage with its girl- and boy-victims still exists to a large extent, I knew Miss Mayo's accusation to be absurd. My intimate knowledge of Bengali home-life was enough. For in many groups—Brahmo, Kshatriya, and even Brahmin as well—marriage is being and has for over fifty years been, deferred, especially in the case of men. Many of these Indian youths, as Brahma-charyas, are under strict and sincere religious training and voluntarily refrain from sexual experience far longer than do most Western youths. This fact is well known to every outsider who has really studied Indian life beneath the surface. This is the aspect which will govern the future attitude, once caste and joint family have lost their hold.

In married life also there is, in some ways at least, great restraint. In obedience to religious injunctions for instance, pregnant women are never approached by their husbands, and it is a very general custom, wherever circumstances permit the expense of the trip, to let the young wife go back to her own mother at the beginning of pregnancy and remain with her until some time after delivery. No matter how Western authorities on psychology and sex may agree or disagree as to the advisability of such separation, these same authorities nowhere testify to a like almost universally observed restraint on the part of Western men.

There are still other aspects. Since, in India, sex functioning has always been considered an essential part of every person's experience, and a prime means of development, Indians are free from such inhibitions against the mention of sex as Christian virgin-worship and priestly celibacy has imposed on us in the West. They speak of all natural functions with an utter lack of self-consciousness which at first appals the Westerner accustomed to consider such things unmentionable. " My sister can't come, she is unwell," is said as simply as " let us go for a walk ". I confess that I for one have come to consider this attitude more healthy and pure. It also finds expression in other ways. Where we permit all sorts of base or flippant sex innuendoes as the mainstay and bulk of comic entertainment on the western stage, while prohibiting innocent sun-bathing, Hindus have not hesitated to depict in their art physical facts with a frankness that nonplusses all Westerners, lewd joke-lover and sun-bather alike. But few take the trouble, before expressing condemnation and indignation, to attempt to probe deeply enough to understand the Indian point of view. For it is not so easy to understand. How explain, for instance, the apparent contradiction between the excessive stress laid on the veiled modesty

of high-caste women and this frankness in speech and
in art forms ? I believe the explanation to lie in the
fact that the veil had its origin not in any sense of
physical self-consciousness or modesty, but at first
purely as a means of emphasizing aloofness and social
distinction, and later as a method of protecting women
from Moghul aggression. The Hindu is by no means
disturbed when the physical form is revealed, whether
inside or outside the house. Within very orthodox
homes women even now generally wear not even a
blouse, and never use any underskirt under their sari.
Their forms are therefore very often quite clearly out-
lined against the light through the thin material.
This never attracts notice, much less criticism, so
long as the woman observes the convention of veiling
her face before certain members of the family group.
Nor is a single curious, much less lewd glance,
ever cast upon women bathers, though men and
women bathe together in sacred tanks and streams,
and though, on emerging from the water, the thin
soaked sari clings to a woman's body so as to reveal
it in all its details. Nor would a Hindu ever dream
of taking exception at, did he even notice, the partly
exposed bodies of coolie women, or the bare upper
parts of the bodies of the women of the South. He
is shocked only when he sees bodies displayed in such
a way as is adopted by Western women on social
occasions, for he quite rightly interprets this as a
physical, and therefore immodest and disturbing bid
for sexual attention.

Whatever modesty-interpretation has been put
upon the veiling of Indian women is a later imposition,
due to the introduction of Western views of the
physical and moral aspects of clothing, such as are

fostered, for instance, by the missionaries who first brought to the Indian mind the astounding idea that naked bodies were immoral. There is a vast difference between the Hindu and Mohammedan attitudes —in the north of India, the latter has carried physical sex-consciousness to the extreme of insulting and even stoning Mohammedan women who dared to show their ankles from under the bourka, that " walking tent " which completely veils them from head to toe, while the Hindu requires no more than that the convention of veiling the face should be observed.

Despite all appearance to the contrary, there is a core of frank purity regarding sex-matters in Hindu thought which promises great things once the race can shake itself free from the abuses of its crystallized Brahmin-fettered customs. Westerners rarely have the chance of observing Indian life intimately enough to perceive this, and are apt to be prejudiced from the start, even when they are not personally addicted to high-necked, long-sleeved missionary nightgowns.

To illustrate this, let me quote an incident and make a confession from my own experience. My Americo-European yard-stick firmly clutched in my hand, during the second year of my stay in India, I visited the famous temple of the Sun-God Surya, known as the Black Pagoda, in the desert near Puri. It is of Tantric origin, but I knew nothing of that philosophy. The temple is conceived as a chariot drawn by heroic horses and is marvellously executed and decorated. It exhibits to perfection unity of sculptural and architectural motives.

For the first two whole days I fought with a heavy puzzled depression aroused by the fact that so many of its countless sculptures presented phases of the sexual act. I looked upon them as obscene. Slowly, held by the skill and beauty of the artistry and craftsmanship in detail, and the utter 'purity' of other sculptures, I was able to arise from my depression with a freeing conviction that so much love of beauty, so much skill of hand, so much devotion in detail, could not conceivably have been put at and kept in the service of a debased conception. Rather than with these exquisite artists, the fault must somehow lie with me and my Western ingrained preconceptions. I remained for another three days of busy sketching, though I could not bring myself to sketch a single 'obscene' sculpture.

Yet, in the succeeding years, I remembered Konarak as a temple *where the majority of sculptures represented sexual acts, and these mostly in unusual and abnormal forms.*

As the years passed and my knowledge of Indian life and thought deepened, a truer understanding awoke in me. I have come to look upon such things very much with the same attitude as is expressed by Count Keyserling : " the whole of their cult is permeated by the spirit of animal procreation. Here for the first time in my life, I behold the display of sexual activity, not regarded as something unclean, but as something holy, as symbolizing the divine in nature." Consequently what more fitting place for artistic representation than the sun-drenched walls of the temple of the god Surya, the Sun, symbolic of pro-creative power? And I did not fail to contrast favourably the frankness of Konarak with the attitude of mind which, in Western capitals, slyly offers and furtively buys photographs that are really obscene.

But I had not yet done with Konarak ; it had a further lesson to teach me. In the succeeding years

I had seen a great deal of India's art and architecture, and had grown less painfully self-conscious and better informed. Shortly before leaving India, I again spent some days at Konarak. Eight years had passed between my two visits. Now I had occasion to realize to what an extent shyness, surprise, and prejudice have power to warp observation. That first visit had left an unbalanced memory-picture in my mind. Among the thousands and thousands of sculptures, *the majority do not represent any sexual act at all, and among those that do, the greater part portray the normal act!* It was my mental attitude that had distorted my impressions, and my memory that had played me false. The first time I had hardly dared to look straight; this time I observed dispassionately, with wide-open eyes, and verified my own shortcoming! This experience taught me more than any other the reasons for the vast failure of most Westerners to understand India, and shed a doubly significant light on Miss Mayo's exaggerations. For where a person genuinely sympathetic to India, as I had been before ever seeing her shores, could so misunderstand, how much more liable to misinterpret must be observers who come to India with a racial bias, a feeling of superiority, or an imperialistic trend of ideas. Luckily I had not had Miss Mayo's X-ray eyes on my first visit to Konarak, else I should have declared that the sterile mass of sand with which an Englishman had caused the entire temple to be filled within from top to bottom, was symbolic of the worship to which it was dedicated!

But no outsider's observations, false or true, have ever had the stirring and far-reaching effect of Miss Mayo's book. It was a violent denunciation of

Indian claims to independence, and laudation of
British rule. The storms that raged around it were
so bitter that for a whole year afterwards the air
vibrated with increasing racial and political antagonism, till one grew sick of the very name of Mother
India. Even the missionary societies of India, in
whose money-gathering interests it had always been
to paint her black, issued jointly a public denunciation
of the book as harmful and grossly exaggerated.
Indian opinion, quite general and freely expressed,
ascribed its writing to direct Governmental instigation
for the purpose of perpetuating foreign rule. But
prolonged observation has led me to believe that,
quite against all her conscious intention, Miss Mayo
has been the worst enemy of British interests and the
best friend of Indian aspirations. Far more than any
other single factor, the boiling resentment of Indians
against her accusations has determined them no longer
to permit outsiders to misrepresent, interfere with, and
exploit their country. " My country, right or wrong,"
found a new and vehement interpretation. The deep
undercurrent that has persisted since the appearance
of the book, the reports of the voracious eagerness
with which it was being read in the United States
and in England, the news that every member of
Parliament had been supplied with a free copy, was
behind the enthusiastic acclamation and support of
the 1928 Calcutta Indian National Congress Independence Programme.

But whereas the book directly helped to usher in
the non-co-operation war of 1930, the repercussion
from its accusations—as my Indian friend the social
worker had instantly predicted—certainly gave a tremendous impetus to reform. Moreover, it resulted,

against the will of the Central Legislative Assembly, in Government's appointing a commission and in its Age of Consent Report, now published in full. This is the first all-India investigation into child-marriage conditions, and has led to the very significant discovery that even the best informed Indians themselves —for lack of just such a thorough-going inquiry— had had but a partial idea of the extent and hold of this evil practice!

Now that the facts are common knowledge, now that women and mothers are in full possession of these facts and are aware of the terrible extent of the suffering and danger to which Indian girls are exposed, the day is past when each woman will submit in silence behind the shelter of her purdah and family, and look upon her ill fortune as the result of her own evil karma. These women have now learned to think socially, and are fully aware that liberal opinion is behind them; they will not rest, nor let men rest, until the priest dictates no longer, until the evil is uprooted, the tree cast into the fire, branches, trunk and roots. For legislation alone will by no means suffice. A long hard fight, or a great and sudden upheaval, can alone alter conditions within the closed doors of Indian homes. But the greatest women's organizations of India have already pledged themselves to this, each member has taken a vow, and fundamental reform is assured.

So, be it Sister or Maiden-aunt, the coming together of the women of East and West is bearing wholesome fruit.

XIII

SUFFRAGE AND SOCIAL WORK

BEFORE going on to consider woman's part in the national movement, let us pass in brief review the steps by which she gained her civic and social consciousness. The first impetus came from men, from Indians with a preponderance of Brahmin square pegs among them, and a few noble Englishmen. These realized the value of propaganda printed in the vernacular to give it a twofold chance of penetrating into sheltered homes. As early as 1857 the first Hindu woman's journal had already appeared, *Shri-Bodh*, a Gujerati magazine. Shortly afterwards, in 1863, its counterpart was published on the opposite side of India, the first woman's journal in Bengali. Mohammedans were slower to wake up to this need, but in 1886 *Tah-Zibi Niswan*, "Culture among women", was founded in the Punjab by Mohamedi Begum, and is still flourishing. Women are its chief contributors of articles on the needs and progress of education and social reform. Beginning with this century, a number of other women's journals have sprung up all over India, those of the South leading in quality.

But attention was also paid to the need of supplying books suitable for women at this stage of development. The fact that for a thousand years and more the majority of Indian women had been kept illiterate had given Indian literature a particular bent. The indirect, but effective, feminine influence was absent in its composition. Since women would not be numbered among the readers, Indian authors, while displaying the most exquisite literary skill and delicacy of feeling, filled their tales also with unparalleled ribaldry, voluptuous, amazingly detailed and often cynical sex descriptions, and gross immorality. The two were often closely intermingled in the same work —a Milton-Boccaccio mixture which our reformers did not find it easy to serve up as books " suitable for young girls ". There was great need for a new literature to spring into being which should embody present needs and problems, or offer old works in acceptable form. But despite some progress made, there exists even to-day a dearth of good Indian reading matter at cheap prices, in all vernaculars, though the women's journals contain excellent information and are great reforming forces.

The organizing of women's associations also helped enormously to impart to women a civic consciousness, not only to release her forces, but to direct them into social channels. Some of these have already been mentioned in the chapter on education. But as all combine both social and educational reform, and are moreover inevitably interlinked with the effort to gain the power of suffrage, they cannot be separated in a short review. Women naturally first pooled their efforts locally. Permanent local bodies carried out regular programmes of educational and social reform. The most important of these were the *Women's Indian Association* of Madras, the *Nari Siksha Samiti* of Calcutta, the *Stree Bharata Mandal* of Calcutta and North India, the

Seva Sadan of Bombay, the *Saroj Nalini Central Association* of Bengal, and the *Mahila Vidyalaya.* They all established sub-committees to take charge of different lines of work. For instance, Rama Swami Mudaliar had already suggested in 1888 that women should be put in sole charge of female committees to advise on education. These associations bent their efforts to that end with the result that at present they are definitely in a position to influence the curricula of schools. Bombay, for instance, owing to their efforts, adopted a new curriculum in 1931.

The leaders of these women's organizations soon realized the desirability of wider concerted action, and called into being, first Provincial or State, and later All-India conferences. The late Begum of Bhopal organized the first All-Indian Mohammedan women's Conference in 1914. Then the women of all creeds and castes joined together in the National Council of Women in India, and the All-India Women's Conference. In 1926 Women's Conferences on Educational Reform were held all over India, in places as widely separated as Madras, Calcutta, Poona, Bombay, Karachi, Delhi, Dacca, Hyderabad (Sind), Lahore, Allahabad, Cawnpore, and aroused such interest and enthusiasm that the following year saw the first All-India Women's Conference on Educational Reform at Poona. These Conferences demanded the establishment throughout India of suitable curricula for girls' education, the abolition of child-marriage and purdah, women's right to inheritance, and civic rights. What enthusiasm and determination these conferences aroused is seen from the fact that many resolutions aimed at the abolition of even the most deeply rooted customs were carried unanimously. The Mohammedan Women's Conference took the lead in condemning polygamy, and every mother present signed a pledge not to give her daughter in plural marriage. In the All-India Women's Conference a resolution was unanimously carried in favour of keeping intact the Sarda Act (demanding uncompromisingly that any marriage with a girl under 14 should be *ipso facto* illegal), and the formation of Vigilance Committees was planned to prevent and bring to light any breaches of the law against child-marriage.

How widespread are the efforts of Indian women to-day, can best be seen by quoting their own additional programme, condensed in a synthesis of the Social Resolutions passed in the latest All-India Women's conference. They are in favour of developing maternity and child-welfare work ; of encouraging indigenous industries and obtaining facilities for industrial training for women ; they demand inquiry into and means for bettering the conditions of women and children employed in labour and mining areas ; they deplore unnecessary expenditure in connection with marriages, births, and funerals, seek the curtailment of such expenses and the abolition of the dowry system ; they are in favour of the establishment of social centres and the training of social workers ; they wish for the abolition of the dedication of girls to temples and immoral modes of life, immoral traffic in women and girls, brothels and commercialized prostitution ; they resolved that steps be taken to prevent the sale and manufacture of illicit drugs ; they are in favour of establishing Rescue Homes for girl minors and for destitute women and children ; they demand recreation grounds for girls and women ; they call attention to the insanitary condition of cities and plan to work in this sphere in conjunction with the municipalities; they ask for the abolition of compulsory caste and community designations in educational institutions as well as in the coming Census; they are in favour of separate Law Courts for juvenile offenders and of women magistrates in such courts; they favour employment of women in jails, lock-ups and waiting-rooms in railway stations; and one constituency desired that the work of the All-India Women's Conference should be carried on in the Hindi language!

The intense interest shown in these conferences, and the practical manner in which work is tackled and plans are laid, are a very hopeful sign. For instance, though the Sikh community is small, the first Sikh educational conference was attended by 2,000 women, and a single one of these collected over one lakh of rupees to be used for the furtherance of reform. Mohammedan women have the hardest road to travel, for their men are on the whole as uniformly opposed to change as are the Brahmins, while they have fewer square pegs among them.

The struggle for the suffrage received the stamp of public approval by liberal Indian men as early as 1917, when they declared in that year's Reform Conference that "sex . . . shall form no disqualification to woman entering any position or profession for which she shows herself capable". At the Bombay and Delhi National Congresses also, 5,000 delegates from all over India declared in favour of the removal of sex disability and have done so in all later Congresses. To press this widespread desire for the suffrage on the attention of the authorities, an All-India Women's Deputation was sent to the Secretary of State for India, led, as previously stated, by India's outstanding poetess, Sarojini Naidu. Government responded by appointing the Southborough Franchise Committee in 1919. But as in the case of social and educational reform, Government did not seem eager for change. The Committee imposed sex disqualifications on women. " In the present conditions of India . . . it is not practical to open the franchise to women ", was its verdict. It might indeed not have been ' practical ', for this was the time when the Montagu Reform Scheme Bill was initiated, and the women's vote might have weakened the reactionary forces. It is a very significant fact that only one member of the Southborough Franchise Committee dissented from its expressed opinion, and that this member was the only Indian on the Committee, Sankaran Nair.

A few further facts in the struggle for women's suffrage deserve consideration. When the various Legislative Assemblies of the States and Provinces were called upon separately to decide on the extension of the suffrage to women, Madras, Travancore, Cochin, Mysore, Jhalawar, and Bombay were the first to vote in favour. A glance at the details of the fight in these two progressive provinces—Bombay and Madras—is also illuminating. No less than nineteen organizations took part in the Bombay campaign of 1921 to win the municipal vote for women, testifying to the keenness of Indian interest. On the other hand, when it came to the question of the provincial vote at Poona (for Bombay) five Westerners opposed the bill in their speeches, though they had the grace at the last moment to refrain from voting. In Poona, 50 white women helped in the propaganda work, as against only three in Madras—yet Madras was the first to win, voting twice as heavily as Bombay in favour of woman suffrage. Only three men gave dissenting votes against women's suffrage in the Madras Legislative Council, and one of these was an Englishman. The victory in Madras is doubly illuminating if we bear in mind that it is in this province that the power of the Brahmin was first publicly challenged and broken in a previous protracted fight by the lower castes for social and political power. It points to the fact that women at the present day profit socially in proportion to the progress of Indianization in the administration and to the defeat of Brahmin power.

Everywhere in India Mohammedans opposed as a body, and purdah States and Provinces also lagged far behind. While Cochin, for instance, removed all forms of sex-disqualification absolutely, purdah-Calcutta did not grant even the municipal vote until 1924, and then on taxpaying qualifications which debarred a disproportionate number of women, since very few Hindu women own property in their own name.

But by 1925 every province but one, Bihar and Orissa, that blackest of purdah provinces, had given to women the vote for the Provincial Legislative Assemblies, and even this last followed suit in 1928. But though thus the women now have a qualified vote, the battle is by no means finished. Theoretically, the civic status of Indian women is to-day on a par with that of the advanced nations of Europe. But in practice they still face many a heavy handicap which must be removed. Property qualifications operate far more heavily against Indian women than men. What is still needed has been formulated clearly in the mandate given by the three leading women's organizations to their representatives at the Round

Table Conference in London in 1931. This defines the ultimate status they have set themselves to attain, and will no doubt attain within a measureable time. First of all, in view of the communal conflict between the men, it is most interesting to note that women declared against preferential or special treatment under the new constitution to be evolved. They merely want the assurance of " equal rights and obligations for all citizens without any bar on account of sex ". The Memorandum sums up the situation and requirements. No disability is to attach to any citizen by reason of his or her religion, caste, creed, or sex in regard to the holding of any public office, or in the exercise of any trade or calling. This means that representative Indian women have at last come out definitely in protest against the Brahmin caste-edicts. They hold

" unqualified and unconditional adoption of the principle of adult franchise to be the best and most acceptable mode of assuring and securing political equality between the men and women of this country. They unhesitatingly consider all conditions or qualifications or tests for the exercise of this right, whether based on property or literacy, to be needless impediments in the way of the enjoyment by women of civic equality ".

They also protest against making the elementary rights of woman contingent upon her relationship to a man. " Every man or woman of the age of 21 should be entitled to vote and to offer himself or herself as a candidate at any election to an Administrative or Legislative Institution."

This is the embodiment of the ultimate aim of Indian women. That it is not an idle or unattainable goal has already been demonstrated by Cochin. To sum up, through its spokeswomen, Indian woman-hood has declared against caste distinctions, communal divisions, polygamy, purdah, child-marriage, and sex discrimination, and in favour of compulsory and free education for both boys and girls, of equal rights of inheritance, and of divorce.

That they still have a long hard road to travel in a country with less than 3 per cent. literacy among its women, is clear. But with the determination and quiet strength acquired, through ages of suffering and work-ing against heavy obstacles, the Indian woman is certain not to be deflected and to reach the goal she has set herself. That it will take generations to bring all her plans to fruition she well knows. But Brahma's seconds are vast, and there is time! Moreover, the educated Indian woman is herself the last to make the mistake of placing too much importance upon the criterion of mere literacy. That is not the only test of culture. Her age-old training in service and self-lessness has marked her deeply and given her im-mensely valuable powers of self-discipline and of spiritual aspiration. As much promise lies in this aspect as in the various movements towards her educa-tion. It is this side of her nature which has been touched and called into the open, to function in free expression through the nationalist movement. Here-in lies the strength of this movement and its special danger to the foreign power.

XIV

WOMEN AND THE NATIONALIST MOVEMENT

ONLY a very minute fraction of India's women has as yet any conception of the intricate workings and problems of administration, or any realization of the great difficulty under which a Government not of the people must of necessity struggle. Had India been autonomously governed during, say, the last fifty years, reform probably would have been much accelerated, but there would have been no lever to use to precipitate interest or action from below, no means of bringing the question of Government into any vital relationship with the average uneducated Indian, woman or man. All change would have been but a slow trickling downward into the masses from the thin advanced intellectual stratum of population above. Generations would have been needed to arouse political consciousness in the masses of men, and still longer for the women subject to these men. But with the sharp awakening due to foreign rule of political consciousness and ambition among the intelligentsia, there came inevitably the keen desire to get the administration into Indian hands, to win freedom.

For a while, politically minded India pinned its

faith to constitutional means by which to attain autonomy, in fulfilment of British promises. But the majority soon felt this means of progress far too slow, incalculable, and uncontrollable; the dead weight of Imperial opposition seemed too heavy to lift by constitutional means. Rightly or wrongly, India lost faith in British political sincerity and promises to lead her to self-government, or at least began to suspect deliberate and intolerable delay. While constitutional reform had called the intelligentsia only into action, a direct drive for independence needed the force of all classes behind it to give it sufficient impetus and weight. What was simpler, in order to gain the masses, knowing so little of administrative intricacies and ponderousness, than the cry "Swaraj!"? For everything that was hurtful, restricting, chafing in the ailing body of Indian life, Swaraj was the cure, the foreign raj was to blame. What more easy for even an illiterate peasant woman to grasp, or what more effective for immediate Indian aims? That much of such agitation and tactics was unfair to the constructive aspects of the alien Government is undoubted; but it is the harsh answer which imperialism must needs call forth at last in every subject nation at some point or other. Moreover, the foreign Government had provided the nationalists with some most convenient levers. While the peasant understood nothing of administration, he did understand when he was told that all the elected Indian members of the Big Delhi Council wanted cheap salt, but that the White Sirkar, over their heads, had doubled its price. The peasant knew he needed salt and wanted it cheap, and he naturally felt more confidence in the lead and promises of one of his own race than in a *mlechche* sahib. But this desire for economic gain would not in itself have been enough to win over the masses and impel them, especially the deeply religious womenfolk of the masses, to action. Another higher motive was needed, and it found embodiment and expression in the person of Gandhi, typical Indian saint and leader. A message of service couched in his words and backed by his life made a direct appeal to the simple Indian heart : the idealistic call to regeneration and suffering !

Serve the Mother, free the Mother, *Bande Mataram*, —it was a cry to appeal as could no other to all the mother-complexed youth of India, and to all the women whose only hope and consolation lies in mother-hood. " Serve the Great Mother ! " That cry supplanted the old call to the worship of ancient goddesses with a vital flaming immediacy and directness ; it supplanted in the minds of women the old duty of service and adoration of the husband. The Mother is in chains—sacrifice for her, suffer for her ! This was a tremendous idealistic appeal to the very heart of the agelong oppressed—to Indian youth and Indian womanhood. The simpler the mind, the more the appeal. They were ready to march forth in defiance of all edicts, as the women of antiquity had done who stormed the gates of their own city and went forth to greet the coming Buddha.

Gandhi's profound knowledge of the heart of his people was never better shown than in his special appeal for women to come and serve. He knew that the strength of India lies in its women because of their great power over their sons, and because of this idealization of the mother. The ground had been made ready for the final appeal during many

previous years. Gandhi has exerted enormous influence by his advocacy of the abolition of purdah over
a long period.

He called upon the women of India for the special
service of fighting the evil of drink, and of boy-
cotting foreign cloth, both causes with a peculiar
appeal to high-caste Indian women. Except for that
small and temporary group of foreign influenced
imitators of Western ways of living during the latter
part of last century, the opinion of Indian high
castes has always been solidly set against the use of
intoxicants of any sort. The high-caste home is
exceedingly rare in which alcohol is kept in any form
even for medicinal purposes. But unfortunately,
with increasing impoverishment, low castes have
turned to the solace of toddy. It was easy to win
over women crusaders to a determined fight against
this evil, still more easy when the blame for it could
conveniently be laid at the door of the foreign raj.
As for the boycott of foreign cloth, it was more
difficult. Many intellectuals in India have no real
faith in the *khaddar* or home-spinning movement.
But on the other hand, during the years of this
century, there has been a marked tendency among
educated Indian women to a renewed appreciation of
Indian textiles, and a preference for saris with the
old genuine Indian woven border, instead of the
strip of lace or machine embroidery sewn on imported
silk which for a short time had been " fashionable ".
This, and the fact that they considered themselves to
be in the service of the Mother, " soldiers of the
cause ", induced even half-hearted *khaddar* supporters
to come out and picket foreign cloth shops.

Women revealed incredible powers of endurance

and determination in this business of picketing. For instance, on September 9, 1930, the Legislative Assembly Elections were to take place in Bombay; the Gandhi party wanted them boycotted, as they were a form of co-operation with Government which it did not wish to tolerate at the height of the non-co-operation movement. Seventeen inches of rain fell during 36 hours, yet women went out in hundreds to all the polling booths to picket, despite the torrential rains. They did this so effectively that the election had to be postponed for that day. The next day they did another twelve hours regular picketing, fresh contingents continually replacing the old in a smooth-running and perfect organization. But by now the police were ready for them, and four hundred women were arrested, only to be met with immense jubilation the moment they were released again.

On the day of the liquor licence auction in Bombay, women formed an unbroken line round the entire building in which it was to be held. Their boycott was so successful that Government obtained the merest fraction of former revenues. The following year the same auction was announced three times, because the bidders, remembering the previous year's experience, were afraid and did not attend. Private treaties of sales behind closed doors had at last to be resorted to, for the boycott by the women was so effective that the auction could not take place.

For the boycott of goods, women who had before been secluded, went unattended to all parts of towns at all hours, unhindered. It is significant cases of their molestation by men were exceedingly rare. Though they had often to go into the most disreputable and dangerous quarters, the only risk they ran was from the police. Not only so, but the very shopkeepers, whose business they ruined, frequently sought to save the women from arrest. When runners came to announce the approach of the police, shopkeepers very often shut their booths to protect the women, much to the disgust of the latter. The women, courting arrest, would argue with the merchants, "You hypocrites, shame on you ; keep open now the police are coming, or else keep closed for good or get rid of the foreign cloth!" One woman picketer told me that a shopkeeper, before whose shop she had stood for hours shooing his customers away, actually pushed her into his booth and closed the door on her from the outside, to preserve her from arrest as the police approached. What could better reveal the power free Indian women are able to exert to bring out the best in Indian men?

Gandhi's preaching of non-violence was taken very seriously by his female followers, but although they could not retaliate, violence did not daunt them. In Borsad, for instance, 1,500 women were going quietly along a street in a peaceful procession. The police met them with a *lathi* charge. The woman leader was wounded, but with bloodstained sari pressed on again, until disabled by further beating. Luckily, women did not always fare so badly in their new ventures into public life and open warfare. For instance, during a raid on the Darsana saltworks, Mrs. Sarojini Naidu was leading. Stopped by the police, she calmly sat down in the dust of the road, with all her followers, and refused to budge. They could not go on in face of the wall of police barring the way, yet they would not go back. Without water or food, they sat there throughout the long burning hours of the day in the scorching dust, calmly twirling the thread on hand-spindles and good-naturedly chaffing the helpless policemen. Now and then the women were called upon to endure great suffering without provocation on their own part, and in such cases they showed the same unflinching patience. At Viramgam, 200 of them took water to the railway station to relieve the thirst of volunteers, a simple act of human kindness. The police set upon them and beat them mercilessly on all parts of the body.

Yet all this did not deter the women; it only served to give an enormous impetus to the entire woman's movement for freedom. The same women who had suffered, were again ready to offer themselves for further service the moment they were healed from their wounds or released from jail. Not only that, but their example acted irresistibly on others. I know of one case which was typical of hundreds of others. A woman living in a purdah town had been strictly forbidden by her mother-in-law to take any part; though several of her relatives and many friends were in the midst of the fight. One day the police attacked a procession of women as they passed by her house. She watched from a shuttered window in agony, and could not bear the sight. Suddenly she gave a cry, dashed out of the room and house, and joined the women in the street—the first time she had shown her face in public. In the ensuing domestic turmoil, the husband actually took her part against his own mother, a most unusual proceeding. New days are indeed dawning for India when such things can happen.

Every day of the non-co-operation fight brought fresh chances of freedom and self-expression to women. Unparalleled opportunities arose for them to demonstrate their organizing powers and endurance out in the open, in public work, those powers which ripen quietly inside the great joint families. For instance, before the Indian National Congress was declared illegal, a thousand people on boycott duty were daily fed at Bombay Congress Headquarters. The whole of the work was done by women, most of them of high caste; they did not scorn to scrub and cook, serve and wash up with their own hands, nor did any question of caste ever enter their minds regarding the people whom they served or those with whom they ate. It was splendid, communal, unitive training and work. Such training will not be lost, nor such experience forgotten when the time comes to apply it to peace-time work.

It is also interesting to see the effect which prison experience has had on women. Hundreds passed through the jails, though most of them but for a night or two, to be released again as soon as possible as the authorities could no longer cope with the thousands courting arrest. Many were sentenced for long periods to serve as first-, second-, or third-class prisoners. That the sentences were sometimes savage cannot be denied. The sister-in-law of Gandhi's first successor, a woman of 65, was sentenced to nine months' rigorous imprisonment in the third class for peaceful picketing. Third-class prisoners have two meals a day, at 10 a.m. and at 4 p.m. In the morning they receive *puri* and *dal* (unleavened bread and pea-soup), in the afternoon *puri* and one vegetable, with nothing but water to drink. Mrs.

Hansa Mehta of Bombay vouches for the following facts : women were often kept overnight in lock-ups level with the ground, without beds or bedding, on stoneflagged floors, behind shutterless iron-barred windows where people from the streets could see in at all hours. When she and two others went to jail, there were eight women in an 18 by 18 feet room in the first class. In the next cell of the same size there were 10 women, in the third 12. For these 12 prisoners only one latrine was available. This was during the torrential rains which drove in through the shutterless, paneless windows, making heavy puddles of water on the floor on which they were supposed to sleep. Great sections of Bombay were flooded ; yet that day no one came near and the doors were not unlocked until 10 a.m., despite the danger of floods. The toilets were out of order, yet no one appeared but two *chaprasis* until 5 p.m. and there was no redress for the unspeakable conditions arising. A letter sent out asking for help was confiscated. At the same time, at Poona, under like conditions, women were kept locked up from 5 p.m. to 6 a.m., without being permitted to go to the latrine, and even then the time allotted was so short that serious illnesses resulted. In one barrack a woman, absorbed in reading, failed to notice and salute the jailer ; all the women in that barrack were deprived of all reading-matter for a fortnight as a punishment. Yet hundreds of women not only went through such experiences once, but courted arrest again as soon as they were released. These examples are not given with a view to questioning the rights or wrongs of such prison conditions, but as an example of the metal of which Indian women are made and the amazing powers of determination and endurance they have acquired in the past.

Of the unprecedented numbers who broke purdah because of the Gandhi movement, one figure will give an indication. In Meerut alone, 5,000 women came simultaneously out of purdah as a protest against Gandhi's arrest, and never returned to it.

The temper of these people, and the supreme control voluntarily exercised over their own feelings, is clearly revealed by a single well-known incident. On "Black Saturday" in Bombay, five hundred injured were taken to hospitals, and thousands were beaten by the staves of the police—yet not a single policeman was injured in return.

One aspect of the non-co-operation war was amusing, or annoying, or portentous, according as one cares to look at it. This was the participation in the struggle by the *bandar* or monkey army—the thousands of children who insisted on doing their share. Barely more than a generation ago, Indian children were still very timid, afraid of whites, and usually scuttled for shelter at their approach, or stood in wide-eyed shrinking embarrassment if forced to remain near. But to-day taunts have taken the place of awe, dislike that of respect ; children, during boycott days, quite commonly jeered at the foreigners as they passed by in their motor-cars and did all they could to annoy them ; and when they take to that sport, Indian children can be just as devilishly exasperating as any Paris or New York urchins. Nor was that all ; their enthusiasm and agility were of use in the actual picketing. Where buyers resisted, defying all pleas not to purchase foreign goods, and started to walk away from the shops with their purchases, the peaceful picketers offered no resistance, but the *bandars* started a hue and cry. A few of these little scurrying demons would run along on all sides of the harassed purchaser, screaming, taunting, insulting him, proclaiming him at the top of their lungs to the whole world as a backslider, a traitor. The *bandars* followed many an offender right up to his own front-door, and took good care that his immediate neighbours learned of his offence. Not many a buyer cared to repeat such an encounter with the *bandars*. Voluntarily, these young-sters burned their own foreign toys and refrained from buying more; they also boycotted festivals which those who did not join in the Gandhi move-ment tried to hold as usual. They declared, for instance, that there should be no Devali lamps while India was in mourning, and made their tour from one offending house to another to blow out the festive oil lamps. A sense of public duty and of burning patriotism was thus ingrained in the coming generation.

As for women's part in the non-co-operation move-ment, it is for later historians to determine whether they would have done better to pin their faith to constitutional reform than to rebel. Whether these women were ill-advised politically in their attitude, is not a point for us to settle; what concerns us here is the realization that during the Gandhi movement, Indian women have shown unprecedented courage, self-control and determination out in the open, in a public cause. It is an indication of the tremendous power they will henceforth exercise in public in all things to which they choose to turn their hands. Their sustained and dogged power, when employed in social betterment, will go on working untiringly from year to year, as we have seen in the case of Lady Bose or Mrs. Ranade. The future of India not only seems safe in such hands, but we can see on the horizon the dawn of another of the great illuminating periods of which Indian history in the past has shown such outstanding examples.

True as it is that it was the wave of patriotic feeling which called women out into the open and directed their courage and work against the foreign raj—an easier thing for them to attempt concertedly than an attack on the evils of their own society—yet it is none the less the case that this movement dealt a most serious blow to the social power of orthodox Brahminism. Never can it regain its lost hold, or erect once more the walls it has so carefully built up through thousands of years. Nor will the Brahmin any longer be able as of old to deny to woman direct spiritual aspiration or religious knowledge. One intensely significant thing occurred which had a direct bearing upon this question. A young Gandhi volunteer, seeing that no protest by the boycotters prevailed upon the drivers of a motor lorry which was carrying foreign goods, made the supreme protest of throwing himself before it and letting its wheels crush out his life. His funeral was attended with all the honours the nationalists could bestow, and a great crowd were present—but it was a Brahmin woman who kindled the funeral pyre! This may have been the first case in more than two thousand years when a woman has dared to perform this ceremony, hitherto always consecrated to men alone. So in the present great awakening that is sweeping over India, woman is even resuming that part in the religious rites which she held in Vedic days, her right to act as sacred priestess.

Thus the fight against the conqueror from without and the tyrant from within goes on side by side in the Indian woman's struggle for freedom. Their ultimate formulated demands are very much the same as were those of Western women in the days when they were fighting for their rights. But it must not be overlooked that there is a significant fundamental difference in aim and direction between the two. The Indian woman's motive power is rooted in spiritual emotion far more than in any material consideration. She is on the whole more tender, less selfish, more considerate than the Western woman. For those who have her cause really at heart and are glad to see what is best and most distinctive in any nation remain untarnished, it is a matter of great satisfaction to realize that she is emerging from this struggle without embitterment. This is to a great extent due to the very form taken by her participation in the Nationalist movement, and to the purifying influence of Mahatma Gandhi. We must be clear as to the spirit in which these women fought ; for them the Nationalist movement was a religious movement, and, still more significant, it was a mass-, no longer a class-movement. It broke the stifling bonds of will-less obedience to caste rules and elders for young men, it opened wide a door of escape from their ancient prison to women. To break the rules of purdah and caste, in the service of non-co-operation and boycott, was now no longer the reprehensible and severely punished act it formerly had been ; it was suddenly seen in the glorified light of service to the Great Mother, a means of acquiring merit ! This was as constructively significant for Indian womanhood as it was annoying to the foreign Govern-

P.   R

ment, for with this impetus women could overleap in one bound the walls of age-old custom without violation to ingrained feelings, either their own or those of their surroundings. They were not giving dreaded offence to father, son, or husband ; they were sacrificing their privacy, their goods, their shelter at the altar of the Mother ! No blame, but only merit stood to be gained ; all the blame was on the head of the foreign raj ! Is it any wonder that millions of suppressed women should take this glorious chance of escape ? Yet even I, who knew so well the most backward sections of orthodox India, had not been prepared for the extent to which this new impetus became active in out-of-the-way corners and villages.

Outsiders may find it difficult to realize how deeply idealistic and emotional was this attitude and this reaction of sheltered unlettered Indian women to the call of Swaraj, the call to action outside the home, unless they remember to what an extent Indian women have for ages been forced to sublimate their personal desires and inclinations, to spiritualize their aims in selfless service. Consequently a call to suffering and service could reach them as could no other, could make them brave the streets and receive *lathi* blows with folded hands in the spirit of a religious sacrifice. Nor was this all, for not only women, but men also, were unconsciously glad that this door of escape to women had been suddenly flung open. Millions of young husbands, who years ago would have liked to see their wives and daughters enjoy a larger measure of freedom, but who lacked the force, courage and economic independence to brave their mother or mother's mother, their joint family, and their caste, were inwardly deeply glad when fate took the decision out of their hands and acted for them—when their women no longer even waited for permission to come out into the open to serve.

Still another factor pregnant with meaning was this : the call for service to Swaraj cut away the ground of opposition from under the orthodox priestly objection to women's freedom. What priest dared thunder anathemas against the breaking of purdah or of caste when it was done at the call of the Great Mother, the goddess supremely worshipped? At last, the goddess had made common cause with her earthly sister !

Thus, the womanhood of India gained the following inestimable advantages from the Nationalist movement and its sharp accentuation into the Gandhi and boycott war : Millions of women broke in one short year fetters which normally it would have taken generations to shake off ; they broke them not in rebellion against their own guilty menfolk who had forged them, but against the alien Government at whose expense India was thus saved from the deep internal conflict and bitterness which the fight for emancipation had called forth between the sexes in Western countries ; moreover, they have the escape-hungry, caste- and joint-family suppressed, mother-adoring youth of India solidly behind them in their support.

All these factors, though undoubtedly unfortunate for, and to some extent undeserved by, the foreign raj, hold untold promise for the future development of India. That her men and women have struck off the fetters of slave-mentality, of hampering custom, while standing shoulder to shoulder in the fight against a common enemy, has linked the younger generation in a bond of sympathy which will immensely favour the realization of women's plans of reform. It has also linked castes and classes which formerly were divided by insurmountable walls, and has given women of all religious communities the chance of working together in deep sympathy for one common aim. Moreover, it has instilled in all who took part the high spirit of a great crusade, and a new hope and pride in India's greatness. Such a movement will not die out without leaving lasting effects, any more than will the women who have once broken purdah return to it, or if a few should return, be again contented in its shadows. All this, with the added spur of international criticism, the stinging memory among the intelligentsia of the Mayo disgrace, will drive the generation which fought the Gandhi fight on and on in ceaseless endeavour for every kind of social as well as political betterment. With heightened consciousness and courage, the stain and sting of abject submission and slave mentality washed away, the Indian youth of to-day offers a very different outlook for India from that of past generations. Many observers have noted this tremendous change in mental attitude.

And one last factor must not be overlooked, the *bandar army*—those girls and boys who have helped their grown-up sisters and mothers in the boycott movement. Theirs is a psychological predisposition and conditioning never before met with in such a form in Indian history. It is bound to colour deeply the social and political history of India in the coming generations. The younger leaders of Nationalist India assert that an autonomous India will abolish purdah by one stroke of the pen, as did Turkey, and with it polygamy, *devadasis*, and all the trailing evils of the old régime. If they should fail in strength to make these promises good, the *bandars* will do so when their turn comes to rule.

We may be genuinely glad on behalf of the British administrator that he is at present exerting all his efforts towards evolving an Indian constitution, that full Indianization is in sight, and that therefore he will not have, as alien ruler, to face these *bandars* when grown up. For anyone who knows child-psychology will realize that a generation of youngsters who have taunted, defied, and mocked an alien ruler in the streets, have had a passionate adoration of swaraj and motherland ingrained in tender years, have seen their sisters and mothers dare and suffer imprisonment, will not grow into men and women who can be kept under an alien hand.

Strange fate; "Educate a woman and you put a knife into the hands of a monkey." The Brahmins —brown and white—will soon be faced with a whole army of *bandars*, male and female, with the new and gleaming knives of education and ambition in their hands. Woe to the Brahmins—and a good deal of pity for them, too, for many of them have honestly done their best and have acted in all good faith.

Yet no one who has the genuine interest of Indian womanhood at heart, can but be glad of every opportunity for advancement, whether it comes from English lives and books and history, or from Indian political hatred or spiritual aspiration. No other factor equals in promise the slow sure growth of a national spirit, nor has any other given, within so short a space of time such chances of liberation to women as the Nationalist war.

The consolation is that future generations will surely see more dispassionately, more fairly than the present possibly can. That future will probably fully realize that the " white Brahmin ", in actuality though not always in intention, has been the Indian woman's friend, the needed " wholesome irritant "—a kindly blue-eyed godfather!

XV

PERSONAL OBSERVATIONS

IN our day, as we have seen, the very foundations of the ancient customs most deleterious to Indian women's interests have received the rudest shaking. The Unchanging East is no more. Age-old walls are crumbling rapidly towards final dissolution. The most promising sign of all is the wholesale disappearance of purdah and the sound beginning made towards the abolition of child-marriage, the two most far-reaching evils.

The entire intricately woven fabric erected by priestly interests is irredeemably doomed, as is the social structure which particularly favoured it. Modern methods in industry, science, and administration are, for instance, strongly favouring the break-up of the joint family system. Not only do these tend to draw trained men away peaceably from the joint family, and induce them to set up separate homes, but the restlessness astir in the youth of India has made bitter and determined attacks upon this stronghold of orthodoxy and group domination. All over India, an ever-increasing war of litigation is being waged in which individual members compel the disruption of the joint family by insisting on their present legal right to obtain separate shares of pro-

perty. This furthers the emancipation of escaping
members along every line, for it breaks the moral and
economic stranglehold of the aged on youth. But
this disruption of the joint family particularly favours
women, for in each instance it frees a whole group
of them at the cost of the power of only one. It puts
an end to the tyranny of the mother-in-law over the
helpless other inmates of the zenana and also with-
draws her adult sons from her direct and excessive
influence. Young women who suddenly find themselves transplanted into separate homes of their own,
gain thereby a tremendous impetus towards initiative,
independence and responsibility—a rounded self-
development.

The breakdown of the joint family system also
tends steadily to raise still further the age of marriage
for girls. Men planning to set up their own homes
naturally want girls capable of running them efficiently ; this puts a premium on training and maturity
in brides. Maturer girls are in turn no longer so
likely to seek a father-substitute in their husbands as
are cowed adolescent brides. Given a chance to
develop both their bodies and their individualities,
they are more fit to become mates not only on the
physical but also on the mental and spiritual planes.
Such true matehood in turn will prevent women from
becoming dwarfed, twisted and frustrated wives.
This again will react favourably upon their relationship to their children. Daughters will tend more and
more to become as cherished as sons, and sons will be
spared the terrible emotional exploitation and dependence to which their unfree and unsatisfied mothers
have up till now inevitably subjected them. Instead
of remaining their whole life long emotionally segre-

gated and dependent upon their mothers, the emotional force of sons will in early youth undergo the normal, desirable socialization which forms the best basis for civic and national welfare. At the proper time sons will therefore also be free to become attached to and centre their affection in a normal way upon a freely chosen mature girl whom they will then honour as a mate and cease to regard as a mother-substitute.

Signs of this adjustment are already visible all over India, and it is bound to take place to an ever-increasing degree in the future. At long last the Indian race, to the infinite gain of both mother and wife, will definitely break through the vicious chain of unreal mother-worship and real wife-degradation. This freeing from the deep-rooted inhibitions and frustrations which are the inevitable outcome of the almost universal mother-complexing of sons and the resultant excessive introversion, will have undreamed-of significance for and influence upon Indian life. The vaporous idealization, the endless taking refuge in speculation and volubility which was so marked a feature of the Indian educated mentality in the past few centuries, will give place to direct concern with actual social problems and wholesome remedial action. Dispassionate philosophic observation and " karmic " explanation of suffering and misery will give proportionate way to determined interference for amelioration. The resulting new social conscience and consciousness will be no longer confined within the family or caste group alone, but will extend its beneficent influence to succour all who suffer. It will operate until the last shackles of artificial segregation and limitation have been struck off from all Indian women within the home and society, and will extend outward to embrace all castes as well as outcastes, and to the terrible suffering of animals.

With the increasing liberation and education of women, the teachings of individual regeneration and purification which Gandhi has so powerfully launched will also find ever richer, more receptive, and widening fields for sowing and reaping. For whereas in the first great revolt, in Buddhist times, women turned nuns and wasted their forces in abnegation of life, Gandhi, in the present revolt, has called on Indian women to function as a social force, to the heightening and elevation of their primary function of motherhood and the lasting gain of the race. Likewise, vivid indications abound of late years that the ancient wholesale escape of men into religious life is lessening; after the care for their own progeny is removed from their shoulders, more and more male square pegs now turn their matured energies to whole-time and whole-hearted social service.

The day has come when Indian men and women, parents and children, are once more jointly placing their feet with fresh vigour and dedication upon the Vedic road of individual and national freedom, of great mutual support in socialized work and aims.

*   *   *   *   *

The road still to be travelled is long, and progress will be uneven up and down through the vast masses and stretches of India. But everywhere the leaven is stirring, as observers cannot fail to see. The following personal experiences may serve to illustrate trends and variations. I myself have had hundreds of occasions to observe one specially significant sign. Nowadays old customs keep their hold on individuals no

longer as principles but from fear of social obloquy.
Where fear of detection is removed, many even of the
most orthodox have no scruple about breaking caste
and purdah, and often do so with great zest. If, in
addition, some special stimulus or general impulse
stirs a larger number of people simultaneously, as in
the Nationalist movement, then with mass-momentum
they sweep away restrictions like straws upon a high
tide ; when and where public sanction cuts through
restraint, minds adjust themselves with unbelievable
ease and readiness. I do not hesitate to say, on the
basis of the surprising number of caste men who have
broken caste rules unknown to their fellows under the
protection of my roof, that not more than one out of
ten orthodox Hindus sticks to old customs as a matter
of principle ; the others are all motivated by fear of
material loss and social prestige.

A foreign Government cannot take the risk, but a
national Government may soon abolish purdah and
caste and cause them to vanish overnight, for the huge
number of restless and cowed youths would hail with
joy a change, a law, which would remove the danger
of public ostracism and break for ever the tyranny of
the aged.

A striking example of the ease with which change
may occur under favourable conditions can be tellingly
illustrated by a certain instance, as it exists in full force
within the orthodox fold itself and does not even
involve a question of reform. It shows how slight a
shifting of the angle of vision is needed to make
radically different conditions acceptable to all. The
sacrosanct temple of Puri, shrine of the Lord of the
World, Jaganatha (Juggernauth), is in a section of
India where Buddhism retained its hold longest, and

some unique traits of its teaching still survive, their
origin unrecognized by the people in general, in full
force.   Within the precincts of this town and temple,
as in Buddhist times, caste and purdah, in opposition
to the usual Hindu custom, are still not observed.
No matter from how orthodox a village the worshippers may come, men of all castes may here partake
together of *prasad*, the food of the gods, and women
who have been strictly secluded all their lives here
fearlessly and unhesitatingly throw off their veil.
They do not question or reason about the why and
wherefore of this unique custom; no principle
actuates or hinders them; simply because it is a state
of affairs invested with public sanction, restrictions
melt like mists before the sun.   With the light ease
of children tossing outworn toys into a fire they cast
off lifelong habit, yet the moment these worshippers
again leave Puri to return to their homes, they once
more submit to purdah and caste with ready willing-
ness and unconcern.

Not only so, but up to most recent days, they were
at once ready again to criticize bitterly any woman who,
away from Puri, strove, however faintly, to stir the
folds of her veil.   Just eleven years ago, in a town
a short distance from Puri, I had invited about forty
of my husband's friends and their wives to come to
my " housewarming ".   This was in the early days of
stubborn and often ill-advised attempts at forcing
reform.   I had argued that since my husband's
Western- or Indian-college-educated friends professed
distaste of purdah, and so much enjoyed coming to us
to talk with " my husband's wife ", they ought in turn
to let him see their wives.   Hence I had sent joint
invitations, instead of arranging a separate purdah

party for the ladies on another day, a proceeding which
would have been much wiser.   But I made the gesture
on principle, because I disapproved of social segregation.   I knew quite well that in this strict purdah
town not a single wife would or could come, but I
counted on the form of my invitation at least giving
occasion for many future discussions which might
lead to social ferment and make for ultimate change.
Moreover, I had a special surprise in store for my
guests.   A young Brahmin girl from Calcutta, who
was out of purdah, was visiting me with her uncle.
She—under Tagore influence—was one of the few
women who sang and played an instrument, the *esraj*.
When the guests were assembled, she sat down with
quiet ease and after general acclamation, she and her
uncle began to sing.   It was a rare treat for our male
guests, who practically never had the chance of talking
to, much less of hearing music from, a cultured woman
of their own kind.   Just as with their own women
at Puri, so here too they accepted cordially and without
criticism the fact that this girl from another province
should be unveiled ; for it offended none of the conventions which immediately concerned them.   I could
see genuine enjoyment on the faces of all as they
listened to the rendering of some of the loveliest of
Tagore's songs for which the poet had both written
the works and improvised the melodies.   There was
at least the hope that among the younger generation
present, some would come to wish that their own
young wives or daughters likewise could have the
added joy and charm of these accomplishments, and
might feel a faint regret that they were deprived of
this afternoon's pleasure.   For, of course, not a single
wife had come—I had been snowed under with some-

what shamefaced apologies for their absence on the part of the husbands.

Against advice, I had also sent an invitation to a woman whom I had not yet met, but who had sent me word that she would like to see me sometime—a widow with sons and daughters for whom she still managed the home. I cherished, from hearsay, a high regard for her, as I did for every little sign of rift in the purdah-walls of this most orthodox of towns : I had been told she was "a little mad"! From what I could gather, the madness consisted in her reading vernacular books and papers, and questioning men visitors to her house from behind her purdah about matters that "concerned no woman"; moreover she had let male relatives beyond the proscribed limit actually see her face, and was keeping her daughter unmarried after the age of twelve.

Of course, I never expected that she would come. But suddenly, when the entertainment was in full swing, a tightly shuttered carriage drove into the compound and on beyond our verandah to the sheltered side of the house. A wave of agitation and burning curiosity passed over my guests. Then I was called into the house—the widow had come! I could see that she was struggling between shyness and defiance of the men outside, but was upheld by a sense of elation : she was proving to the white woman, of whose criticism of purdah she had heard, that there was at least one purdah woman daring enough to take up the challenge! I could have hugged her, but sat decorously with her behind purdah in my own room, chatting with her as long as I could neglect my other guests.

Great her daring had indeed been, for though not

one male guest of mine saw her face that day, criticism of her coming to a house where a large group of men were assembled was bitter and stinging for months and months. If it be true that, since then, lack of sympathy and an abundance of obloquy has driven her more than " a little mad ", so much the greater the disgrace to the educated men of the community, many of whom, ten years ago, cordially expressed in private their disbelief in purdah, yet refrained from action in public and, in this instance, did not hesitate to cast a stone with all the rest.

But only a year later, the Gandhi nationalist ferment was having its first effects even in this town. One little purdah woman, whom I knew, was under the influence of some young students who had enabled her not only to acquire an easy reading knowledge of the vernacular, but supplied her with good reading matter. She had become interested in the Gandhi cause, and when his 1922 call came for funds, and women were offering their jewels, she contributed her share. More than that, despite severe criticism, she went in a closed carriage from house to house, visiting all her relatives to pester them with demands for money. In doing so, she met face to face several persons who were beyond her purdah pale. One of these relatives, reputed to be a hardened miser, instead of giving her even one penny, treated her to a most severe lecture on her behaviour. Soon after she had gone, he missed a silver ornament which she well knew he valued. He at once sent word to the minx to return it. " Yes, uncle dear," her answer came, " you shall have it the moment you send me its weight in coins, otherwise it is going to be melted down for Gandhi's funds ! " She got her contribution.

About that time, in the same town, I succeeded in slipping in a wedge against purdah in a certain family. I persuaded a young friend of mine, coming from a huge joint family, not only to bring his young wife and two sisters-in-law to see me, but to let my husband be present. We sat under the trees on the sere and yellow excuse for a lawn, around a tea-table. It was both touching and amusing to observe what a daring adventure this occasion implied for the young women. They had drawn their veils closely over their faces, turned their heads away, and answered in monosyllables, each word carrying a note of struggle and victory over inner inhibitions. At last, after a spell of several minutes' significant silence, during which she had no doubt been gathering all her courage in the hollow of her small red palm, my friend's wife flung a question all her own at my husband like the quick frightened throw of a stone. Her daring was followed by a sharp audible intake of agitated breath and squirming confusion; then suddenly a merry sweet bubble of laughter broke from all three; the Rubicon was crossed.

But for one single woman who took a step towards freedom, there remained hundreds in that province for whom there was still not a ray of hope. How galling purdah and joint family life can be, a very near relative of my husband's was even then discovering. Despite her grief and pleading, despite the fact that her own people offered to fetch her and bear all expense, she has never since the day of her marriage, over fifteen years ago, been allowed to revisit her family; possibly fearing to have the tale of bitter unhappiness made known, the mother-in-law could not be induced to let her go.

Considering what a backward state of society these conditions present, one fact has tremendous significance. Only nine years later, in this same town, at the next call of Gandhi, dozens of women crossed these terrific barriers of caste and purdah as if they had been mere low mud-walls. Nor did they wait any more for leave from men, but found that male approval trailed in the wake of their action. These men who were mentally timid, lacking initiative, and emotionally over-dependent on women, felt relief when the necessity for action was taken out of their hands by the brave defiance of the women themselves. One of these latter not only broke through purdah, but has become an effective public speaker; another has shown supreme organizing capacity and led hundreds of villagers. That this could happen in a seemingly hopeless purdah town within so short a time is a vivid indication of the range and power of the new regeneration sweeping over India. Such change is penetrating into the most sheltered nooks and corners. In the very same jungle State where that mother-in-law had the power to keep a young woman captive against her whole family's desire, a social earthquake took place a short time ago. A certain girl had been widowed when little more than a child, but the very idea of widow remarriage had not yet penetrated there, and would have convulsed the orthodox with horror. The girl was very poor, but unusually intelligent. Somehow, before she married, her father had managed to let her have one year of schooling in another town, in itself a step of radical advance. In that one year she had learned the elements of reading and writing in her own vernacular, and a little sewing, and had had just a glimpse of

further possibilities of development. She had, for
instance, seen some paintings and colour-boxes, but
had never had a lesson in this art. Yet somehow, on
that meagre one year's school foundation, she managed
to go on developing herself. Instead of forgetting,
as is so usual, the little sewing she had acquired there,
she went on experimenting on her own initiative with
new stitches and patterns, until she could turn out
really lovely decorative work of her own design.
Meanwhile, she had also somehow managed to procure some elementary colours, and with these painted
quaint pictures on any bit of brown or yellow scrap
she could lay her hands on, for she was too poor to
buy paper. Some were intricate geometrical designs
such as are used in the ancient powder tracings for
holy days ; others were more ambitious, though sometimes pathetically inadequate—renderings of gods and
epic heroes. But her untutored work showed a surprising feeling for decorative quality and fineness of
line, undoubtedly worth training. The girl longed
ardently to be given the chance of further education,
and her father, far too poor himself to help, could have
been induced to let her go if only someone had come
forward with the slight financial help required. But
who was there in that orthodox group with any
tolerance, far less backing, for such sinful impenitent
widow's thoughts ? Just one young uncle, trained
for a clerkship, sympathized with her ambition.

It was this young man who brought her to me the
day after my first arrival in the town. He had exerted
all his efforts on her behalf, but to no purpose save
to draw sharper criticism and antagonism upon himself
as well as the girl. No doubt, this had thrown the
two young people closer together, and given him that

strong sense of responsibility which I felt in him from the first minute. Shy, simple and eager, they approached me for help. I could read them like a book, and saw what they themselves, who were bred in an environment that knows no premarital romance, had no doubt not yet fully envisaged and deciphered. His every gesture and glance was eloquent of reverent protective love, and hers of the most tremulous adoration. But he was married, having been compelled to marriage by the family against his will. Though his small clerkship brought him in a pitifully inadequate income, he would gladly have given it all to send this girl to school. But as member of his joint family, he was forbidden the free disposal of even a small part of it. He saw no way out.

I gauged the nature of this man's love for the little widow by his intense interest in her getting a chance of further education. Where many an Oxford graduate does not trouble to impart to his wife even the rudiments of education, this young clerk had taught her to perfect herself not only in her own vernacular, but in addition began to teach her Bengali so that she might have access to the printed riches of that language. Unfortunately, to my bitter regret, I was in no position to give any financial help, but I tried my best to procure it from outside. I wrote on her behalf to a great painter who taught in an institution famous for giving girls an equal chance with boys ; I also wrote to a patron and critic of art in Bombay ; weeks passed before I received any reply, then came apologies, profuse excuses, but nothing more. When I went to Calcutta, I tried again in other quarters.

But fate acted far more quickly than I. Suddenly I received the news that the town was seething over

the elopement of this uncle with the young widow.
Shortly afterwards I had a letter direct from him.
Seeing no other way out, both to protect and free the
girl, he had run away with her to Delhi, married her
there as second wife with the rites of the Arya Samaj
society which advocates widow remarriage, and then
immediately placed her in a school. His family could
now no longer deny him the right to contribute to her
support. But they could outcaste him, and he now
doubly dreaded to forfeit his post. He hurried back
at once, and, to the great honour of the raja under
whom he served be it said, he was not dismissed,
though the community with few exceptions was
ablaze with indignation.

The significance of such daring is fully appreciated
if we recall that never before had a single case of
widow remarriage even been thought of in that community. In such ways is the ferment working
throughout India. Yet orthodoxy and reaction raise
their heads at times in the most unexpected places.
A great national leader, member of a society advocating remarriage, wrote to his widowed daughter from
abroad assuring her of his fullest approval and support
should she decide upon such a step. Back came the
most indignant answer, no matter what her honoured
father's view or that of the society he sponsored
might be, she, a Hindu woman, could and would never
dream of so running counter to ancient tradition.
Nothing on earth would ever induce her to marry
again! In case he should be motivated on his part
by any unwillingness to bear the burden of having her
back again in his own home, she went so far as to
remind him that her widow's maintenance share was
large enough to make her economically independent.

Thank heaven, even her reform-mad father would no longer have the power to drive her to so wicked a deed as remarriage!

But between the extremes of the radical and orthodox attitudes, we can at present find every shade and degree of compromise. Since India has little by little slipped into her age-old bonds by ever intenser degrees of restrictive Brahmin legislation, this same road can be travelled backwards, towards freedom. In any extremity, the orthodox can always, by turning to old enough sacred writings, rely on finding some religious text to sanctify the breaking down of an ancient wall. The very orthodox mother of a dear friend of mine bitterly opposed his marriage to a girl who not only did not belong to the same august subdivision of the Brahmin caste, but, horrors! even came from another province. She had tried everything in her power to frustrate his intent, doubly harassing because he devotedly adored his mother and hated to give her pain. It took him nearly two years of constant effort to win his way at last. But when the elders realized that they must either give in or lose this brilliant member of their caste, they found priests ready to bring forward ancient texts that, strangely enough, covered and permitted just this exception! So the marriage took place, with due religious rites. But though they gave in, they had failed to win him over. He continued his lone way.

Outspokenly against all hampering ancient customs, he had built a separate home for himself and his young wife and further had defied all conventions. His wife observed no purdah, nor either of them caste rules. The well beside his house was thrown open even to untouchables—all bitter tales for the old

orthodox mother to swallow. But her longing to see
the little home and the first baby, then almost a year
old, at last conquered and she came for a visit.   Over-
whelmed by the genuine love poured out on her, her
defences crumbled still further.   It was not many days
before she stopped toiling through the weary hot sand
to the river's edge to fetch water ; orthodox Brahmin
of the deepest dye but a few short years ago, she was
now actually brought to the point of voluntarily
touching the water of that polluted well—though she
did take the comforting precaution of sprinkling into
all she used a few precious drops from her sanctifying
jar of Ganges water!   Only those who know India
well can realize what an enormous change of inner
attitude and adjustment is here implied.   It seems as
if Hinduism is fast bursting its shell and regaining its
ancient elasticity.

Where old age can be found making such touching
readjustments to modern days, such vast concessions
of hoary principles for the dear sake of human love,
it is regrettable to find so many instances of educated
youth sacrificing theirs for mere material gain.

While in the capital of a native prince, I was the
guest of one of its chief Hindu state officials, who
belonged to the group which comes under court rules.
One of these was strict observance of purdah for their
wives.   My hostess's car being well known in the
town, we sat behind tightly drawn curtains and
scarcely dared to push them aside a bare half-inch to
watch the gay glitter and movement of that vivid
northern bazaar.   It was an odd sensation, this peeping
out, and made me realize that one of the lures of
purdah must be this sense of tasting forbidden fruit.
But the moment we cleared the massive guarded gates

of the city walls and swung out on to clear roads, my
hostess with a merry little laugh signalled to the driver
to stop, threw open the door, and flashed out,
" Come along, now I'll show you speed ! " A
moment afterwards the stately turbaned driver sat
with imperturbable unsmiling dignity within purdah,
while we were outside and my friend's two little red-
tipped jewelled hands drove the car at a steady sixty
miles an hour. But with my amusement was mingled
a regret that this girl, brought up in non-purdah
Bombay, was compelled through material interest to
observe a custom which she loathed, instead of being
able to use her forces to further its breakdown. It is
this everlasting compromise on the part of some of
India's educated youth that so retards progress. But
this is merely a transition-phenomenon.

The rising Mohammedan generation likewise is
often forced to just such compromise. During my
stay at some rockcut caves, a very illustrious party of
about 14 to 20 came for one day's visit. The head
of the party was a dignified old Mohammedan close
to a throne. There was only one lady in the group,
the wife of the old man's son, because husband and
wife had not come with the others straight from the
capital, but joined them on the way. Purdah rules
within the old man's family were strict, so she kept
veiled even from her own father-in-law. She was
not permitted to see the caves in the company of the
men, yet craved for a good look. So I was asked
and gladly proceeded to take her under my wing.
We two modestly kept four caves behind our august
lords, and thoroughly enjoyed being together and
chatting at our ease. She spoke faultless English,
was altogether charming and intelligent—and her

grandmother had been English! Whenever, in the
caves ahead of us, the floodlights were being used and
the indefatigable curator held his visitor engrossed
with tales of the frescoes on the walls, several of the
bored young men, including her charming husband,
slipped back to us for a few moments' relaxation and
talk and puffs from cigarettes which they did not
dare to smoke in the presence of their august elders.
No smallest fragment of purdah was observed then!
Respect and love and a generous mixture of pity for
the old induced this young group to keep up a show
of observance. Once the grey heads are underground, nothing on earth will keep these young people
in outworn chains.

But in the face of all such subterfuge it is refreshing
to come across people such as the Parsis, who are free
from caste and purdah, and consequently have a far
greater chance of living fully and simply, forced to no
compromise. Once as I travelled towards Delhi, a
Parsi woman, Dr. C., entered my compartment at
Agra. Quite independent and alone, she was touring
a certain district of North India to organize welfare
exhibitions, and was just then on her way to Delhi
to arrange there a hygiene-course and baby-show.
She had in her charge dozens of exhibit boxes. Full
of cheer because of the response she was eliciting
from even quite illiterate women, and tremendously
hopeful over the possibilities of educating through
visible demonstration, she expressed the sure belief
that it would be fatal to wait to impart literacy first.
Only wide publicity, in which the willing helpfulness
of men was essential to spread the news, was needed
to have the effect of bringing hundreds of women to
visit a show, and then to induce them to come regu-

larly to hear simple chart-illustrated talks on hygiene
and sanitation. For the life of zenana women is so
lacking in interest, that these welfare exhibitions with
their vividly coloured contrast-charts of good and bad
ways of living offer them entertainment as novel and
welcome as the cinema shows unattainable to the
majority. My travelling companion was middle-
aged, unmarried, and, being a Parsi, came from a
group which has always respected and encouraged
every form of education and individual enterprise for
women as well as for men. So she was inwardly free
from the many fetters under which Hindu women
labour. She regretted bitterly that more Hindu
widows could not be induced to come forward to
help in the work. The better placed, and the more
highly educated the family, the more reluctant they
seemed to let their widows take to independent
work.

As we neared Delhi, she inquired where I planned
to put up. When I replied, she pressed : " No, don't
go to a hotel, come with me ! I always stop with old
friends of mine near Delhi Gate, Mohammedans,
interesting people. You'll enjoy meeting them. It
is a big joint family ; the women are strictly secluded,
but very advanced." " Strictly secluded, but very
advanced "—this was still rather new in my experience. I had not yet met with it in Hindu families,
and I was curious to get a glimpse of it in a Mohammedan house. Still, I demurred, it seemed too great
an imposition to inflict my presence unannounced
upon absolute strangers. " No, no, that's perfectly
all right, I assure you. Take my word for it, they'll
be delighted to see you and have a chance to talk to
you. There's a whole house always set aside for

guests, and it's certainly not full now, I know—do come ! "

A young man, a driver, and a big car were waiting at the Delhi station, and shortly afterwards we drew up before a huge wooden door in a blank wall. We entered a courtyard wholly surrounded by houses. As soon as the gates were thrown open, we saw some women step out from one of the houses, cross over, and wait for us in the shadow of a verandah. The moment our baggage had been deposited in some rooms and the two men were gone, these women came forward with a warm welcome. My presence was accepted as though long and cordially expected, with the most winsome, quiet, undemonstrative courtesy. One of the women was of Junoesque build, about thirty-five years of age, the younger two were girls of sixteen and eighteen. These latter were a curious blend of shy gracefulness and ease, the oldest a gracious self-possessed hostess.

First came a flood of questions on the part of Dr. C.—" How is your mother keeping ? When does X. expect her baby ? Have you been able to induce your uncle's mother to call in a trained woman doctor instead of one of those awful midwives ? Has Y. been persuaded to send his girl to school ? " It seemed that Dr. C. had her finger on a hundred pulses in that widespread family relationship. She was consulted on dozens of problems, and our listeners apparently were the vital educative intermediaries between the new knowledge of the world and scores of little sheltered hinterland families. Dr. C. was questioned as to the news and progress of her work in nearby towns, and about similar work in other parts of India. I could see that these purdah women

had thrown a web of keen interest in welfare work
not only over their own immediate surroundings, but
over the whole of India, Mohammedan and Hindu
alike; a rather surprising revelation to me who
mourned over the lack of civic interest and the devotion to tea-parties of many of the cultured society
ladies of Bengal.

In a large dining-room we were served with a
sumptuous dinner by two menservants. The three
women did not share it, but hovered about with
gentle insistent urging to take, " oh, just a little more !
Or don't you like it ? " I would have thought the
quantities of delicious food we had already demolished
could have left no room for the question. Now came
my turn. I was put through a full catechism about
the West, keenly, sympathetically, quaintly. A glance
at the rooms we were in had shown me the usual
hotch-potch European furniture common to most
well-to-do Indian homes—rose-splashed carpets,
wretched framed lithographs, cats embroidered on
pillows, lace curtains, everything that was fashionable.
But my eyes over and over again returned to the three
women, for nothing in their costumes was Westernized. One of the girls wore a Hindu sari, a dress
increasingly adopted by Mohammedan women of
late years, the other the trousers and loose tunic which
are the fashion among young Mohammedan girls,
while our hostess had donned vivid voluminous
trousers of stiff flower-sprayed silk brocade, a blouse
of gold tissue, and the filmiest rainbow-hued head-and
shoulder scarf. I could not fill my eyes enough.
Never had I seen a woman more the picture of health,
ease, contentment, and unworried yet lively and intelligent interest. Nor could I believe my ears when

told that this radiantly youthful, luxuriantly relaxed creature was the mother of seven children. I never saw her husband, but before I left the next day, Dr. C. and I were asked to visit the zenana buildings surrounding another inner court. There was not the shadow of a man around, but a full assortment of women of various ages and qualities of dress. With special deference we were here introduced to the real head of the house, an old woman who spoke not a word of English, but had the most astounding flow of Hindustani ; a shrewd masterful face and humorous twinkling eyes, yet the same smooth grace so pleasing in the younger women.

No contortion of thought could ever afterwards have made any of these women into purdah-martyrs in my memory, and as for our young hostess, I knew beyond a doubt that she was a fulfilled contented woman, knowing a depth of peace such as few women in the Western bustle are ever blest enough to experience. Only one other woman in India, a Brahmin mother whom I knew intimately and who had been married at thirteen, radiated an equal amplitude of joy and restfulness. This showed zenana and family life at its best, with all its rare but actual possibilities of wide sheltering security and loving peace, of fostering a happy serene expansion untroubled by material worries.

While I could feel glad sympathy with the wholesome completeness of such family life, there were yet always certain differences of manners and ways of looking at things which reminded me continually to beware of undiscerning comparisons in details. Quite often exactly opposite habits will shock Indians and Westerners.

It would hardly occur to us to belch in order to express to our Indian host how wonderfully we think he has fed us, nor could we be expected to read at first sight the meaning of the startled look of an orthodox villager when he sees us take hold of a drinking-glass with our left hand.

I still remember how indignantly I resented my first meeting with an ultra-orthodox visitor of my husband's. I happened to be in the room when he was ushered in. For a whole half-hour he never spoke one word to me. To a direct question which I at last put to him, he answered by looking at and directly addressing my husband as if it were he who had spoken. Nor did our visitor once favour me with even a fleeting glance. Aha, I thought, so this is how the orthodox show their disregard for women —and I exploded as soon as he was beyond earshot. I received the laughing explanation that I had been paid the greatest of compliments, had been treated with the most delicate form of politeness. Since I had committed so incredible a breach of etiquette as to expose my face to a man not entitled to see it, he had acted as if unaware of my guilt and even of my presence !

One has continual occasion to refrain from trying to impose one's own ideas, or attributing blame where no offence was intended. For instance, as practically no Hindu woman ever has a room to herself, as many rooms have only curtains at the doors and all are used indiscriminately during the day, she sees no reason on earth for any privacy within the zenana, while we resent intrusion into our rooms.

Concerning this, I had a number of startlingly revealing experiences. Once, exhausted after a hot dusty railway trip, I had taken a bath at noon and lain down in only a flimsy nightgown on a cot. My Hindu hostess had sent word she would come with her daughters and some other women to have tea with me. Already at two o'clock I was startled from the depths of sleep by a noise in my immediate neighbourhood. There, just beside my bed, stood an old woman, and three others were near the door, all gazing at me with huge interest. A small boy of about seven was righting a flimsy stool; its toppling over no doubt had wakened me and cut short their inspection. I was frankly annoyed, but could not show it. The first glance told me that these simply dressed women could hardly belong to the expected party; but such parties are always very elastic, and I wondered if they might be poor relatives. It took me some time to make them understand, politely, that I would rather they left me for long enough to give me a chance to dress, and that I would then join them post-haste in the room downstairs. Despite my interrupted sleep and weariness, I hurriedly dressed, and went below. There was not a sign of any women anywhere, neither of these simply dressed ones nor of the gorgeous glint of silk and gold which I knew would herald the approach of my hostess. It took some ferreting before I discovered that my visitors had been merely the wife and female relatives of the caretaker, eager to have a good look at the stranger.

The second experience threw light not only on the absence of privacy, but also on the custom of polygamy. I had occasion to stop for reasons of work in a wealthy Hindu home. The palatial house had recently been completed and fitted out from top to

bottom by English firms with English furniture.
Though it stood on an arid plain where white heat
beat down from a furnace of sky for many pitiless
months of the year, and choking dust-storms blinded
and penetrated everywhere, engulfing upholstered
chairs balefully beckoned on every hand throughout
the wide rooms.

Yet I knew, for it was common knowledge, that
amidst all this appalling modernity, somewhere in
the maze was an old-fashioned room in which lived,
sulking and purdah-hidden, the first unlettered orthodox wife of the owner of the house—a keen business
man who had risen to sudden wealth. As there had
been no son, he had not hesitated to marry again, but
chose this time a much younger and more accomplished wife, whose only partial observation of purdah
made her a more presentable mistress of this palatial
home—an important factor, since, for business
reasons, this Hindu determined to stand well with
Westerners and with a certain liberal Indian group
with official powers.

On the evening of my arrival the young hostess
and her children had been present at the great dinner
given to two other white women, myself, and a number of Indian men. During the weeks which followed
I had frequent chats with my hostess, but my food
was brought on a tray to my own room, evidently
one of the best rooms of the house. One broiling
afternoon, when the servants had cleared away, a
glance from my window which overlooked the drive
through the garden had shown me that the young
wife and her children did not mind braving the heat,
for they stepped into a closed car and drove off.
Shortly afterwards a humbler horse-drawn carriage,

a tonga, arrived; from behind its billowing curtain
issued four women and one young girl, none of whom
I had ever seen before.   They had the appearance of
villagers, I had no idea who they were or what they
wanted, but was certain that at any rate their arrival
did not concern me.

The afternoon was young, the heat very old, stale
and annoying.   Fully dressed for the occasion in my
spectacles only, I prepared as usual to enjoy my siesta,
luxuriating under a fan on an airy rattan chair.   In
happy alternation I now absorbed a page of *Jud Süss*,
now spat out some chewed fibres of sugar-cane on to
a shining brass plate, now counted the drops of per-
spiration—one every five seconds—which fell from
the bend of my elbow on to the cool marble floor—
just the sort of ultra-tropical comfort and relaxation
which one glories to have known and to know no
one else has beheld one in.

The sound of some shrill excited talking reached
me from outside, from the direction of the inner
courtyard, over towards the gorgeous plant- and
flower-set swimming pool—in which no one ever
swam.   Then I heard the soft patter of bare feet;
suddenly my door was thrown open without a pre-
liminary knock, and in walked a fat lady in a gorgeous
swinging orange skirt, purple shirt-blouse, and
magenta head scarf—a lady whom I had never before
beheld.   In her wake there trailed into my room the
four humble ladies and the young girl.   One horror-
struck glance at me, then for some seconds a stony
staring at the floor, during which I threw a kimono
over myself.   None of us knew what to do; dumb-
founded, I did not speak, and no one spoke to me!
But there was no immediate retreat; the towering

purple and magenta presence took a few uncertain
steps forward, uttered some phrases to her following,
and made an uncertain gesture with her hands as if
showing off the room.   All threw furtive glances at
walls and ceilings, glances whose vanishing tail-end
did not fail to take me in once more with horror and
curiosity ; then, still without a word to me, my
visitors were gone again !   There could be no mistake
—I had at last met my elusive senior hostess !   Taking
advantage of the absence of her rival, she had left her
" chamber of anger ", and for one lone hour played
the rôle of proud lady of the house to show off to her
poor relatives the undreamed glories of the newly
built mansion.

I never again saw her in that part of the house, or
for that matter, anywhere else, but my ears burned
for many a day afterwards, for I knew that Hindu
women never fully undress even in their own sight
while bathing in utter privacy.   How could she have
known that somewhere in the vast world outside
such a silly custom as knocking on doors existed, or
have dreamt of the fathomless shamelessness of white
people !   I was too embarrassed and pained, for their
sake, not for my own, ever to mention that gaudy
tragic figure and its fleeting visit, to the other wife,
or to anyone else in the house.   Yet I could not get
the discarded wife out of my thoughts.   She had been
like a sombre tropic sunset fighting with futile flames
the sudden and hopeless eclipse of blackest night.
Whenever I heard the bright gay laughter of the
children of the other woman echo through the halls,
I knew that she too heard it, shut away brooding
somewhere in her lonely room ; and I loathed this
palace and I blessed divorce, and wondered when the

day would ever dawn for India when women, like men, could marry a second time.

I came across two other cases of polygamy in India. One of my friends was the only white woman I knew who could boast of two simultaneous mothers-in-law. Her father-in-law had studied in England as a young man. Upon his return to India, the family pressed for the completion of a prearranged marriage. Though bitterly opposed to it, but economically dependent still, he at last gave in, as most educated sons, when prevailed upon by their orthodox and lovingly merciless mothers, do almost as readily as the vast mass of illiterates. Yet, in the final scene with his father before his giving in, he flatly announced that nothing would deter him from marrying again, should he ever fall in love. Smilingly the father assented, neither impressed by, nor fearing, this fantastic Western notion ; it would soon wear off in the safe atmosphere of India, where no man of his group had any chance of meeting the women carefully hidden behind purdah. Yet some years later he did fall in love, in a most unexpected and disconcerting manner. Riding over their lands one day, he saw in the fields a lovely peasant girl planting rice. He saw her again and again, and insisted on marrying her. No persuasion availed ; he held his father immovably to his ancient promise. Luckily, the girl was of the same caste as the man ; the family gave in, and he married her. My friend's husband was the child of this second and favourite wife. But whatever the state of affairs had been at first, by the time the English daughter-in-law had been added to the interesting family circle, the treatment meted out to the two wives by their husband seemed to have mellowed down to exquisite impartiality : he whipped them both ! My friend had heard his harsh voice and the swish of a whip before she had even had the pleasure of a *darshan* (blessed beholding) of her father-in-law's august face.

Of still another case I gathered details from a friend who was closely connected with a court. The senior rani, who came from a great and wealthy dynasty, was in time supplanted, for lack of issue, by a princess of a poor though princely house. The Maharaja became very infatuated with her young fresh beauty, to the intense humiliation and grief of the senior rani. She could not resist the temptation of grasping a fine opportunity to humble her timid little rival. But it had been too bold—a bitter public insult during a great official function. The Maharaja, in punishment, confined the senior rani to her room ; and there the proud queen was compelled to remain for days and days, until her spirit was broken enough to apologize.

But after no very long period the Maharaja's fancy was caught again elsewhere, this time by a non-Hindu girl of some culture and intelligence ; in her he really found his first woman " comrade ". The two equally neglected ranis now joined together in mutual execration of the latest intruder ; the palace reeked with intrigues. But though discarded in affection, certain inescapable duties to their lord and master still devolved impartially upon the two wives. One of them was summoned at a certain hour to attend His Highness in order to give him the daily massage—(a treasured duty of a Hindu wife), and whatever other accommodation he might demand. It often happened that this summons came when the two ranis were together in my friend's presence.

T*

Pleading, cajoling, demanding, each tried to induce the other to take over the now distasteful duty. " Please, *please*, you go to-day, I don't feel well." " No, I went yesterday, it is your turn to-day." " Yes, but you made me go twice in succession just before ! "

To-day, I am told, the two ranis are no longer allies. Once more at loggerheads, the State now feels the full brunt of their discontent in poisonous intrigues for power. Consideration for the public welfare has been completely lost sight of in the craving to oust each other's favourites from official seats at whatever cost.

But for every tale of extreme selfishness or fruitless misery, one can bring forward another whose motif has power to kindle the spirit of man. One woman, now well over sixty years of age, gave me a personal glimpse of early reform days. Her father was indefatigably striving for change against bitter opposition. He had had the courage to marry a widow, and, though stones were often thrown at them at first, to keep on taking her out into the open air. He was above all else eager to have the women of high castes set free from all ancient bonds, for he realized the tremendous social force which there lay dormant. But he also saw the need of physical building up. In those days high-caste girls of her town saw very little outside the walls of the zenana, and after ten years of age were completely secluded. Open ridicule was poured on anyone who failed to conform.

There were three sisters and several brothers in the family. One of the sisters was by nature very indolent, detesting exercise ; the second was indifferent towards it ; the third, my friend, adored it. But none of their opinions was ever asked, and every morning, without exception, the whole small brood was led forth at five o'clock sharp for a brisk walk of never less than three miles over the *maidan* before the school tasks—equal for both boys and girls—were taken in hand.

All three women are still living. The lazy one, since the moment she escaped from her father's authority by marriage, has never set foot outside her home except to step into her carriage, and has done little social work. Of the other two, one is still an enthusiast for all things Western, and is at the head of an establishment which furthers education along English lines. She has long given up strenuous exercise, and replaces it by inveterate cigarette smoking. The third has remained like her father, a most indefatigable reformer throughout her life, and even at the age of sixty could and often did tire me out walking up and down the steep slopes of a hill-station, or through the crowded bazaar of her town. And, where her father had been able to see only to the full physical development of his own children, she, in turn, is now influencing physical education in half a dozen schools.

A few years ago, the young daughter of the Mohammedan Prime Minister of one of the greatest native States, after her studies in India were completed, declared her intention of going to England for the purpose of taking a course in nursing. Her friends and relatives expostulated, pointing out with horror that it would mean her doing a sweeper's work— she would actually have to handle bed-pans ! Again, since she had not to consider either time or money, if she must keep to her decision to do work of a social nature and in the medical profession, then why stop at nursing ? Why should she not take a degree in medicine ? Then, they pointed out to her, as she knew perfectly well, she would not have to be at the beck and call of doctors and patients, but might easily some day herself be in charge of a hospital. She quietly kept to her decision with the explanation, hesitatingly given lest it might sound like boasting, that it was just because a nurse was required to do a sweeper's work that she proposed to train for it. For, as she went on to assert, " no work is degrading ; that prejudice must be broken down, or we can never progress. If some of us from the highest ranks give the example, it will carry more weight ".

She went to England, and was the first Indian girl to graduate in that work from a great English training school. While her attitude showed both splendid courage and nobility, it no longer implied such hardship as reformers had to be prepared to face at the beginning of the present Indian renaissance.

What sacrifices those Hindus had to undergo who had the courage in the past to defy their own society, few outsiders realize. No tribute is too high to pay to many of these pioneers. One Brahmin friend of mine, married to a spirited girl, realized that she was slowly being broken in his joint family. Pleading and interference by him on her behalf only made conditions worse for her during the long hours when he could not be near to protect her. So, despite bitter opposition and the public disapproval which leaving a joint family brings on the offending member, he took his wife away. In punishment, his father withdrew financial support ; except by resort to law he could enforce no claim to his rightful share in the family property. Enforced legal division would have been hurtful to the entire group ; he was too high-minded to have recourse to it. Consequently the young couple had to put up in a tiny dark flat on the ground floor of a dirty narrow alley in the midst of slums. Then he succeeded in getting work as a bookkeeper, that would keep the wolf from the door. Yet despite these unaccustomed deprivations, he took upon his shoulders still another burden. His wife's sister became widowed, and as she had born only a daughter, her fate in the husband's household was unenviable, to say the least. My friend unhesitatingly welcomed both mother and baby into his tiny flat.

Not long afterwards, another rebellious male cousin also left his family and joined this little island of refuge in the rough sea of Hindu orthodoxy. Together they lived and shared an abject, genteel poverty. The widow was still voluntarily observing much of the asceticism prescribed for her kind, and kept in purdah. Consequently, as the two tiny front-rooms were level with the terrible alley where street urchins were continually peering through the window-bars, she remained confined to a small dark back room. Nor could his wife, though she had broken purdah, get out into the fresh air. The slum streets of that city were still not fit for high-caste women to venture into without risk ·of insult; and they could not afford carriage hire to take an airing on the distant *maidan*. So for years the two women and the growing girl lived a dismal life, deprived of exercise, fresh air and sunshine, as hundreds of thousands of middle-class women are forced to pass their entire life in purdah cities. My friend's wife soon developed

tuberculosis, but he withstood with stubborn pride
the pressure of his friends who urged him to appeal
to his father for help.   Nor did his father, though
undoubtedly acquainted through others with the
pitiful state of affairs, volunteer relief by paying over
even the smallest part of his son's share of property.
The family were unrelenting in their belief that the
young wife was a disgraceful creature, a mischief-
maker, who had stolen their son; they probably
rejoiced over the news about her health—*karma* was
overtaking her!   In the appalling humid heat of her
fanless room she lay helpless for months before death
released her.   Soon afterwards the father arrived,
expressed his condolence and urged his son to return
to the comfort and freedom from care of his family
fold.   But too pained over the poverty-induced death
of his wife, and unwilling to accept aid conditional
on his abandoning her helpless widowed sister, he
chose to remain in his slum and go on carrying his
burden.   He spent his spare time teaching the little
niece, had her trained in music, took her out for
walks, and sent her to school and college.   There
should be at least one woman in the world who
through his efforts could taste the full freedom of
life!   But unfortunately, early privation had weakened her constitution also, so that at best he succeeded only in forcing the blossoming of a colourless
lily on a very drooping stem.   Yet his defeat was
in essence nobler than many a loud-sung victory.

This short description of the dreariness and deprivation involved in their condition and surroundings
is typical of the unhealthy life to which the great
majority of middle-class purdah women in cities
are condemned.   Mercifully, low-caste women are

spared this ultimate misery—and as they are purdah-free, have also been spared appearance in these pages.

I will conclude these stories from my own experience with that of a very dear friend of mine who stands out in my memory as embodying the best, both in spirit and action, of Hindu life and thought. His case is doubly significant, as he is orthodox in religious belief, though not in observance of caste, and has lived all his life in a most backward purdah and caste community. He has never been in Government service, has never striven for worldly success, has never posed as or considered himself a reformer, has never been politically active. On the one hand, his mind is singularly free from the inner uncertainty and taint of the slave mentality engendered by ages of political subjection; on the other, his daily life is serenely untroubled by fear of caste or priestly edicts. Yet no one has ever taken exception to his quiet undemonstrative frequent infringements, because the radiant purity of his motives is too clear for challenge. Though he still stands at his post in the world, he is universally known by the reverent nickname " Swami-ji " in recognition of the quality of his spirit. He is a widower with a young daughter to bring up and provide for; nor is this all, for his roof shelters several poor young village boys attending the near-by schools and college who, but for his help, could not dream of obtaining an education.

Beside this steady drain on his resources—and he is not rich—his house shelters a floating population of visitors and village relatives who come to him for help, comfort, advice, or even only for relaxation. There is no hour of the day or night when Swamiji's door is not open to the unexpected guest or the

distressed petitioner. Should too many come suddenly unannounced near evening meal-time, when the
time and strength of the servants will not allow of a
second inevitably lengthy cooking-process, Swamiji
and his servants announce quietly and convincingly
that they have just finished eating, and set their own
cooked meal before the guests, who have no inkling
from their cheerful faces that host and servant will
have to fast till the following noon.

If all beds are occupied, the host gives up his own ;
for him there is always room, peace and rest on any
floor. Morning and evening, no matter how crowded
the house may be at times, how noisy with discussion or laughter, or whatever the attitude of his
visitors towards devotional forms, Swamiji, without
even the need of physical withdrawal to solitude,
quietly composes himself on the floor with crossed
legs, folded palms and closed eyes to collect his
thoughts in prayer and meditation. All this is done
without a trace of self-consciousness or of demonstration, done easily, gently, as one picks a flower
while passing by a blossoming hedge.

As a young man, Swamiji had seen within his
family group in the distant village-home a lately
adopted girl, then still a child. Like a visionary
flash, the thought came, " we belong to each other ".
When the time came and his parents insisted on his
marriage, he announced that he would take no other
than this girl and would wait for her. The marriage
took place before she was thirteen, and became a
deeply tender beautiful intimacy which lasted for
four years and ended with her death in childbirth,
leaving him alone with his infant girl, the only child.
Swamiji lived on to " do his duty " and to fulfil the

prescribed number of years that are to be devoted to family cares. He gave all his thought to the up-bringing of the child—no son could have been more loved—to assisting young relatives, no matter how distant, and cheering of friends. But he steadfastly refused to marry again; his life is an open book and no other woman has figured in it. With simple belief and expectation he looks forward to the day when he may drop all the cares of worldly life, with-draw into contemplation for a last ingathering of forces, and then cross the final threshold towards reunion. His is the same pure belief in the mystic affinity of souls which of old inspired the voluntary *satis*. Despite all Brahmin teaching to the contrary, he feels that, where such affinity exists, it must be manifest in equal purity, steadfastness, and faithful-ness for man as for woman.

Many a month had passed and our friendship was a deep one, before I learned that the objectionably dust-ingrained punkah-cloth above his bed would never be touched or removed by human hand while he lived—his wife's own hands had pinned that worn-out sari there.

Yellowed and tattered by age, just such a veil of deep affection and reverence yet floats through the dreams and aspirations of India; its fibres spun, its textures woven by gentlest hands may yet outlast the strong machine-made yarn of Western aims.

All the experiences above recounted—fragments cut from the vast tapestry of Indian life by my blunt scissors—illustrate the immense complexity of the Indian woman's problem. A thousand-faceted glit-tering ball of gold which revolves unceasingly, casting now dazzling rays of light, now ink-black shadows . . . how difficult for foreigners—Governments or individuals—to understand her status deeply enough to help rather than hinder her in her onward path!

Meanwhile, Brahma's vast clock ticks off another of its immeasurable seconds; soon even the British occupation—that wholesome irritant—will have become a memory of the past, a fleeting image in a fitful dream towards the dawn of India's new day.

But one thing will remain; the age-old search! The woman of modern India will merely alter its outward form; instead of the ancient path of abnegation, she may find fresh ways of approach, a new and joyous realization of the ancient ideal—" Be thou a Sita—a perfect wife and mother!"

LIST OF BOOKS

Ali, Syed Ameer, *The Legal Position of Women in Islam.* London 1912.

All-India Women's Conference Report, Fifth Session. 1931.

Bader, Clarissa, *Women in Ancient India.* London 1925.

Bhattacharya, P., *Ideals of Indian Womanhood.* Calcutta 1921.

Butler, C., *Pandita Ramabai Saraswati.* New York 1923.

Cousins, Margaret C., *The Awakening of Asian Womanhood.* Madras 1922.

Dutt, G. S., *A Woman of India.* London 1929.

Field, Harry H., *After Mother India.* London 1929.

Frazer, R. W., *Indian Thought, Past and Present.* London 1915.

Garratt, G. T., *An Indian Commentary.* London 1928.

The Indian Year Book. Bombay 1930–31.

Kelman, J. H., *Labour in India.* London 1923.

Macnicol, Nicol, *Pandita Ramabai.* Calcutta 1926.

Mayo, Katherine, *Child Marriage in India, Volume Two.* London 1931.

Mulla, D. F., *Principles of Mohammedan Law.* Bombay 1912.

Murdoch, J., *The Women of India.* Madras 1895.

Natarajan, K., *Miss Mayo's Mother India.* Madras 1928.

Progress of Education in India, Quinquennial Reports. Calcutta 1930.

Radhakrishnan, S., *The Hindu View of Life.* London 1927.

Rai, Lajpat, *Unhappy India.* Calcutta 1928.

Rapson, E. J., *Ancient India.* London 1914.

Shajahan Begum, *Why Purdah is Necessary.* Calcutta 1922.

Urquhart, M., *Women of Bengal.* London 1925.

Wingfield-Stratford, B., *India and the English.* London 1922.

Winslow and Elvin, Jack, C., and Verrier, *The Dawn of Indian Freedom.* London 1931.

INDEX

For Product Safety Concerns and Information please contact our EU
representative GPSR@taylorandfrancis.com
Taylor & Francis Verlag GmbH, Kaufingerstraße 24, 80331 München, Germany